SUFFERING AND
THE THESIS OF PURGATORY

WITH PROPHETIC WARNINGS FOR OUR WORLD

As revealed by The Blessed Virgin Mary to

IVETA *CLEOPHAS* FERNANDES

SUFFERING AND THE THESIS OF PURGATORY

First published in 2021

 A catalogue record for this
book is available from the
National Library of Australia

ISBN: 978-0-6451071-0-4 (pbk)
ISBN: 978-0-6451071-1-1 (ebk)

Typesetting and design by Publicious Book Publishing
Published in collaboration with Publicious Book Publishing
www.publicious.com.au

In conformity with the directives of Pope Urban VIII, we have no intention of anticipating the judgement of the Holy Apostolic See and of the Church on Apparitions, reported by us, but not yet recognized; indeed, we submit to, and accept her final decision without reservation.

In thanksgiving to Our Lady of Salvation

and to the Archangel Saint Michael

This Book is dedicated to His Holiness Pope Francis I,

and to His Holiness Emeritus Pope Benedict XVI

"Now I rejoice in my sufferings for your sake,

and in my flesh I complete

what is lacking in Christ's afflictions,

for the sake of his body, that is the Church."

(Col 1,24)

"These are the words of the Apostle Peter in his First Letter: "You know that you were ransomed from the futile ways inherited from your fathers, not with the perishable things such as silver or gold, but *with the precious blood of Christ*, like that of a lamb without blemish or spot."

And the Apostle Paul in the Letter to the Galatians will say: "He gave himself for our sins to deliver us from the present evil age", and in the First Letter to the Corinthians: "You were bought with a price. So glorify God in your body."

With these and similar words the witnesses of the New Covenant speak of the greatness of the Redemption, accomplished through the suffering of Christ. The Redeemer suffered in place of man and for man. Every man has *his own share in the Redemption*. Each one is also *called to share in that suffering* through which the Redemption was accomplished. He is called to share in that suffering through which all human suffering has also been redeemed. In bringing about the Redemption through suffering, Christ *has* also *raised human suffering to the level of the Redemption*. Thus each man, in his suffering, can also become a sharer in the redemptive suffering of Christ."

(Pope John Paul II, Salvifici Doloris, n.19)

PREFACE

Mons. Anthony Alwyn Barreto,

Bishop of Sindhudurg

Once we finish our journey in this world, we return to God; for God created us that we may live with Him. Sin creates a void in our relationship with God and it brought disruption in God's beautiful plan for us. The punishment of sin is separation from God (CCC 1035). Adam and Eve experienced this separation when they committed sin and they were thrown out of the garden.

Death is not the end of life but the beginning of a new life with our God. The place after death is decided for us by the way we live our lives here on Earth. We know that we cannot help ourselves after death. Once a person is thrown in Hell, he or she cannot redeem themselves. The Catholic Church says, this is a state of definitive self-exclusion from communion with God (CCC 1033). On the other hand, a person who reaches Heaven is a person who attains the purpose of God in their life. They die in God's grace and friendship, and are perfectly purified to live forever, for they see Him as He is, face to face. (CCC 1023). They intercede for us so that we may find ourselves in their company to praise our almighty God.

The Church always reflects on those who had not been perfect in the sight of God or those who had done good but needed purification. The Church believes that the mercy and compassion of God gives them yet another opportunity to come into His presence after their purification. The place of purification is called Purgatory. (CFR. CCC. 1030-1032)

We have a responsibility towards them. We are taught in our families to pray for the Souls in Purgatory and we are encouraged to offer masses and pray rosaries for the Souls in Purgatory. We are also taught to make sacrifices for them. The example of Job in the Holy Scriptures tells us that Job's sons were purified by their father's sacrifice.

The personal insights of Iveta Fernandes which is compiled as a *thesis on the Purgatory* will help us to pray and make sacrifices for the Souls in Purgatory. It is a noble task. We need to pray for the Souls in Purgatory because they cannot pray for themselves. Our prayers for the Souls in Purgatory are based on the mercy and compassion of God who will never turn down our prayers. We show His mercy to them through our prayers.

May the work on the topic of Purgatory help the readers to return to our merciful God who eagerly awaits like the father of the prodigal son. May we walk blamelessly in the sight of God to see Him face to face.

† Bishop Alwyn Barreto

Bishop of Sindhudurg (India)

January 5th, 2021

INTRODUCTION

"But the Woman was given the two wings of the Great Eagle"
(Rev 12,14)

This book is the fruit of a life of prayer and suffering of Iveta Fernandes. It will be a precious gift to whomever it is given to.

Felix Xavier and Iveta Fernandes, a married couple, both born in Africa and both immigrants of Indian origin, are now Canadian citizens. Iveta was a hairdresser earlier in life. After experiencing a deep conversion and following a decree of nullity of her first marriage, she married Felix Xavier. They together live a very simple and mostly hidden life dedicated to much prayer. They also devote a lot of their time in helping the poor through the Saint Joseph Community Center, Foymont, Canada.

Felix Xavier and Iveta are both Catholic and are deeply attached to the Pope and to their Bishop. They have a great love for the Eucharist and foster a deep devotion to Our Lady and to Saint Michael, the Archangel.

For many years now, Iveta, also called "Cleophas" in this book, reports having received a true spiritual education, given to her supernaturally by the Virgin Mary through patient teaching - often repetitive - through locutions and intellectual visions, mostly in the utmost discretion of their modest home in Canada. Iveta also describes apparitions of the Virgin Mary in an extraordinary way and relays Her messages, often spoken aloud in the presence of others, mainly at Mount Batim, in the Diocese of Goa, India - their country of origin.

On reading the transcripts of the recordings made by Felix Xavier during these locutions or visions, one is reminded of Catherine of Siena or Bridget of Sweden. The spiritual manner of teaching that Iveta shares is from an immense love of the Virgin Mary who looks after Her children - and more so in our days in an extraordinary manner - which is very similar to that described in the 'Treatise on True Devotion to the Blessed Virgin' of St Louis Marie Grignon de Montfort.

Of utmost significance is Iveta's account of her participation in the Passion of Our Lord, wherein she undergoes episodes of extreme physical, psychological and spiritual suffering. These acts of spiritual offering are requested of her in advance and are in conformity with her will, and with her husband's will. It is always revealed to Iveta in advance as for whom she would be offering the suffering for. Her most significant moments of suffering are during the Holy Week of each year, wherein Iveta sees within her Soul moments of the Passion of Christ and, as she unites with Him in her suffering, Jesus often speaks to her. She also sees interiorly the continuation of the Passion of Jesus in the current and forthcoming persecution of the Church.

This book mainly consists of the messages that Iveta received in suffering during the period 2010–2021, and they are the continuation of the preceding book: *"The Mercy of God and the call to return to the Harbour of Truth."*

This Book underlines how the culture of death in our modern world deeply offends God, thus opening our eyes to the inevitable consequences of our choices.

As a follow up or continuation from the messages of Fatima, this Book describes how the Virgin Mary, *Our Lady of Salvation*, has received a particular and essential mission for our times from the Most Holy Trinity. Here, Our Lady appears as 'Mediatrix of All Grace, Co-Redemptrix and Advocate.' The term "Co-Redemptrix", not yet welcomed by the Magisterium of the Catholic Church, is here without ambiguity: Our Lord Jesus is the *only* Redeemer, and Mary is Co-Redemptrix along with Him who is also Her Redeemer. This ability to Co-Redeem is also extended to all those who consent to offer their suffering, as *little vessels of Co-Redemption* along with Our Blessed Mother. As expressed in this book, the request of Our Lady that those titles be proclaimed Dogma by the Pope is not for Her need but for our need. The Church's 'yes' to such a gift will allow a torrent of Grace to be released, of which we are much in need!

This book 'Suffering and the Thesis of Purgatory' shows the splendor of God's Mercy that is inseparable from God's Justice, and it foretells of a disaster that will happen if we do not choose conversion and if we go on 'playing God'. It also describes the great danger of the schism of the Catholic Church - that originates in the refusal to accept the ministry of Pope Francis - as well as the extension of the persecution of the Church with all of its horrors!

The messages contained in this book also provide us with an understanding of the signs of times, especially of the Covid-19 pandemic, which appears as the *first birth pang* of the coming *Great Apostasy*.

These insights are meant not only to call us to a deeper conversion and to prayer but also to offer up our suffering with Our Blessed Mother, united to Our Lord's Passion.

*

On several occasions, particularly in 2018, Iveta received precious insights in the mystery of Purgatory.

The insights offered to us in this "Thesis of Purgatory" are presented as deeply necessary for our times – times in which faith in the reality of Purgatory has become so weak. Deeply necessary, because the loss of faith in our modern world is also a consequence of a great lack of prayer for Souls in Purgatory - as now we do not benefit from those Souls who, had we prayed for, would have entered Heaven and interceded for us.

All through this part of the book, we are also given to contemplate the beautiful project of God, the wonderful exchange of love, which the Catechism of the Catholic Church explains in this manner: "In the communion of saints, 'a perennial link of charity exists between the faithful who have already reached their heavenly home, those who are expiating their sins in Purgatory and those who are still pilgrims on Earth. Between them there is, too, an abundant exchange of all good things'. In this wonderful exchange, the holiness of one profits others, well beyond the harm that the sin of one could cause others. This recourse to the communion of saints lets the contrite sinner be more promptly and efficaciously purified of the punishments for sin." (CCC 1475)

It also underlines powerfully the Co-Redemptive ministry of the Blessed Virgin Mary as well as the ministry of Saint Michael, the Archangel. Our Book describes in more detail what Saint Catherine of Genova had described - thanks to her own spiritual experience. This present edition offers footnotes of several extracts of Saint Catherine's "Treaty of Purgatory".

For a fruitful understanding of all these insights, it is important to realize that they were given on Holy Saturdays, a few hours before the Easter Vigils, thus making the immense fecundity of the Eucharistic celebration more impressive!

*

This book as well as all the writings of Iveta's are the fruit of her prayer and suffering. These collections of writings have not yet received formal ecclesial approval, being too early. They remain for private use.

As you go through the pages of this book may you marvel in thanksgiving amidst the Mercy and Justice of God and may you accept the invitation to pray and offer yourself for the conversion of sinners and for the Souls in Purgatory!

Fr. Antoine E.
December 25th, 2020

PRESENTATION OF THE BOOK

This book comes into being at the request of Our Holy Mother, the Blessed Virgin Mary, the Mother of Our God.

The Mother of God reveals that we are entering the purification before the era of a thousand years of Peace.

Jesus said: "I will be with you till the end of time." We walk now hand in Hand with the Mother of God, of whom Scripture reveals as "the Woman clothed in the Sun", who will take us through these moments of deep darkness of various spiritual kinds.

In these messages, the Mother of God, Our Holy Mother reveals how and what we must do: "TOTAL TRUST," the only way, God's way through these times.

Here, the Mother of God also reveals Her Supreme role in Salvation that God has entrusted Her with, as *Mediatrix of All Grace, Co-Redemptrix* (with Jesus The Redeemer) and *Advocate* before Jesus Her Divine Son, the Divine Judge.

Unto Her is given all Power, all Grace, all Gifts to bestow upon Her children, God's children who will Consecrate themselves to Her and call upon Her in each moment and decision of their lives.

Iveta *Cleophas* Fernandes

THE BLESSED VIRGIN MARY REVEALS HER ROLE FOR THESE CURRENT TIMES

Iveta Cleophas Fernandes, a simple woman, married to Felix Xavier Fernandes has been chosen by Divine Providence to be an 'instrument' through whom God through the Immaculate Heart of Mary wishes to make known His Salvific Plan for Our World in 'these times - this period of history'. This is in the context of the predicted times and the strategic role of the Immaculate Heart in obtaining peace for the world through the fulfillment of the Fatima Message and the proclamation of the 5th Marian Dogma.

As a Victim Soul, Iveta has been called to suffer, to co-redeem with Our Blessed Mother the Co-Redemptrix, united to Jesus the Redeemer, to bring back Souls to God. In this union and for this purpose, Iveta offers her prayers and suffering for the Domestic and Universal Church.

This book also details the Suffering of Our Lord for the sins of our contemporary world, for which Christ Our Saviour, died for! For He has traced the path of suffering that we may understand that this is the requirement of reconciliation with God the Father: To pay the debt of Divine Justice that sin requires. *"I have paid the major part of your debt, but you are required to do reparation for some of the offences in a small amount known as Divine Justice." (Message of April 7th, 2017)*

And in this Book, as Christ redeems, He reveals the Co-Redeeming role of His Blessed Mother Who 'walks the way of the Cross' with Her Beloved Son. *'See how My Blessed Mother Co-Redeems for you. She carries my Cross in Silence for your sake, for your world today.' (Message of April 18th, 2014)*

The book *'Suffering and the Thesis of Purgatory'* also brings to the fore the understanding of Purgatory and the necessity of praying for the Holy Souls who are *'paying the debts of Divine*

Justice.' Through our prayers and once purified, these Souls are released to *'Praise, Worship and Glorify God unceasingly for us and thus obtain for us the necessary Grace and Faith through their prayer.'(March 31ˢᵗ, 2018)*

However, fully aware of our plight, Our Blessed Mother comes out with a road map for these critical moments; for Her role is to prepare Her Children for the times of the Great Persecution against the Church before the second coming of Christ. *(March 30th, 2018)*

She comes to request us to Consecrate ourselves to Her Immaculate Heart and that *'should we invoke Her and consecrate ourselves and our children each morning to Her Immaculate Heart and teach our brethren to do the same, She will not abandon us and will lead us through these moments of the persecution that is fast arising.' (Message of 13th October, 2015)* This Spiritual Battle against the forces of darkness, Satan himself, is Hers, She says. She will be the one who will crush him in the end. Our position is to stay under Her Mantle and protection and assist with prayers, sacrifices and with the practice of The First Saturday Devotion made known by Our Lady at Fatima, namely: Recitation of the Rosary, a good Confession, adoration of the Most Blessed Sacrament, Holy Mass, Consecration and Communion of reparation to the Immaculate Heart of Mary. Here Our Blessed Mother's whole purpose and mission is to bring Souls into union with her divine Son, Jesus. So, when we consecrate ourselves to Her, its full meaning is 'to Jesus through Mary'. It is important to note that: *'The prayer most efficacious is the Holy Rosary; it will dismantle the darkness of the mind and the heart restoring the conscience back.' (Message of April 13th, 2017)*

Our Blessed Mother has also given us the 'sacramentals' of the scapular and the Mediatrix of all Grace Medal to assure us of preservation from all temptations, supply us with graces for protection and martyrdom, and an assurance of defending the

Church, the Holy Father and of being led into the era of Peace! For 'In the end, My Immaculate Heart will Triumph and the era of peace will descend upon Your World and the reign of The Immaculate Heart and The Sacred Heart of Jesus will flourish for a thousand years of Peace.' (Message Sept 6th, 2018)

May you understand these moments, and may the Holy Spirit open your heart to receive the Messages that are contained in this book!

Christopher Dias[1], December 28th, 2020

---

[1] Christopher Dias is the editor of "Mother of God, Mediatrix of All Grace Magazine" published online at www.mediatrixofallgrace.com, and ex-Graphic designer of the Messenger of the World Apostolate of Fatima, The International Magazine of the World Apostolate of Fatima.

Table of Contents

YR 2014: DO NOT SEEK EASY COMPROMISES WITH THE WORLD, RETURN TO GOD!

YR 2015: IT IS THE DESIRE OF MY SACRED HEART TO BRING YOU RELIEF SHOULD YOU PROCLAIM MY MOTHER AS MEDIATRIX OF ALL GRACE, CO-REDEMPTRIX AND ADVOCATE

YR 2017: I COME TO INVITE YOU TO CO-REDEEM WITH ME, I WHO AM THE CO-REDEMPTRIX, UNITED TO "JESUS" THE REDEEMER

YR 2018: ONLY SHE ALONE AS MEDIATRIX AND THE MOTHER OF GOD, THE WOMAN WHO IS CLOTHED IN THE SUN, WHO WILL CRUSH THE HEAD OF SATAN IN THE END CAN HIDE YOU AND RESCUE YOU

YR 2019: I AM THE MEDIATOR BETWEEN YOU AND MY FATHER, BUT MY MOTHER IS THE MEDIATRIX BETWEEN YOU AND ME

YR 2020: WHEN SHE IS PROCLAIMED, I WILL OPEN THE FLOOD GATES OF HEAVEN THAT ALL MY BELOVED CHILDREN WILL BE ABLE TO UNDERGO THIS SUFFERING OF THE PERSECUTION OF MY CHURCH

YR 2021: ONLY TRUST IN GOD THROUGH ME!

YR 2010: TAKE COURAGE,
HOW THEN MUST SCRIPTURE
BE FULFILLED? THESE ARE THE
THINGS THAT MUST HAPPEN

1. FATHER LET THIS CUP PASS ME BY, BUT NOT MY WILL, BUT THINE BE DONE.

A vision:

They come marching closer and closer. Every Church door is closed. They have barred the Church doors, and yet they march. They have a warrant. They have some kind of a document that they can enter. Every city in the World is in an uproar. The Military kick the doors open and they find so many Priests. They do not even speak to them, they just grab them and they ... Oh My God, My God, asking them to denounce Jesus of Nazareth as True God in the presence of The Holy Eucharist.

A beautiful vision:

Each of these Holy Priests look up to Heaven, they see the beautiful Face of Our Holy Mother in The Eucharist, holding The Monstrance close to Her Heart and they look back at the Military guards, they say not a word. They will not denounce Jesus...Those that will not open the doors and in Third World countries, their churches are set ablaze! I see Sacred Statues and religious articles brought outside and battered and broken as though to put fear in the faithful. You see rejoicing in those who are following the antipope, the antichrist. They shout out that the 'Gods have come down on Earth and peace and prosperity is ours.'

I see Jesus staggering and holding on to the trees. Peter is in a sitting position, in a deep sleep against a tree. The Lord comes and finds no consolation from the Apostles. Peter hears His footsteps but cannot open his eyes or stand up. Jesus returns and falls against the rock. Anguish, anguish in Our God! I see an Angel descending with a cup, and as though tries to console Jesus. The Angel is Our Blessed Mother's Angel. Heaven is shut completely, complete silence! All Heaven's weeping ... Jesus is leaning against the Angel and holding the Chalice. He is ready to drink the Cup. He gets up and is ready to go to the Apostles. This is that moment ... when I see the Holy

Father. Jesus prays for Our Holy Father. As He draws near, Peter's eyes open. Peter says, "Is that you Lord?" Jesus says, "are you still sleeping?" He tells them to get up, "the hour is at hand when the Son of Man will be betrayed into the hands of sinners."

This is the same betrayal we are about to experience now. Even family members will betray one another. Brother against brother, father against son, mother-in-law against daughter in law, this is that hour, sorrow ... sorrow!

Peter tries to get up, "What's the matter Jesus, are you feeling okay, why is there Blood all over You, did something happen?" Jesus says, "Peter, wake up John and James, the one who will betray Me is at the door." It is dark, the moon is shining, and they have torches, but it is very dark where they come from, as though it is the darkness of sin. The night itself is bright. Shadows, shadows ... the smell of death... of the Innocent One is in the air ... They wipe their eyes and ask, "what's going on?" The Lord says, "It is time." James asks, "Time for what, Jesus?" Jesus in all His anguish. "You have no idea what is about to happen." (April 1st-2nd 2010)

2. SHE HAS A SUPREME GRACE

Jesus is taken to be Crucified; they tear His Garments ...

I see Our Blessed Mother. She's going into that area and She sees His Blood. With Her own Hands She wipes it. They do not allow Her to come close, but She is in the Praetorium, it's a pretty rough place! It's like a rich man's back garden with rocky stones and only a pathway ...Jesus is beaten. They give Him a reed in His Hands, and they put this purple Garment on Him. They slap and punch His Face.

He has a severe bruise on His left cheek that is bleeding, the cheek that Judas kissed ... crying ... Not a protest Jesus makes! They do not allow Our Lady to come close. She sees all the Blood. There is *a woman looking at Our Lady, she is Pilate's wife. She comes with towels in her hands, many little hand towels, and says to Her, "His Mother?" Our Blessed Mother looks at Her with tears in Her Eyes and nods. The woman also has tears in her eyes, and she gives Our Lady the towels. Our Lady motions to her that She wants to go where Jesus is right now and pick up The Blood from there, but She can't. The woman says, "I'll take you there." She takes the veil out from her head and puts it on Our Lady. It is of Royalty!*

Jesus is led out and the Cross waits for Him. It is like up a ramp that they are bringing Him through. And you see Satan in the crowd mocking Him. Our Lady goes and begins to wipe the blood quickly because She wants to follow Jesus. John and Mary Magdala wait outside. Our Blessed Mother is wiping the pavement stones quickly, gathering all the Blood. She has a Supreme grace, all the blood seems to be coming, the stones remain. She bows and thanks Pilate's wife and walks out to meet the crowd. She hands the towels to Mary Magdalene, who passes it to another Mary who puts it in her mantle and holds it. Mary Magdalene has though two veils. In one she is carrying herbs and spices to be placed on the Body of Jesus. She has prepared them with Our Blessed Mother. This is in accordance with the Jewish Law or Tradition. These spices are to scent the Body and to decompose it quickly.

I see the Vatican - Blood, blood, blood and screaming! The Cardinals are preparing to take a vote. There is a majority of the black smoke of Satan!

Jesus has arrived at the bottom of this long winding ramp. They are dragging Him and mocking Him. Our Lady is far away, but She is coming quickly. The kind people who are with Jesus make way for Her. They go in front and are beaten by some of the people though. They are pushed down. They are saying to the faithful - who are saying "No! No!.. what has He done?" - "Have you not heard, have you not seen what He has testified to? He calls Himself the Son of God, He is only a mortal. Is He not the Son of a Carpenter? And that is His Mother, miserable ..." (April 1st-2nd 2010)

3

3. TAKE COURAGE, HOW THEN MUST SCRIPTURE BE FULFILLED?

Our Lady speaks:

"My beloved children, do you see how much is the suffering of your Saviour? He has prayed for this hour that will befall you when they will drag you and hand you over to the authorities. You will be beaten and flogged, and many will be put to death. Take courage, how then must Scripture be fulfilled? These are the things that must happen."

They are walking again. Our Blessed Mother seems to be walking ahead of Jesus. They won't let her walk behind Him, so John and Mary of Magdala take Her, pushing Her through the crowd ahead of Him (I'm tired …) Jesus has no feet left, they are bruised, and bleeding and pieces of flesh are falling from them, from our Master already. The little Angel who was consoling Him is picking up these pieces of Flesh and putting Them in a large Ciborium with His Blood. He is holding this Chalice which is like a Ciborium.

Now I see Jesus coming towards His Mother "Oh! Mama, Mama" … crying… She stretches out Her arms. The soldier who is near Jesus stays back and allows Her to come closer, but She is not allowed to touch Him. The others will not let Her touch Him. They push him aside and say 'What are you doing? No one is allowed to come close and no Women!' 'That's His Mother, the poor Woman' 'Yes pity Her', he says 'She must see the criminal Son She brought forth' These are the cruel words the soldiers utters to the good soldier whom one of them pushes, his name is Mel … Jesus sees Her in all this suffering. He smiles at Her as She returns the smile, the smile is one of consolation. "It is alright" She says to Him, "Son, worry not about Me, I am well, we must do The Father's Will for which We have come into this World for."

These are the moments now when I see sons and daughters that will be dragged out of their homes of the faithful and will be put to death in the presence of their parents. We must draw courage from this moment. This is what they were born for, to do The Father's Will. In the fidelity to their faith, the Catholic Faith, they now give up themselves to bring forth the fruit of this suffering. Their life is like a seed that must die. Parents ... Oh! what suffering ...

My head is tormented in pain, I cannot bear it Blessed Mother... (April 1st-2nd 2010)

4. THIS WILL BE THE STRENGTH THAT ALL MOTHERS WILL DRAW FROM HER

I see Jesus. Pilate washes his hands, and he lays the sentence on Jesus. He says, "His Blood be upon you", and he releases Barabbas and they are happy and are screaming their praises. This, Pilate did to keep his newly found ties and peace with Herod and with the King, out of fear of men, but Jesus looks at him with loving Eyes, bows His Head and walks. He glances into the crowd and His Glance falls on Our Blessed Mother. He looks at Her with what Love. She raises Her Arms. He draws all His strength from Her Glance.

This will be the strength that all Mothers will draw from Her, as Mediatrix[2] of all Grace. She will give them the Grace to endure that moment. She Herself will come. They will see the Son of God sitting at the Right Hand of God The Father. He Himself will receive their Souls and their blood which is united to His, the blood to bring the fruits of the Renewed Church. (April 2nd, 2010, Good Friday)

---

[2] See "Treatise on True Devotion to the Blessed Virgin" of St. Louis Marie Grignon de Montfort, nn. 83-86

5. EVERY SIN IS PARADING IN FRONT OF THE LORD!

Jesus stretches out His Arms and takes the Cross. They place it on His right Shoulder, which is bruised already. His left Hand goes up to hold it. He is bowed already under the weight of it, yet it is not the weight of the cross but the weight of our sins. Every sin is parading in front of the Lord!

The journey begins for Jesus. He is carrying His cross and is exhausted ... so many He sees as He looks on through His eyes full of Blood that is dripping from His thorn crowned Head and from His bruised Forehead and eyebrows that are torn. He sees their faces. He prays for them in His suffering and they will repent and be saved!

This is that hour, those that will decide to follow the antichrist or the faithful, those who will take the 'mark of the beast.'[3] These are our own brothers and sisters, own kin - blood kin and spiritual kin, it is a horrible moment! (April 2nd, 2010, Good Friday)

6. YOU SEE THE HORROR OF NATIONS WHO HAVE LEGALISED ABORTION. THIS IS THE WORSHIP OF THE ANTICHRIST!

I see so many children, so many little children being killed ... crying... crying and suffering ... Jesus dies here and suffers for those committing these crimes. He prays for them that they return and be saved!

You see the horror of Nations who have legalised abortion. This is the worship of the antichrist! These children are sacrificed to him! Pregnant mothers - this is a time of great suffering for pregnant mothers! Mothers and children in their wombs are being taken to be

---

[3] Rev 13,17

killed because they will not take the mark of the Beast, they are put to death! It is illegal, yet it is made legal because they are declared deformed and then killed! This is the sacrifice of the desecration of the Holy of Holies, Jesus in the Eucharist.

I see Russia leading in this. It is for this reason says Our Blessed Mother, "I had desired that Russia be consecrated to My Immaculate Heart. Russia has spread its errors and abortion has been legalised in other Nations, but Russia will still be converted and consecrated to My Immaculate Heart, though it will be late, late for she has spread her errors! Little one, do you understand what I Am saying?" (*April 2ⁿᵈ, 2010, Good Friday*)

7. THE FALSE REFUGES

Jesus is dragging Himself. I can see Our Master. He cannot carry the Cross. Simon himself is not there. He is tired! John tries to hurry holding Our Blessed Mother as She hurries to give Jesus strength, as though She wants to carry the Cross, but the soldiers pushed them back. They do not fall, but they almost do! The crowd is so large that you can barely move. Jesus staggers ... staggers and staggers with the weight of sin and thinks of all the suffering He must still undergo, and He falls ... crying ... suffering ... He can barely move. It is as though He is dead. The soldiers are afraid. They try to open His Eyes, "He's still breathing", *says one of them,* "give Him a little while and we will pull Him up."

This is that little while, this is that fall that Jesus takes as He is praying for His Priests who must undergo great suffering, even for those Elect who must go into exile! They will suffer the fear of this moment and know about those of their brethren, dying for the love of God.

There is rejoicing in the camps of the wicked, in the false refuges under God's name. You see people eating and drinking because they think they are saved. They have killed the fatted calf, they are killing lambs and roasting them, and they are rejoicing that they are saved, but woe to such! They will see the horror of this moment; it won't be long!

There are those, even the Elect are among them, who are led astray. They have chosen this, because of their own will. They did not surrender! Although God elected them, they chose not to hear the Divine Spirit. Their human reasoning led them to these camps. These are those refuges of human origin, and now their leaders, out of fear will give in to the adversary and they will all be slaughtered. Terrible martyrdom! Some will take the mark of the Beast like their master who led them. Some will realise that they have chosen wrongly and will try to run, but they will be killed!

And in honour of those who did not take the mark of the Beast, during the thousand year of reign[4], on these sites, the faithful who will live, will reach these sites of pilgrimage and place a small Cross and erect a small Chapel in remembrance of those who died and in spite of their human weakness, did not take the mark of the Beast. They will burn the images of the antichrist and dig a hole and put the bodies of those who had taken the mark of the Beast – those that had been slain, slaughtered, because they took the mark of the Beast! (*April 2nd, 2010, Good Friday*)

8. THIS MARKS THE CHASTITY OF PRIESTHOOD

Jesus comes up the hill. They grab the Cross. I also see two others serving the same sentence on either side of Jesus. They have placed Him in the centre as though He is the biggest of all the criminals! They throw the Cross on the ground and strip the other two criminals who are screaming and wailing, yelling, cursing and swearing at the guards and also spitting

---

[4] Rev 20,3

and kicking! Their feet are being tied. Jesus makes no protest as they pull the Garments off him. Crying ... crying ... Our Blessed Mother comes quickly. "No" She says, as they were undoing the area most private. They return to tie it back on Him. They obey Her. She thanks them and walks back. Mary of Magdala says, "Mother, they would have killed you, why did you do that?"

This marks the chastity of Priesthood, sacred to God and sacred to all Men. Jesus died for them and has borne the suffering even for the areas that they will keep their vows for. Those who have fallen are many that I see, and they do not know how to rise.

"Only repent, repent and confess your sins to your confessors, to your Spiritual Fathers, sin no more this way, for what profit is in it?" (*April 2ⁿᵈ, 2010, Good Friday*)

9. THE TEARING OF THE TEMPLE CURTAIN, THE DIVISION IN THE CHURCH!

Jesus whispers in His Heart

"Mother, Mother" ...

Our Lady ... Spirit to Spirit: "I'm here Son I'm here." ... *crying ...*

I see Rome and Our Holy Father declaring what this will mean. The division of the Church, the tearing of the Temple Curtain when Jesus expires! It is that moment now, the declaration of Our Lady as Mediatrix *of all Grace, Co-Redemptrix, the tearing of the Temple Curtain, the division in the Church! Jesus has died for that moment!*

I see the soldiers have taken His clothing. They are sitting and throwing dice and are gambling His Robe away. Jesus looks down at them and they cease. He looks up to heaven. "Father forgive them for they know not what they do."[5]

These are those who gamble their faith away. Jesus prays for them, that they repent and return!

I see only the one who wins the Robe of Jesus. "What am I to do with it?" *says he.* "Well, keep it for good luck. They claim Him as a King don't they?" *says another.*

This is the one who will repent and be saved - the one who wins the Robe.

This is the Robe of Martyrdom, that is washed in the Blood of The Lord[6], the purest Lamb, the Blood of The Lamb on this Coat and upon all Priests, who will wash themselves in the Blood of Martyrdom.

The soldier takes the Coat and runs down. There is a man there Domiscus? ... Demetrius ...my eyes are tiring ... he throws it at him and says, "hold it for me."

"I'm not your servant, I'm the servant of the Man dying. That is my Master." *(It seems like he was his servant once)* "We'll talk about this later." *says this soldier. The servant looks at this Robe and realises ... This is The Robe of his Master, his true Master.*

He looks up at Jesus and says "Thank You Master, You gave me a gift, I am free! Your Blood is on this Robe, I shall protect It with my own life." *And he runs away to hide it. (April 2nd, 2010, Good Friday)*

---

[5] Luke 23,24
[6] Rev 7,14

10. THE HOUR IS COMING WHEN THEY WILL INFLICT UNJUST ACCUSATIONS AGAINST MY PETER

They have reached the Courthouse. Jesus is thrown down... while He waits for His private encounter with Pilate...

Jesus speaks to my Soul:

"Know that the hour is coming when they will inflict unjust accusations against My Peter, My Peter who suffers so much for my Church, My Peter who bears My heavy Cross! He will not compromise and so they will inflict Him with unlawful accusations. They will order him and command him to leave the Seat of Peter. They are those of the anti-christ who will support the anti-pope who is already among... You will see him, be not afraid, it is not the hour, but these are the birth pangs before the hour.

Pray My children, pray, pray that My Peter will proclaim My Blessed Mother as your *Mediatrix Of All Grace*, unto whom I have bestowed All Grace and All Power[7], *Co-Redemptrix*, who has suffered this Holy Night with Me and continues to suffer greatly especially in these days that mark the closeness of My underground Church. She will lead My *Remnant* into these hours, and She will continue to intercede as your *Advocate* for those who return and for those who will die, whom you must pray much prayer for! Pray in the manner She has made known to you. ..." ... *(and Jesus falls)*

Jesus continues: "Jesus of Nazareth, as Man-God in your anxiousness I have taken this fall, and as God-Man I rise that you may rise! Jesus of Nazareth, I am with you My flock, My sheep and My lambs. Amen. Amen." *(Holy Thursday, April 1st-2nd 2010)*

---

[7] See "Treatise on True Devotion to the Blessed Virgin" of St. Louis Marie Grignon de Montfort, n.76.

11. THIS IS LIKE THOSE WHO WILL ACCUSE THE PRIESTS FALSELY FOR CRIMES OF IMPURITY

Jesus carries His Cross and is staggering ... suddenly Mary of Magdala leaves Our Blessed Mother and Mary Cleophas says to her, "What are you doing? You cannot leave Her." Mary of Magdala replies, "Take care of Her, take care of Her, I got to go, I got to go." She moves with great love and hurries through the crowd who push her. "Woman, get back!" say the soldiers, "You will be killed!" She is not afraid and runs to Jesus. She finds an opening under the guards and runs to Jesus under His Arms. She takes off her veil and presses it against the Master's Face under His bowed Head and pulls it back. They hurriedly pull her and ask her what she is doing. "Get out of here you wicked witch", they mock her saying "Is that not the one, the prostitute that He saved? See how much love she has for Him! What business does she have with Him if He says He is God's Son?"

This is like those who will accuse the Priests falsely for crimes of impurity.

Mary of Magdala looks at Her Veil and kisses it. She sees the features of Our God on It and places it close to her heart. She hides it and runs back to Our Blessed Mother. "What did you do? You could have been killed", says Mary Cleophas. "Are you worried?" Mary of Magdala replies, "Do you not see what they are doing to our Master? What are our lives, if we die, we deserve death!"

We will see the sinners and prostitutes[8] turning to God when they see the great illumination that will befall upon all men as an outpouring of God's final Grace. (Holy Thursday, Good Friday, April 1st-2nd 2010)

---

[8] Mt 21,31

12. JESUS BESTOWS UPON HER THE FULLNESS OF GRACE AS CO-REDEMPTRIX UNITED WITH HIM TOTALLY

Our Lady is close to the Cross now. She looks up at Jesus with what Love... Jesus draws all His strength from His Mother. Jesus is only in great sorrow at this time. He whispers Soul to Soul: "Mother, Mother if I could spare you from this, You know I would." *She looks at Him, Her Soul speaks to Him:* "Son, worry not about Me" ... *crying ... what Love, unconditional Sacrifice! ...*

Then Jesus looks at His Apostle, His favourite Apostle, John: "Son, this is Your Mother"[9] *John looks at Him and weeps.* "Yes Lord - he whispers - I'll take care of Her, give me the strength!" 'I've prayed for you too.' *Jesus says, Soul to Soul.*

Jesus looks at His Mother with such Love - the emptying of His entire being even of His Mother for us now. He says to Her "Woman, behold Thy son.[10]" *She looks at Him with Joyous tears rolling from Her Eyes, warmth with no malice in Her Mind. She takes us all into Her Immaculate Heart, the whole human race. Yes, She is truly the Mediatrix of all Grace. Jesus bestows upon Her the fullness of Grace as Co-Redemptrix united with Him totally. He whispers to Her.* "In this way the Son of God is Glorified, The Son of Man Glorifies God! Amen."[11]

He speaks of their hidden understanding "I Am in The Father and The Father is in Me." *Even at this hour, it appears as though the Father has abandoned Him, but He draws strength from His Father's Will, the Spirit of The First Person resides in Him to undergo this moment! It is a Mystery... suffering (April 2nd, 2010, Good Friday)*

---

[9] John 19,27
[10] John 19,26
[11] John 13,31-32

13. OUR LADY SHOWS THE IMPORTANCE OF THE 'MEDAL' OF THE MEDIATRIX OF ALL GRACE

Our Lady shows the importance of the 'Medal' of the Mediatrix of all Grace[12]. She gives us the promises: After these 'Medals' have received the Blessing of a Consecrated Priest obedient to The Holy Father and an understanding of these times they will carry:

1. The Grace of being preserved from all temptations, temptations of impurity that will rise into the Church and streets that no man can resist, except with the Grace of the Immaculate Conception in them.

2. As *Mary Mediatrix of all Grace,* they will carry the Grace of protection for the Elect and the protection of the Cover of Her Mantle, The Blue Mantle of the Immaculate Conception to lead them to the places of safety.

3. They will carry the Grace, those who will suffer Martyrdom. There will be Joy in their faces and they will bear no fear!

4. These are those who will stand to testify that the Holy Father still lives, and that the Church of God is still alive! They will be put to death as men go mad! A further promise of this 'Medal': That the faithful take courage and they will see the True Pope. If they believe the elect chosen for those times and stay faithful, She will provide everything for them that is needed.

5. And the final promise: This 'Medal', as the Mother of God, the Immaculate Conception of Mary conceived without sin, Mediatrix of all Grace, that it stands for, She will lead the church out into the era of Peace ----The Triumph of The Immaculate Heart.

These are its five promises. (*Good Friday, April 2nd, 2010*)

---

[12] The Unveiling of the Medal occurred on 14th October 2016 at Ganxim-Batim, Goa

YR 2011: IN THESE TIMES OF THE GREAT PERSECUTION

14. ALL POWER, ALL GRACE, ALL GIFTS HAVE BEEN ENTRUSTED UNTO ME

Our Lady Speaks:

"… I desire with great desire that every hour you keep the invocation of what My Jesus has made known to His servant Faustina "Jesus, I trust in Thee. Amen." Now add to it "Mary I trust in Thee. Amen."

With this invocation you will keep temptation away from your mental thoughts." … *"I am the Mother of God, Our Lady of Grace, Mediatrix of All Grace.* All power, All grace, all gifts have been entrusted unto Me to dispose according to My Will, which is the Will of God for His plan on Earth in these times of the great persecution. I Am your Mother Who loves you dearly. Amen." *(Sunday June 15th, 2011)*

YR 2012: MY CHILDREN ARE NOT PREPARED, FOR THEY HAVE NOT CONSECRATED THEMSELVES TO MY IMMACULATE HEART!

15. TO THOSE WHO WILL WEAR THE MEDAL

Our Lady Speaks:

"My beloved children, I thank you for this coming, to honour My request to come this day on the feast of Divine Mercy. It is most fitting that the Holy Mother, the Church celebrates this Holy Feast of God's Mercy for your world, a world deteriorating and with sin increasing, yet I Am the Woman Clothed in the Sun.[13] I am the Mother of God, I Am the *Immaculate Conception* ... Jesus, My Divine Son the Redeemer. I am the Co-*Redemptrix*, the *Mediatrix of all Grace*.

I come today to bring before you what I have entrusted to this little one of Mine and My Jesus, Cleophas, your beloved sister, known as the Medal of the *Mediatrix of all Grace*. I Am Our Lady, Mediatrix of all Grace. This, in which you will understand the fullness of Truth, the Catholic Church, the Bride of Christ.

Rejoice little ones of mine, for today, before I Am proclaimed the *Mediatrix of all Grace*, to those, who will wear this Medal after it is blessed by a Priest, My beloved chosen son, a Catholic Priest, will receive this privilege before time like in Cana[14], the privilege of conversion, the privilege of praying for those in need of conversion and the promise of the heavenly host of the army of God, Michael the Prince to entrust your Soul in the last hours of agony safely to God. Amen.

I love you dearly, I am the *Mother of God*, I am your Mother. I desire that you pray the Rosary united with the chaplet of Divine Mercy each day for the intentions of My Immaculate Heart, that the Bishop of Rome His Holiness, your Holy Father

---

[13] Rev 12,1

[14] John 2,4

Peter the Rock, the Pope of My Jesus, Pope Benedict the XVI proclaim me as *Mediatrix of all Grace*. On that day, the gates of Heaven will open to release the Grace that is awaiting with the promise to fulfill the promise of this Medal.

It is enough for now beloved children. Now many of you will have the privilege to see Me. I Am the *Mediatrix of all Grace*, your Mother who loves you dearly. Amen." *(April 15ᵗʰ, 2012, Hour of Mercy Sunday, Visitation of Our Blessed Mother, Batim, Goa, India)*

16. BELOVED CHILDREN, SOON COMMUNICATION WILL CEASE

Our Lady Speaks:

"My beloved children, I thank you for responding to My request to pray at this hour for the needs of your world through the St. Joseph's Community Centre at Foymont, through God's Salvific Plan: Charity and Mercy with Justice for your world!

Your world is deteriorating terribly children, and prayer has ceased to rise for the needs of saving of Souls! My Heart is sorrowful, for many of My children are plunging into darkness, many are walking the path of eternal darkness!

Prayer has taken another path, a selfish path where all seem to want to clothe themselves with bodily needs. Make known to them beloved children that when they recite the prayer taught by Jesus, the Our Father, there is no more that can be granted, for the Father that sees all will bestow upon them all that they need each day, each minute, each hour! You need no more, except to live God's Holy Will!"

… "Beloved children, it is your Heavenly Mother's desire to begin to take small steps of praying together for each intention and in receiving a 'Yes' or a 'No' from My Divine Spirit, My Spouse the Holy Spirit, God's Holy Spirit.

Beloved children, soon communication will cease, and it will bring great distress! I have already made known how you must communicate through your Guardian Angels. You have known this path but now you have fallen away! Begin to practise each moment with each other and make known this path through the Angels and Saints to reach to all your loved ones.

I will help you, Amen. Pray My children pray for the completion of My 'Medal' as *Mediatrix of all Grace* that My children may receive it and begin to pray for its fulfillment. I love you dearly, I thank you for responding to My request. Only obey, all will be clear! I Am the *Mother of God*, I Am the *Mediatrix of all Grace*, I Am the *Immaculate Conception*, I love you dearly, I Am Your Mother, Amen." *(August 1ˢᵗ, 2012)*

17. I DESIRE ALL MY CHILDEN TO KEEP BLESSED CANDLES

Our Lady Speaks:

"My beloved children, pray, pray much prayer for the Holy Father that he may proclaim Me *Mediatrix of all Grace*. Only then am I able to open the floodgates of Heaven to let fall upon all My children the Graces they are in need of to withstand these moments of tribulation.

The calamities of the Earth will increase. Nature will shift at an even more alarming speed. Fear not, at this hour I desire all My children to keep blessed candles, candles that you must light when a storm of nature presents itself in the place you are dwelling.

All My children on Earth, this is for you, pay no heed to anything else except keep your eyes on the Holy Father. He will make all things known. It is enough for now. I will return on the fourteenth day of the ninth month of the year two thousand and twelve at the hour of Divine Mercy to entrust unto you what God desires. Pray My children pray! Amen.

I Am The Mother of God, I Am the *Immaculate Conception,* I Am Mary Virgin of Nazareth, I Am the *Mediatrix of all Grace, Co-Redemptrix and Advocate* before the Throne of God, before the Divine Judge, I love you dearly, I Am your Mother, Amen." *(September 12ᵗʰ, 2012)*

18. THOSE WHO HAVE EMBRACED PAGANISM AND THE CULTRE OF PAGANISM

Our Lady Speaks:

"My beloved children, I thank you for responding to My request to come before Me this day at the hour of Great Mercy known as Divine Mercy ...

Now beloved children, this is what I desire to make known this day to you that what I had made known to this little one of Mine, many days gone by known as the requirements of fifteen days,[1] (endnote) a preparation for all My children, for much is unfolding in the form of persecution, calamities and suffering that will be inflicted by My adversary on My children. These are none other but those I have already made known. Now they are coming to pass. Know and understand only prepare as I have asked. Amen." ...

... "Beloved children, this day there will be much weighing on you. I have already placed a heavy suffering in the early hours of the morning on this little one of Mine and My Jesus, My beloved daughter Cleophas. It is for those who have embraced paganism and the culture of paganism on this day. They embrace this manner, some in ignorance, some who have sold themselves to be Satan's advocates. Pray for them beloved children! Pray for them, for they are only mounting on many sinful behaviours known as mortal sins, sins of impurity, sin that lead even to the culture of death! Only pray!

This[15] is the day that your ancestors used to prepare for Sainthood in understanding of the Resurrection, praying for those who are serving Divine Justice, serving in Purgatory. Today it is no longer (observed); it is only a passing obedience if one desires. Make it known that it is the desire of your Heavenly Mother that all Her children must understand this day to be a preparation for the two days of the Great Feast.

The Feast of The Resurrection: To pray for those who are serving Divine Justice who will enter the Resurrection for all Eternity in Paradise before God to pray for you, if you should now pray for them.

And the preparation of all those in remembrance of those gone before you, known as Saints, which the Church has proclaimed, that you must follow those who have already paved the way for you. This is in remembrance and to understand the pondering of your call to holiness to sainthood! Amen." ...

"I thank your Spiritual Fathers, My beloved chosen son who prays for you. I love him dearly, Reverend Father James Duffy and My beloved Bishop, My Chosen Son, His Grace

---

[15] October 31st, vigil of All Saints and November 2nd, commemoration of all the faithful departed

22

Bishop Alwyn Barreto who prays for you and is in need of your prayers for him.

Pray for your Holy Father, in need of much prayer in these hours! A great weight weighs upon his shoulders, a great decision weighs upon his heart. It is enough for now. I love you dearly.

I Am the *Mother of God*, I Am the *Mediatrix of All Grace*, Pray for this intention that My children receive the Medal. I Am your Heavenly Mother Who loves you dearly, only remember to entrust all to My Immaculate Heart[16]. Amen." *(October 31st, 2012)*

19. WHEN THIS MOMENT BEFALLS YOU, YOU MUST TURN TO PRAYER

Our Lady Speaks:

"My beloved children, with great rejoicing, with great love and with great desire, I desire to thank you for your fidelity to fast and pray, to abstain and to be present here before me in the three consecutive days that I had made known to you.

It pleases The Eternal Father to see such fidelity, even though you are creatures with a fallen state, My Grace in you helps you rise when you entrust all to My Immaculate Heart. Of most importance

---

[16] *The Mercy of God and the call to return to the Harbour of Truth, pp.70-71. "My beloved children how often have I made known to you about your anxiousness. As a good Mother I desire to help you walk the path of holiness, but the first rule of our walk towards this path of holiness and on this holiness towards God is to entrust all to My Immaculate Heart. It is there all darkness will be separated and you will see the path more clearly. Be not troubled, I Am here. I am asking of you to, please My beloved children, entrust all QUICKLY to My Immaculate Heart."* 25 January 2012

is your Consecration to Me in the early hours of the morning, the opening prayer of your day and to walk with Me each day in this manner. Make known to all My children of this manner.

This day, God The Father is well pleased and much content of your service as slaves of Mary for The Eucharistic Jesus. Jesus living in you and through you with Me be made known to all your brethren who will come before you. Amen.

Now beloved children, this is of great importance and I desire to make known to you: There will come a confusion, what has already been made known to you, of the three days of darkness. It is not so. It is My adversary to whom power has been given, even over Nature, to bring forth a darkness upon the Earth, a darkness that will frighten many, a darkness for which many of My children are not prepared, for they have not consecrated themselves to My Immaculate Heart - by this, those who were baptized in the Faith and have wandered away! Know and understand I am Queen of Nature!

Even in such, if you pray to Me, I alone can prevent such a misery. There is not much prayer rising except a great confusion. I am making this known to you now before it happens, that if those who I have made known to, prepare for the fifteen days they will draw much from this moment. It will come upon all mankind for God shall allow such. Know and understand, this is the preparation! If prayer does not rise so that I Am unable to prevent this moment, it will mark the preparation for the *One World Government*, the order that will bring great distress upon all My children!

Know and understand beloved children many are confused about wood. Do you not understand, when the sun does not give light, there will be no warmth and when all will no longer be, where will your warmth come from?

Know and understand that My children will have to come together, and those that can provide for this moment when it befalls you, you must turn to prayer. Pray beloved children, pray! The candle will be your warmth, the Blessed Candle, that I have asked for. This is only an understanding of the first birth pang of what is yet to befall. Be not anxious, be not troubled! Consecrate yourselves to My Immaculate Heart, I will clothe you with My Mantle to bring the Motherly warmth that you are in need of.

Beloved children, those who under much medication, you must resort right now to prepare for these days; fifteen that I have asked. It is only an understanding when it happens. Amen." ...

"I love your dearly. I Am The Mother of God, I Am your Heavenly Mother, Who clothes you with My Immaculate Mantle. I Am The *Mediatrix Of All Grace, Co-Redemptrix* and *Advocate*. I love you dearly! Go in the peace of My Jesus through Me. Amen." *(December 18ᵗʰ, 2012).*

Endnote

1. FIFTEEN DAYS PREPARATION: While in prayer I (slave of Mother Mary for the Eucharistic JESUS) asked our Lord JESUS to help me write this letter of preparation so that you may not loose sight of what is more important. Amen. This is about what is asked of us the faithful - preparation of food, salt, candles, warm clothing, wood, batteries, plus 15 days supply - for the chastisement that is about to befall on humankind and all living creatures on Earth and in the Seas.

"Take care that you set your minds on the things above, your Soul, in The Words of JESUS: "Take care! Be on your guard against all kinds of greed, for one's life does not consist in the abundance of possessions", (Lk: 12- 5).

Therefore, keep your hearts and your Souls open that you prepare for neighbour as self, bearing also in mind that we might just be the sower that others may reap. Ask for our Heavenly Mother Mary's help in this preparation, to guide your path, so no greed may enter you to bring condemnation upon yourself and your dear ones, your people. Amen. May no one of you in this preparation be caught in greed, to hear the Lord JESUS say: "You fool! This very night your life is demanded of you. And the things you have prepared, whose will they be?"

Always be rich towards God, in charity of Love, forgiving as CHRIST JESUS even unto death. How happy the Soul who sees this path and embraces his cross to prefect life in CHRIST JESUS. Amen."

Note: This message was given in August 15ᵗʰ, 1998. In October 31ˢᵗ, 2012, Our Lady revealed this message is now coming to pass and that what was asked for 7 days is now for 15 days, referencing to a supply of any medicines that one might be taking. Etc. Amen. See part of message of October 31ˢᵗ, 2012 to understand this message. Amen

YR 2013: BELOVED CHILDREN MAKE KNOWN THE SCAPULAR AND SPREAD THE DEVOTION TO THE HOLY ROSARY

20. SOULS WHO REFUSE TO ACKNOWLEDGE GOD AS THE CREATOR

She Speaks:

"Beloved children, today I desire to make known that the suffering this little one of Mine and My "Jesus" Cleophas is enduring, is an offering towards reparation against God as The Creator from the beginning of time, for Mankind has grown amiss, and the negligence of thanking and acknowledging the Creator has brought about darkness to Souls who refuse to acknowledge God as The Creator and have embraced Satan's manner of thinking, known as the theory of 'creation'[18]; scientifically an ingenuity of Man's wicked plot against God, Amen." *(March 26th, 2013)*

21. I WILL TAKE YOU INTO THE HOURS OF THE PERSECUTION KNOWN AS THE DESERT

"Pray beloved children, pray that I be proclaimed *Mediatrix of All Grace, Co-Redemptrix* and *Advocate*. It is in this manner I will take you into in the hours of persecution known as the 'desert'[19], the desert that has been made known in the book of Revelation. I Am the Woman clothed with the Sun.[20] Unto Me is entrusted All Power, All Grace for your sake by the Most Holy Trinity. My desire is to make known to you the Redeemer, Who lives with you in the Holy Eucharist, My Divine Son Jesus.

Pray, pray, pray for the conversion of all God's children, for many are led astray and it sorrows My Immaculate Heart. Amen.

---

[18] A theory that "refuses to acknowledge God as the Creator."

[19] Rev 12,14

[20] Rev 12,1

I love you dearly. I Am the *Mother of God*. I Am *Our Lady of Fatima*. I Am the *Immaculate Conception*. I Am your Heavenly Mother, the *Mediatrix of All Grace*. I love you dearly! Amen." (13*th* *May 2013, Batim, Goa, India*)

22. BELOVED CHILDREN MAKE KNOWN THE SCAPULAR AND SPREAD THE DEVOTION TO THE HOLY ROSARY TO MANY OF MY CHILDREN

Our Lady Speaks:

"My beloved children, how it pleases My Immaculate Heart to see such fidelity. How I desire that many of My children will come to be in this manner. Make known this manner of prayer, your love for Me, to those who ask of you how to pray. It is simple, entrust all to My Immaculate Heart and I will do the rest. Only I can help!

Beloved children make known the Scapular and spread the devotion to the Holy Rosary to many of My children. It is of most importance, in these hours of the battle that's weighing against the faithful!

Prepare little one of Mine, prepare! Always be joyful in carrying your Cross, the Cross of Jesus, upon your shoulders.

I desire with great desire to thank your Spiritual Father, My beloved Chosen Son, Reverend Father James Duffy, who continues to please Me much and prays for My intention even in his suffering moments, entrusting all to My Immaculate Heart, that only I be glorified and that through Me, God will be Glorified, Honoured and Worshipped throughout your Earth. Amen.

Beloved children now be at peace, I Am close at hand. Entrust all to My Immaculate Heart and do as I have asked. I love you dearly, I thank you for responding to My request to pray at this hour for the needs of your World through the St. Joseph's Community Centre at Foymont, God's Salvific Plan that will be understood in due time.

I Am the *Immaculate Conception, Mediatrix of all Grace, Co-Redemptrix and Advocate,* your Heavenly Mother Who loves you dearly, Amen." *(September 26th, 2013)*

23. THE MIRACLE OF THE EUCHARIST

While Iveta is in suffering, Jesus speaks:

"My Church, to You I speak as True God and True Man present in the midst of You in the Holy Eucharist, the Consecrated Bread and Blood through the hands of My Priests in the line of Melchizedek[21], of I who am the High Priest, Jesus, True God and True Man.

Unless you eat My Flesh and drink My Blood, you have no communion with Me.[22] I have spoken of this already. Now through this little one of Mine, I reveal what has come to be known as the Miracle of the Eucharist, Flesh and Blood present, I Who Am God in the Second Person of The Holy Trinity, in the Holy Eucharist.

Through this little one of Mine, Cleophas, I have revealed My Flesh and My Blood. As the body consists of white flesh and red flesh, known to man as white meat and red meat, I have revealed Myself in this manner in what has come to be

---

[21] Psalm 110,4 – Heb 5,6 and 7,17

[22] John 6,53

known as the *Miracle of the Eucharist* in the fulfillment of My Word spoken in Holy Scripture.

Unless you eat My Flesh and drink My Blood you have no Communion with Me.[23] I Am Jesus of Nazareth, True God and True Man present in the midst of you desiring to come to dwell in you,[24] that you may have Communion with Me and through Me with My Father, for We are One, The Father in Me and I in The Father.[25]

I have made all things known plainly through My Blessed Mother, Mary, Virgin of Nazareth.

I desire that the last and final dogma, as it has come to be known, that My Mother be proclaimed the *Mediatrix of All Grace*, for I have bestowed all Graces unto Her for your World in these times of the persecution of My Church, My Bride known as the Bride of Christ, I Who Am He as the Redeemer and Judge. My Holy and Blessed Mother, *Co-Redemptrix* and *Advocate*, pleads before Me, for each of you My little children who have fallen to the ways of the World and with the father[26] of this World into eternal darkness.

Through the suffering of Victim Souls united with My Suffering as the Redeemer and at the call of My Blessed Mother to serve in such a manner, those Souls are redeemed and brought back to God by the *Co-Redemptrix and Advocate*, My Blessed Mother, the *Immaculate Conception*.

I Am Jesus, True God and True Man of Nazareth Amen, Amen."

There is silence and Jesus speaks again:

---

[23] idem
[24] John 6,56
[25] John 10,38 – 14,10 – 14,20
[26] John 8,44

"I Am present now in this little one of Mine through My Flesh and Blood, the Holy Eucharist, Who speaks to you all My beloved children, children of God, children of Light.[27] Amen. Amen." *(Iveta had just received Holy Communion prior to this message) (September 27th, 2013)*

---

[27] 1Thess 5,5

YR 2014: DO NOT SEEK EASY COMPROMISES WITH THE WORLD, RETURN TO GOD!

24. AND SO MANY SOULS ARE FALLING INTO HELL

"I will let you know … you comfort My Immaculate Heart pierced with so many thorns of ungrateful men who continue to blaspheme God and plunge many of God's children into perdition. Know and understand, many of the faithful even are walking the path of perdition![28] They have abandoned their love for God and are following a false understanding of God.

Beloved children I come this day to call all the faithful to return to prayer. Pray, pray, pray many Holy Rosaries! - of great importance in these moments! Men continue to offend God and the cry of so many oppressed, innocent Souls have come up to God Our Father. If you do not pray, I will no longer be able to hold the Hand of God, from bringing down His wrath to annihilate Nations!

There is confusion and distress over all the Earth. Creature and creation are groaning in pain like a mother groans and cries when she is about to give birth. Know and understand, the threat of World War III is not far. Pray beloved children pray, pray that this must not come to be!"

Vision: … Now, She opens Her Garment with Her Right Hand and stretches it out and a part of the Earth opens and so many Souls are falling into Hell … Oh!... (Cleophas) … crying Oh! … it's frightening … crying …"

Our Lady continues to speak: "Only prayer can suffice to render Souls back to God. These Souls are lost forever, but there are many that will fall if you do not pray!"

Vision: Our Blessed Mother looks up to Heaven and She speaks:

---

[28] Mt 7,13

"You must pray for the Holy Souls in Purgatory. Many do not pray for their loved ones. Pray My children, pray! They need your prayers to ascend into all Eternity and Paradise with God. They are paying the debts of Divine Justice. Your prayer is important. They will come down as Souls to help you, as Angels..." *(March 25th, 2014)*

25. THEY WILL DRAG YOU LIKE THEY HAVE DRAGGED ME

Good Friday Morning: Jesus is suffering: ... bound and dragged, they are taking Him .

"It is in the same like manner they will bind My Priests and drag them like criminals. Know My Priests, take courage I have suffered this, it is needed for My Church. This suffering of yours will bring you the Crown in Paradise, with Me. Amen. Amen."

Jesus speaks: to my Soul...Ah...Ah... "Truly I tell you, this generation has become a perverse generation and now I tell you before it comes to pass, they will inflict you with all anti-god laws, and men will become like decayed bodies, the stench of sin will be all over your streets, but know My faithful *Remnant* that I have prayed for you in these moments of My great Suffering. Take heart, I Am through it all with you. They will drag you like they have dragged Me when you stand for the Truth! Take heart and do not grow anxious! Submit yourself that you may gain your life in All Eternity with the Crown of Glory where I will Crown you. Do not succumb to what they will impose upon you. Guard yourselves against all lawlessness that is coming to be. I weep for you, those who will fall away, I weep for you and even now I implore you to take heart and amend your ways. I have Suffered for you too, return to Me!

I Am Jesus of Nazareth, True God True Man. Amen. Amen."

"My Priests and Nuns, all Religious and many of the faithful who defend the Truth, this is how you will be mocked and driven like a beast. Take heart, some of you will escape this, know that it is I Who has permitted so! Pray, pray, pray that you may not be overcome by grief and fear to denounce Me and fall into the hand of Satan. He will do everything he can to ask you to denounce yourself and serve him. I have Suffered and prayed for you ...I Love you..." (*Good Friday, April 18th, 2014*)

26. DO NOT SEEK EASY COMPROMISES WITH THE WORLD, RETURN TO GOD!

Our Lady Speaks:

"War is imminent, only prayer can hold the moments back. Pray My children, pray, pray that the Holy Father proclaims Me as *Mediatrix of All Grace, Co-Redemptrix* and *Advocate*. Only then I can help, for All Grace, All Power has been entrusted by God the Father, God the Son, and God the Holy Spirit - My Spouse unto Me, to help you in these moments! Do not seek easy comprises with the World, return to God! I long to caress you in My Immaculate Heart as a Mother restores Her children back to health. How many of you are unwell! Return to God by repenting of the offences you have committed and be reconciled through Holy Confession; the Sacrament God has left for you.

Many of the faithful have abandoned the practice of receiving the Living Flesh and Blood of My Divine Son "Jesus" in the Holy Eucharist. Beloved children return, for how then will you sustain yourselves against these forces. You are not alone, for I Am with you in these hours!"

She pauses ... and continues to speak:

"Do not seek easy comprises with the World. Know that the One World Government is close at hand. Do not seek to take any debts, for it will plunge you into darkness. Be on guard against every lawlessness and every heresy that is unfolding.

I love you dearly. My desire is to restore you back to God that We may be happy into all Eternity as a Family of God.

I Am the *Immaculate Conception*. I Am the *Mother of God*. This day the Church honours the Divine Presence in My Immaculate Womb, The Annunciation, the Presence of God made Flesh, the First Tabernacle I Am! I Am the *Mediatrix Of All Graces, Co-Redemptrix* and *Advocate*. I Love you dearly, know that when you call on Me, I Am there with you through it all. I will not abandon you! I love you! Amen..." *(March 25ᵗʰ, 2014)*

27. I AM THE REDEEMER AND THOU ARE THE CO-REDEMPTRIX

Jesus speaks to His Blessed Mother:

"Mother, how I desire to suffer you not, this suffering with Me."

She raises Her Head and speaks:

"Let it be done unto Me as You Will. Amen."

Jesus reveals:

"I Am the Redeemer and Thou O Blessed, My Mother of all mothers, is the *Co-Redemptrix*! This night you will suffer with Me. This day you will suffer greatly with Me, but your suffering will not be over. Mine will end and Yours will begin as *Co-Redemptrix*, to bring in all the lost children who will fail to see My Love for them. Will you help Me Mother? Blessed art Thou for such Love! Amen. Amen."

Holy Mama just looks up and again repeats: "Let it be done unto Me according to Thy Will. Amen." (April 17th, 2014)

28. GO TELL MY MOTHER I NEED HER. I THE REDEEMER NEED HER TO CO-REDEEM WITH ME

He speaks Soul to my Soul:

"My Mother, My Blessed Sorrowful Mother as *Co – Redemptrix*, will intercede for you. Invoke Her, it is Her Hour to Protect Her children! Pray, pray, pray that My Peter proclaim Her *Mediatrix Of All Grace*, for I Who Am Jesus of Nazareth, True God True Man, has bestowed all Grace and All Power of My Father unto Her for your sake. Only She can help prepare you for these moments. Amen. Amen." ...

Jesus looks at John and His Soul speaks to him:

"Go, tell My Mother I need Her. I The *Redeemer* need Her to Co-Redeem with Me. Go beloved John of Me, Jesus of Nazareth."

John: "Yes Lord Jesus."

Jesus: "Amen. Amen."

And he runs. Jesus is brought before Pilate in this room and Pilate questions 'Jesus'. He makes no protest and does not answer.

'Jesus' speaks to me Soul to Soul:

"Children of God, you who are My faithful, begin carrying the crosses of those who seek compassion.

See how My Blessed Mother Co-Redeems for you. She carries My Cross in silence for your sake, for your world today. Pray, pray, pray that She be proclaimed *Mediatrix of All Grace, Co-Redemptrix*, by your Holy Father, My Peter, this day called by Me, Pope Francis I. Amen. Amen."

Jesus looks at me – Soul to Soul, He speaks:

"Daughter, daughter, blessed one of Mine Cleophas: Make known your Blessed Mother to all corners of the Earth. Make Her known, because through Her, they will know My Love and My Compassion. Make Her known as the One Co-Redeeming with Me, now suffering and will continue to suffer even after I have expired for the Salvation of My children, Her children" ....

He looks at His Mother again. Soul to Soul:

"I The Redeemer, Thou Art the *Co-Redemptrix, Mother of Salvation*. Thou I beg to Redeem the Souls that are not yet aware of My Mercy."

Holy Mama says not a word, She only nods Her Head.

"Amen, Amen." *Jesus replies.*

He agonizes at this moment and He raises His Head and looks at John the Disciple: "Son behold Thy Mother, Mother behold Thy Son![29] From this hour Thou art The Mother of all The Redeemed as *Mediatrix of All Grace*. All Power and All Grace, I bestow upon Thee. Thou art the *Advocate* of the children yet

---

[29] John 19, 25-27

to be Redeemed who will turn to Thee! Only Thou can bring them before Me! I entrust this Mission to Thee My Blessed Mother. To thee My Blessed Mother I entrust it!"

She has no word to say, She only smiles at Him.

And Her Soul speaks to Him: "Let it be done unto Me, Thy born slave according to Thy will. Amen. Amen. Amen." *(Good Friday, April 18th, 2014)*

29. I HAVE BESTOWED THESE GRACES UPON HER FOR YOUR WORLD FOR THE TIMES OF PERSECUTION

Jesus looks at me now, and Soul to Soul He speaks:

"Daughter, beloved one of Mine, Cleophas, make known My desire for the salvation of Souls, that My Mother, My Blessed Mother be proclaimed *Mediatrix of all Grace, Co-Redemptrix* and *Advocate*. I have bestowed these Graces upon Her for your world for the times of Persecution that are upon you. You will see them increasing.

Know that the plan in which I had entrusted the secrets in the years gone by, are now coming to pass. It is not necessary you know, only pray, all is in place!

Only the day when My Peter proclaims My Blessed Mother as *Mediatrix of All Grace, The Mother of all Humanity, Co-Redemptrix* and *Advocate* before I who am the Divine Judge will mark...who are in the city like Judea must flee to the Mountains.[30] My Church must go underground. My

---

[30] Mt 24,16 – Luke 21,21

Mother and I will be with you through Her. Amen. Amen."
(Good Friday, April 18th, 2014)

30. IT IS FOR THIS REASON I DESIRE THAT THE MESSAGES BE BROUGHT FORTH

Our Lady speaks:

"My beloved children, Oh how great a joy you have granted Me this day to see your love and your fidelity! Inspite of all your weakness, you still desire to follow the Divine Will of God. It is of great joy in Heaven and it will be on Earth if you continue in this manner. You will bear fruit; now only do as I have asked!

Especially, of great importance are the Messages! All that you have asked you will see its fruit when the Messages begin to unfold and are made known to My children who await My Word. There is much confusion, there is much darkness, and many are following false gods, yes even the faithful have been led astray! It is for this reason I desire that the Messages be brought forth. I Love you dearly."

"Continue in this manner. Pray, pray many Rosaries! Pray together, form cenacles that will glorify God and prayer will ascend to God. Do not compromise, only speak the truth!

I Am The Mother Of God. I Am your Heavenly Mother, Who Loves you dearly, the *Immaculate Conception,* the *Mediatrix Of All Grace, Co-Redemptrix* and *Advocate* in Heaven.

I await that day when I shall be proclaimed by your Holy Father Pope Francis I, His Holiness that I may let fall showers of Graces that are necessary for your World. Go in the Peace of My Jesus.

I love you dearly, only remember to entrust all to My Immaculate Heart. Amen." *(June 25th, 2014)*

31. YOU ARE NOW AT THE THRESHOLD OF THE GREAT APOSTASY

Our Lady Speaks:

"My beloved children, I have come down from Heaven... I desire with great desire to make known the desire of God Our Father.

Beloved children, I desire with great desire to thank My beloved chosen sons present here to receive My Graces. It is through you that My Graces will flow upon My Garment, the Garment of Grace as I release today and unveil the Garment of Grace, the Scapular under the title of the *Mediatrix of All Grace*, I Who am She.

Beloved children, I also desire to thank My beloved daughters, present here chosen to lead all God's children into Holiness with God to the virtues of the knowledge that God will entrust unto You.

Know and understand now I desire to make known God's desire and God's Salvific Plan. You are now at the threshold of the great apostasy. I desire that you entrust all of yourself unto Me.

Welcome into the abode of My Immaculate Heart, here I will rescue you from the cruel slavery of the devil that has been spread, for I was not proclaimed, as Russia was not Consecrated to My Immaculate Heart. In the end it will be so, and My Immaculate Heart will Triumph in the days of persecution.

Know and understand I will be with you if you only Consecrate yourselves to My Immaculate Heart.

God desires to bring His Salvific Plan to the World through Me. I Am The *Mediatrix of All Grace, Co-Redemptrix* and *Advocate*, your Advocate pleading before The Divine Judge, My Divine Son "Jesus" present with you in the Holy Eucharist, enduring much suffering through the desecration and the black masses that are rising all around.

Know and understand these times! A great dissension will descend upon Peter the Rock. They will divide and accuse Him of all lawlessness unjustly! Pray, pray, My beloved children, pray for your Holy Father, the successor of Peter, the Rock upon which Jesus, My Divine Son promised to build His Church and the gates of hades will not prevail.[31] Yet the hour is coming now, you must understand these moments!

I desire with great desire to make known to all My chosen sons[32] present here to be in solidarity with the Holy Father with your Bishops and in communion with one another. It is through you the plan of God will be made known.

I desire with great desire to thank My beloved chosen son, The Bishop of this Diocese, who now honours Me and has made Me known in the land of Fatima, I thank Him immensely.

I desire to make known as I have made known in the days gone by that Batim, this Holy Mountain Ganxim, lies *in the shadow of Fatima*. It is the fore runner of the future. Now may you understand: It is the continuation of Fatima after the persecution into the Era of Peace. I Who Am the Mother of God will lead you through these moments. Amen." ... (*October 13th, 2014*)

---

[31] Mt 16,18

[32] The priests

42

YR 2015: IT IS THE DESIRE
OF MY SACRED HEART TO
BRING YOU RELIEF SHOULD
YOU PROCLAIM MY MOTHER AS
MEDIATRIX OF ALL GRACE,
CO-REDEMPTRIX AND ADVOCATE

32. IN THEIR QUEST TO SEEK TO PLAY GOD, THEY HAVE EMBRACED SATANISM

Jesus speaks:

"My Peter, courage, I Am with you, I Am in you! In your moments when you feel empty, turn to the Blessed Mother, She will console you. It is that hour of the persecution of My Church, My Bride. How I wish it was not so! The iniquity of mankind has reached the climax and prayer is lacking to bring it to order. It is imminent that this suffering befalls the good and the bad, all of mankind!

It is the desire of My Sacred Heart that you prepare My Church, My Lambs, My Sheep, Whose Shepherd you are, for these moments to understand them, that they may remain faithful.

It is not time yet for you to abandon the Seat of Peter, however this hour is coming. Fear not, it is The Master, Jesus Of Nazareth, Who has given you the two Keys as the successor of the First Peter.

It is the desire of My Sacred Heart, that you bring forth the last Dogma to Crown The Immaculate Heart of My Mother, My Blessed Mother as in the proclamation that She be proclaimed *Mediatrix Of All Grace, Co-Redemptrix* and *Advocate,* for She is so in Heaven.

I The Second Person Of The Most Holy Trinity in union with The First Person, My Father and The Divine Spirit *(The Third Person)* has crowned Her already in Heaven.

It is Her hour of power to protect Her children, the *Remnant,* though they will be scattered like sheep;[33] yet I will be with them in what has come to be known as the *underground Church.*

---

[33] Mt 26,31

This persecution is none other like the ones that have preceded it nor will any follow like it, for such is the lawlessness and wickedness of mankind! In their quest to seek to play God, they have embraced Satanism!

Peter, My Peter, My Pope Who carries the Cross of My Church, in union with My Peter Who is known as Emeritus Pope Benedict XVI, you Who are Pope Francis I, I am with you, I am Jesus of Nazareth, the Master in union with My Father and My Spirit. My Church will not be an orphan and the gates of hades will not prevail against it[34], for I will dwell Myself with it in union with The Spirit of My Father and My Holy Spirit, The Third Person of The Most Holy Trinity who will dwell with it always, forever and ever. Amen." (*1ˢᵗ Friday of Lent, February 27ᵗʰ, 2015*)

33. PRAY, PRAY, MANY ROSARIES FOR YOUR HOLY FATHER

Our Lady Speaks:

"Now I come before you with great joy to thank you and all My children who have continued to pray the '*Three Thousand Hail Marys*', this devotion to bring forth the fruit that I be proclaimed *Mediatrix of All Grace, Co-Redemptrix* and *Advocate* by your Holy Father, today Pope Francis I. His Holiness is also in need of much prayer!"

… and She pauses … and Her Heart is as though silent: "Oh! what suffering, Oh! What suffering My beloved Chosen Son, His Holiness, Your Holy Father Pope Francis is enduring! Oh! how they charge Him with unlawful accusations! Pray My beloved children, pray, pray many Rosaries for Him; in this way His strength will continue. Amen." (*March 25ᵗʰ, 2015*)

---

[34] Mt 16,18

34. PREPARE MY SHEEP, MY LAMBS, FOR THIS TERRIBLE PERSECUTION

Jesus Speaks: "Little one of Mine, Cleophas make known what I Am about to make known to you.

Make known to My Shepherds, make known to your Holy Father, My Peter known to you as Pope Francis I, make known to My Peter, known to you as *Emeritus Pope* Benedict XVI, My *praying Peter* for your World, for these moments when it begins. I Am Jesus of Nazareth, this day you will understand from that first moment as I reveal to you, I Who Am The High Priest, you who are My Priests who follow in My footsteps: Come follow Me!

You who are the fishers of men[35], you must understand these moments now, the signs of your times! You must understand to prepare My sheep, My lambs[36], for this terrible persecution that is rising and will befall all Nations! Not one will escape this for such is the sin of man and the cry of the innocent that has come up to My Father and to Me, The Divine Judge.

Prepare, prepare, prepare your sheep, your lambs for these moments! Do not be afraid, I Am with you, even unto Martyrdom. Those who are of you must suffer! Do not be afraid! No longer will your Churches as buildings stand. They will take them from you...

Do not be afraid of not pleasing man, for yes, I warn you and I make known before it happens, many will flee, those who are and speak of themselves as the faithful, and I have made known to you that the prostitutes and the tax collectors[37], when they hear these Words will return!

---

[35] Mt 4,19

[36] John 21, 15-19

[37] Mt 21,31

46

Save My children, those I have entrusted unto you wherever you are My Shepherd. Do not fear! I Am with you through it all to the end[38] and My Blessed Mother Who Co-Redeems with Me will be with you as She is with Me to the end. I love you My Shepherds, I will hold each one of you.

Jesus of Nazareth, the High Priest[39] Who you will Celebrate this day your Communion with Me, I The Bridegroom, you My Brides! Amen. Amen." *(Holy Thursday, Good Friday, April 2nd-3rd, 2015)*

35. THEY WILL DRAG YOU, LIKE I AM DRAGGED NOW

Jesus speaks: "My Priests, I have suffered greatly this night for you. My Apostles, how heavy is the Cross that weighs upon you now! Do not compromise, know that I have suffered this night for you.

They will drag you, like I Am dragged now, through the streets. They will drag you and mock your Priesthood. Such is the suffering and the Blood that will purify My Church of the terrible sins of outrageousness and sacrilegiousness and desecration. Take courage, I Am with you! I, The High Priest have suffered for you and for My sheep and My lambs.[40] You My Priests must do the same. Some of you will escape this night as My *remnant*. Pray, pray, pray always. Amen. Amen." *(April 2nd-3rd, 2015)*

---

[38] Mt 28,30
[39] Heb 4,14
[40] John 21, 15-19

36. SHE WILL HELP YOU IN THE HOURS OF YOUR PERSECUTION

Jesus speaks:

"Daughter, make known this: You are much troubled, you are much perplexed, is there no one to help you? Is there no one to pray with you except My beloved, who is weighed down himself with so many worries. You are in need of much prayer.

This I desire to make known to you: My Peter, My beloved Peter Who has embraced the name Pope Francis I and righteously it is so, for such is My desire for My Church. I Am Jesus of Nazareth, The High Priest desiring to make known to You, your journey to Calvary has begun, My Spirit is with you.

It is to You I have entrusted the two Keys of My Church. It is My Blessed Mother that will help You and My sheep and My lambs. It is the desire of My Sacred Heart that You proclaim Her as *Mediatrix Of All Grace, Co-Redemptrix* and *Advocate* for these times. It is through Her many lost Souls will return to the sheepfold; whose Shepherd You are.[41] She will help You in the hours of Your persecution. No greater sorrow will befall You than that of My Grace in You, My Peter Whom I Love."

"My Priests, My Shepherds, My Apostles, it is upon you I charge your Souls to embrace Divine Mercy, Divine of Me Who Am all Mercy, and reveal it to My children without compromise that they may turn and repent for their sins. Even now the hardened of heart can return if only you will make it known to them. I Am with You. Amen. Amen." *(Holy Thursday, Good Friday, April 2nd-3rd, 2015)*

---

[41] John 21, 15-17

37. MOTHER, WILL YOU CARRY MY CHURCH AS CO-REDEMPTRIX?

Jesus opens His Eyes, looks at the thieves, and He looks down. They are dividing His clothes, gambling away. They care not about anything or anyone. They cast lots for His cloak. Jesus looks at them. "Father forgive, them for they know not what they do[42]", *He says and bows.*

He looks at His Mother: "Mother, Mother" - *Soul to Soul, Redeemer to Co-Redemptrix:* "Woman, behold Thy Son." *He looks at His most favourite Apostle, John.* "Son - *Soul to Soul:* Behold Thy Mother.[43]"

Soul to Soul Jesus speaks to His Mother: "My Church, My Bride, My Peter suffers immensely for Me! My visible Peter, My invisible Peter! Mother will You carry My Church as Co-Redemptrix?" *Holy Mama does not hesitate:* "Let it be done unto Me according to thy Word[44]. Yes, My Divine Son." *She bows.*

Jesus speaks to My Soul: (Vision: I am under the Mantle of Our Lady)

"Daughter, little one of Mine, Cleophas, I thank you for giving yourself in this manner to suffer for My Bride, the Church, the Catholic Church and My Peter, Pope Francis I.

Make known this to My Peter, My Peter who carries My Cross in these hours, and walks to Calvary with Me: 'It is the desire of My Sacred Heart to bring you relief, should You proclaim My Mother as Mediatrix of All Grace, Co-Redemptrix and Advocate'. The Most Holy Trinity has

---

[42] Luke 23,34

[43] John 19,25-27

[44] Luke 1,38

49

bestowed this upon Her. You will see speedy relief coming to the faithful whom You care so much for, My Peter. I love You. Jesus of Nazareth, the High Priest. Amen, Amen." *(Holy Thursday, Good Friday, April 2nd-3rd, 2015)*

38. WALK IN HARMONY

St Michael speaks:

"Beloved children of God, with the delight of God I come before you to commend you for your diligent and zealous effort to make up for all that was wanting in you with the Grace and Gifts that Our Blessed Mother continues to bestow upon you; these Graces and Gifts when you seek it of Her, when you ask it of Her and when you call upon Her to finish what you have not finished.

It is Her desire once again to speak to you, yet this I must make known to you to prepare also for your Mission in the Land of your Ancestors, asking each in moment the Divine Spirit of Our God to enlighten you and invoking My presence that nothing that does not belong to God will enter to infiltrate God's Mission. I will be with you constantly and when danger is lurking around you, when you sense it, the Spirit of God will enlighten you at all times. You must invoke My Presence by reciting My prayer, the prayer to invoke Me. Amen.

I Am St. Michael, the Archangel that stands before God at God's right Hand always in His Presence, now before you at the command and as the Servant of the *Mediatrix of All Grace*, the *Mother of Our God*, the *Co-Redemptrix* of all men in need of Her intercession and Advocate before the Throne of God, The

Divine Judge in the favour that God will see through Her a loving Mother interceding for all Her children who invoke Her presence under this title! It is also with the delight and joy of Her Soul that I make known Her joy to you, of all the prayer that is arising for this intention. Amen."

*

Our Lady Speaks:

"My beloved children, I thank you for responding to My request to pray for the needs of your world which is desperately in need of prayer, desperately in need of harmony and desperately in need of peace! Only I can help! Do as I have asked and walk in harmony.

It is harmony My adversary hates, and in harmony you can do all things as I would do"..... "I love you dearly. I am the Mother of God. I Am your Heavenly Mother, always at your side, the *Mediatrix of all Grace*, *Co-Redemptrix* and *Advocate*, awaiting that moment to be proclaimed on Earth, that I may dispense My Grace upon the children of God who are in much need, in this chaos that is arising in all corners of the world, it will increase ever more frequently! Man will rise against man and nations against nations. There will be much bloodshed ..." *(May 13th, 2015)*

39. THE WORLD LIVES IN A WORKING MANNER, IN DISOBEDIENCE TO GOD'S COMMAND

St Michael speaks:

My beloved children, at the salutation greeting of the *Queen of Heaven*, the *Mother of God*, Our Queen, Our Mother, I Am St. Michael here before you at Her command, Her servant. I come this day to bring you the message She desires to make known to you:

"Beloved children you are much perplexed, you are much tired, you are much anxious! You do not yet understand to entrust all to My Immaculate Heart quickly as it comes before you; it is for this reason you are weighing! Many are the deeds I would give you My consent, but the direction would be different from your manner of thinking.

Beloved children, know and understand to keep Holy the Sabbath Day, except for a situation of an ailment that you need to attend to a brother or sister and for situations that are those brethren of yours, closer to enter the Resurrection, known to you on their dying bed. All others must be kept for the next day. Rest on the Sabbath! Teach others in this manner, for how else will they know? The world lives in a working manner in disobedience to God's command of rest, for God rested, so must you! Amen." *(June 17th, 2015)*

40. EVERY TIME THE ROSARY IS RECITED, I CAN BIND THE SPIRITS

St Michael speaks:

"Beloved children of God, how it pleases Our Immaculate Mother today as the World honours Her under the title of *Our Lady of The Holy Rosary.*[45]

The Rosary is this chain that I Am holding. By this, every time the Rosary is recited, I can bind the spirits which are the advocates of Satan and cast them into the bottomless pit. It is in your power to invoke Our Blessed Mother, the *Mother of Our God* and Me, Her servant, to chain these forces of darkness that often you yourselves invite by not entrusting all into Her Immaculate Heart.

---

[45] Feast of Our Lady of the Holy Rosary, October 7th

I come before you this day at Her request to place a Word of love from Our Heavenly Mother to you, Her little children, children of God. I Am St. Michael Who stands in the Presence of God here before you at the command of the Mother of God. Amen." *(October 7th, 2015)*

41. YOU ARE AT THE LAST HOURS OF THE BIRTH PANGS OF HEAVY LABOUR OF THE PERSECU- TION BEFORE THE GREAT APOSTASY

Our Lady speaks:

"Daughter now make known: My beloved children, I have come down from Heaven once again and I thank you for responding to My request to present yourselves here before Me in Consecration to My Immaculate Heart. I will not abandon you! I assure you of My Motherly love. I come today to make known to you the Motherly love, that I desire to restore all My children back to God. You must help Me! I come before you today to assure you that should you invoke Me and Consecrate yourself each morning to My Immaculate Heart and teach your brethren in this manner, I will not abandon you! I will lead you through these moments of the persecution that is fast arising!

Beloved children you are at the last hours of the birth pangs of heavy labour of the persecution before the great apostasy. Be not troubled, be not anxious, be not afraid! I Am with you through it all!

I thank You My beloved chosen sons for coming before Me this day. It is through You that My beloved children will come to know the Mercy of God, that this year will be proclaimed such, by His Holiness, your Holy Father, My beloved Chosen Son Pope Francis I, in union with Emeritus Pope Benedict XVI, the hidden Pope that prays for this

World of yours. Without His prayers you would not be able to endure the suffering.

Beloved children I come before you to ask of you now especially My chosen sons[46] to remain in solidarity with your Bishops in all Dioceses in which God has placed you and you My beloved children to be obedient to your Shepherds. Pay heed to what they say, return to the Sacraments, especially Reconciliation with God of most importance and receive the Holy Eucharist. Spend great moments with My Divine Son Who waits for you.

Beloved children I ask of you, especially My chosen sons and all Religious to remain in solidarity with the Holy Father. He will lead you through these moments."

Vision: O! She is opening Hell Ah! Oh ... so many Souls are perishing ... Ah!

"Beloved children, I desire that you pray for sinners, so many are falling into the bottomless pit and I cannot save them. Help Me beloved children and I will promise you My fidelity to ensure you eternal happiness with God.

My only desire is to restore you to My Beloved and Divine Son, Who I as *Mediatrix Of All Grace, Co-Redemptrix* and *Advocate* in Heaven, am pleading for you and your World. Soon it will come to be a proclamation on Earth and then you will see the power of God descending upon those that are faithful to Me. *(October 13th, 2015)*

---

[46] The priests

YR 2016: IT PLEASES
MY IMMACULATE HEART
TO SEE THE DEVOTION OF THE
FIRST SATURDAY THAT I MADE
KNOWN IN FATIMA

42. THIS COURSE CAN BE CHANGED THROUGH THE POWER OF THE HOLY ROSARY!

Our Lady speaks:

"I have longed for this moment. How I wish that all My children would be faithful in this manner, but it is not so!

I desire with great desire to reveal the anguish of My Heart, My Motherly Heart is concerned, concerned about so many of My children who heed not My request and are walking the path of perdition.[47]

It is not too late beloved children of Mine. Turn from that path and return to God through Me by Consecrating yourselves to My Immaculate Heart. You are in great danger! There is no more time for such nonsense and such mischief that you are embarking on as though you have all eternity on Earth. You are not far from seeing the heavy-laden burden on your Holy Father's shoulders, for the great apostasy is near at hand! The desolate sacrilege[48] will come into being very, very, soon!

Pray beloved children, pray, many of you are neglecting prayer. Pray the Holy Rosary, you know its power! I can help you through it all if only you will recite the Holy Rosary faithfully to Me.

Beloved children, you are at the threshold of World War Three, yet I can help if you will pray the Holy Rosary. Even this course can be changed through the power of the Holy Rosary! It is not God's way, the choice is yours, you must choose God now! How I weep for you and how I long to embrace you, even in your wretchedness, even when you

---

[47] Mt 7,13

[48] Mark 13,14

disown Me! I long to Love you with My Motherly and tender Love. You will never know this Love anywhere else, only I can give you this, for God has given Me all Power, all Grace and all Gifts to bestow upon you. There is no peace in your hearts, there is no peace in your families, there is no peace in the World for there is no prayer and there is no Adoration and Reverence for Jesus in The Blessed Sacrament.

Your Churches are empty. Jesus is alone waiting for you, to answer you and your requests. How He longs to pour out His Love upon you, yet you seek other ways where you will not find Him.

Pray beloved children, pray much for your Holy Father. Oh! How much weighs upon Him! If you only know how much Love he has for you! His Love is such, like the Divine Saviour ready to lay His life down for you, each one of you that form the Church, the Bride of Christ, the Holy Mother, the Catholic Church.

Today I invite both, Catholics and non-Catholics, to come and drink from the Fountain of the Mercy of God; it is for all God's children. Embrace it and you will see its fruit. Amen." (Jan 1st, 2016)

*

Our Lady speaks:

"It pleases My Immaculate Heart to see the devotion of the First Saturday that I made known in Fatima, the devotion that My Divine Son Jesus made known for me, to Me and in Me, where you will find your Saviour. I will take Him to you perfectly and bring many children to this knowledge. This devotion is of great importance in these times for yourselves and for your families and the World. Amen.

I Love you dearly, I Am the Mother of God. Today The Holy Mother, The Catholic Church honours Me and Venerates Me as The *Mother of God*, I Who Am She, the *Immaculate Conception*, Mary Virgin of Nazareth, the *Mediatrix Of All Grace*, *Co-Redemptrix* and *Advocate* in Heaven, awaiting that hour on Earth that I may dispense all Gifts, Grace and Power to resist temptation and fight the Spiritual battle against the forces of darkness, Satan himself.

I Who will crush him in the end! My Immaculate Heart Will Triumph! Amen." *(January 1st, 2016)*

43. PREPARE MY FLOCK, MY SHEEP!

While suffering His Passion, Jesus speaks to all the Apostles:

"My beloved Priests just as I have made known to the Apostles, as I foretold of My Passover, the Institution of The Holy Eucharist, My True Flesh and My True Blood of that day of the false prophets that will come in My Name[49] - to be aware of them! And yet I also foretold of your preparation!" *(As the Apostles asked Him: when will this be?)*

I have made known and now I make known plainly.

These days are surely coming, and they are fast approaching! To all those Apostles known as the Scarlet Red Apostles[50] and known as those that wear the Purple

---

[49] Mt 24,11

[50] The Cardinals. The scarlet red signifies "your readiness to act with courage, even to the shedding of your blood, for the increase of the Christian faith, for the peace and tranquillity of the people of God and for the freedom and growth of Holy Roman Church". (Pope Francis to the new created Cardinals, 28.06.2018)

Garment[51]: Prepare my flock, My sheep, My Lambs[52], for these days are approaching and they are coming like you have seen the weather, at an alarming rate! Be not afraid, I Am with you through it all! My Holy Mother will take you through these moments, make Her known as the *Mother of God*, the *Mediatrix Of All Grace* that will bestow of Me, of Mine through Her, as *Co-Redemptrix* to intercede for all the hardened sinners.

Her suffering is immense now[53] and as *Advocate* She will plead before Me for all your needs and I before My Father - Redeemer and Co-Redemptrix - Now Her Mission begins! Amen, Amen." *(March 25th, 2016 Good Friday)*

*

While suffering His Passion, Jesus speaks to His Priests:

"My Priests, I Who Am the High Priest in the line of Melchizedek,[54] True God and True Man, Jesus of Nazareth, be aware, I warn you of false prophets! Many of you have embarked on such a dreadful journey to betray the Holy Father as the false Pope, it is not so! Return to the *harbour of Truth*, he is My Peter. Your fidelity and obedience to him is necessary for you to become Holy Instruments and to bring your sheep into holiness. I have already traced this path for you!

To you My Seminarians, My Deacons I ask the same, pay heed I have warned you of the false prophets, you will know them by their fruits. Obedience to the Holy Mother, the Catholic Church is necessary! Obedience to the Holy Father is

---

[51] The Bishops
[52] John 21, 15-19
[53] Rev 12,2
[54] Psalm 110,4 – Heb 5,6 and 7,17

necessary, obedience to your Superiors, your Bishops in whose Diocese you are placed by Me. I Who Am the High Priest, you who follow in My footsteps, return, return to the Truth! It is the Truth that will set you free[55], for now you are in bondages and in anxiety, for your road is clouded by many falsehoods!

I have traced the path for you, follow Me! Jesus of Nazareth, the High Priest. Today you will remember the first day when I gave you My Covenant in My Blood and My True Flesh. Amen, Amen." *(March 25th, 2016 Good Friday)*

*

I see the guards coming. They are marching. They pass by the Upper room. The Apostles get up and look through the window and they are frightened. They ensure all the doors are closed. Our Holy Mama's Heart sinks. She knows this moment, She knows who they are. She knows where they are going.

The Apostles come running to Her and say, "What do we do?" She smiles at them in spite of all fear, anguish and pain. "Be not afraid", She says and She tells them to go back and rest.

The Divine Spirit enlightens me now in written Words in front of me…

The role of The Mother of God, Mediatrix of All Grace, Co–Redemptrix and Advocate begins, and they will come for Her children. This is the understanding of how She will protect Her children and strengthen those who must suffer for the purification of the Holy Mother, the Catholic Church.

The Vision closes. *(March 25th, 2016 Good Friday)*

---

[55] John 8,32

60

*

Jesus looks at them and speaks to them:

"Have you come to arrest the Son of Man like He were a bandit, a thief?[56] Know now this is the hour and for that reason the power is granted to you to do so."

Now Jesus speaks to My Soul:

"My Pope, Peter My Peter Francis, Benedict, My Cardinals, My Priests, My Apostles know that you are coming to this moment! Prepare My sheep, prepare one another for many of you will pay the price, know that I have walked this path!

You are those who will wash your robes with My Blood as Martyrs[57], your blood united to Mine for the purification of My Bride, My Church, the Catholic Church. Amen. Amen."

"My Priests, My beloved Priests this hour will befall you! Prepare, prepare and invoke My Holy Mother to be with you through these moments as She now Co-Redeems with Me in prayer. Take courage, I Am with you through Her. Amen. Amen." *(March 25th, 2016 Good Friday)*

44. JESUS OF NAZARETH THIS DAY SUFFERING FROM THAT FIRST GOOD FRIDAY IN REPETITION

Jesus, Soul to my Soul:

"This day daughter make this known, little one of Mine, for this day I was conceived in the Womb of My Mother. Know

---

[56] Mark 14,48
[57] Rev 7,14

and understand this is how My faithful *Remnant* will endure many persecutions, yes even the *Remnant*[58], they will seek them and only those chosen by My Father will remain to carry on the Domestic Church and the Universal Church. They will treat you like criminals, such is the hardness of the heart, even Pharaoh's heart[59] was far softer than these criminals, such is the lawlessness!

I speak to you My *underground Church*: Know and understand My Mother will be with you, My Blessed Mother Who now Co-Redeems with Me, even in this suffering. She is suffering with Me. She prays for you. Take courage! Through Her I will be with you and through My Priests I will be with you in the Eucharist, My True Flesh and My True Blood. I will sustain you, I will not leave you orphans!

Take courage! Pray, pray much prayer, pray the prayer My Mother has taught you, known to you as the Holy Rosary. It is a weapon against the assaults of Hell, for yes all Hell will break loose in the days ahead. Know that I have told you this before it comes to pass. I Am Jesus of Nazareth this day suffering[60] from that First Good Friday in repetition for the crimes committed this day, to this day and to the end of time.

I will be with you, Jesus of Nazareth, the High Priest suffering for His Church as She undergoes Her purification for all the lawlessness that has entered. Amen. Amen." ...

*

Iveta: Holy Mama don't let him[61] take mine, these Souls.

---

[58] Rev 12,17

[59] Exodus 7,13

[60] See Blaise Pascal: "Jesus will be in agony until the end of the world, we must not sleep during that time." (Pensees, Penguin books, 1966, p.313).

[61] Satan

Holy Mama: "he won't daughter, he won't. I Am here. You have captured them[62]. Now they are Mine, his battle is with Me, not with you! You are under My Mantle and protection! No harm will come to you! It is in the like same manner no harm will come to all My children in those days and in the days of the *underground Church* if they Consecrate themselves to Me. I Myself will defend them, Jesus in Me and through Me in these moments!" *(Good Friday, March 25th, 2016)*

45. DO NOT SEEK AN EASY COMPROMISE WITH THE WORLD

Jesus speaks Soul to Soul as they raise Him up:

"Do you see, My beloved people, My faithful *Remnant*, how much I have suffered for you? Embrace My Mercy, repent of the many offences you have committed, yes, My Priests, My Religious, and return to the harbour of Truth! Do not seek an easy compromise with the World. Enter always through the narrow road[63], it is the road that leads to Salvation. It is the road where My Mercy awaits to embrace you and My Mother, Who Co-Redeems with Me this day as in the First Good Friday, waits at the door, at the Gate that leads to the narrow road. Do not enter the wide road - the wide gate does not belong to Me! It is of the father of lies[64], the false prophets who will deceive you! Rise even though you have fallen, rise now and embrace My Mercy!

Your Consecration each morning is of vitality to you and of great importance to understand your path to Holiness, to carry your Cross and follow Me. Amen. I Am Jesus of Nazareth,

---

[62] The Souls Iveta was praying for.

[63] Mt 7,14

[64] John 8,44

Man-God suffering As God- Man for My Sheep, My Lambs, Amen. Amen." ...

*

Jesus speaks to the women:

"Women, do not weep for Me, weep for yourselves and for your children.[65]"

Now they look at Him as though they don't understand what He is saying.

Soul to Soul, Jesus speaks to me:

"Beloved daughter now suffering with Me as the Redeemer, and My Mother as *Co-Redemptrix*, make known to all My beloved children, My mothers, My sisters, that unless they repent of their own offences and embrace My Mercy, they cannot enter into the Kingdom of Heaven. Make straight daughters of Jerusalem, daughters of God, your paths! Repent of all that you have failed to do and … weep for your children that they may embrace My Mercy." …

*

Jesus speaks to me now Soul to Soul:

"Daughter, I Am aware of your weakness, but My Grace is sufficient. Carry it with Me through My Holy Mother. Countless Souls are redeemed this day[66], and many will return when they understand how much you suffered, that is, I in you

---

[65] Luke 23,28

[66] Iveta is undergoing heavy suffering. See Col 1,24

64

and My Mother in you and you in Us. It is Our suffering that you carry for love of your brethren.

Make known now, it is in like same manner many of you must carry others to protect them and so that they may be the *remnant* and you - My Priests, My faithful - will be the Sacrificial Lambs. Amen. Amen.

Jesus of Nazareth Man-God, God-Man. Amen. Amen."
(Good Friday, March 25th, 2016)

46. RENOUNCE THIS MANNER OF LIVING AND EMBRACE MY MERCY

Soul to Soul, Jesus speaks:

"Beloved Children of God, many of you have fallen into a state of immorality and live in impurity, defiling the Temple of God. Know that I have suffered[67] this for you and have embraced your shame. Renounce this manner of living and embrace My Mercy by coming to Confession to be reconciled to Me through My Priests. My Blessed Mother Who Co-Redeems will cover you with Her Immaculate Mantle and help you rise from your shame. There is no time to continue in this manner of living.

I love you and I suffer for you! Embrace My Mercy, which your Holy Father My Peter in union with My hidden Peter, Pope Francis and Emeritus Pope Benedict, as you know them, have declared this year as the year of Mercy. They understand

---

[67] The Agony of Our Lord Jesus

the importance of this moment, do not waste this return, beloved children of God. Return children, all of you of various faiths, embrace My Mercy and live in the order of sanctity, even now it's not too late! Amen, Amen."

-----*Jesus pauses*-----

Soul to Soul, He speaks again:

"My *Remnant*, My faithful, do not seek easy compromises with the World. I warn you, do not be enticed with the glamour and the easy living that the World parades before you. My adversary has convinced many of My children to embrace such living as a means of happiness! It is falsehood and false happiness! It won't be long before they are all thrown into the wayside! Pray for such Souls and do not look upon them as a model to follow, but may they see you as a model to embrace truth.

Jesus of Nazareth now embracing the engulfing moment of My Agony, True God, True Man. Amen, Amen." (*Good Friday, March 25th, 2016*)

47. THE LAST DOGMA

Jesus speaks Soul to Soul:

"My Peter this day, my hidden Peter too, Pope Francis and *Emeritus Pope* Benedict XVI as you have come to be known on Earth and in Heaven, take courage when you see the situation that you do not understand how to solve, I am with you through it all. I prepare you for the impending moments for the *underground Church* and the continuation of building My City known as the *City of God*.

I am Jesus of Nazareth, the High Priest Who appointed you as My Peter through My Spirit. My Blessed Mother continues to hold you, as She is here with me. She is ever so close to you!

I earnestly ask that the *last Dogma*, as it has come to be known, that She be proclaimed *Mediatrix of all Grace*, *Co-Redemptrix* and *Advocate* that She will be able to dispense the Graces to all My children to endure these moments with ease. Amen, Amen."

Jesus speaks Soul to Soul with His Mother:

"Mother ...Ah! Ah! I would have spared You this moment, but You must carry My *Remnant*. You must carry My Children into the desert[68] and prepare ... and walk with them to Me, You understand it all."

She nods and asks Him not to speak. "Let it be done unto Me according to Thy Will." *(Good Friday, March 25th, 2016)*

48. THIS IS THE ELEVENTH HOUR OF MERCY

Suddenly the thief on the right rebukes the thief on the left to be silent, saying to him, "We are deserving of this crime, this Man is innocent.[69]"

He looks at Our Lady and he draws his strength and then he looks at Jesus. This is Mercy as he understands it. "Jesus, remember me when You come into Your Kingdom."

Jesus smiles

---

[68] Rev 12,14
[69] Luke 23,41

"This day, you will be with Me in Paradise."

Agony ... and Jesus speaks Soul to Soul:

"Daughter, little one of Mine, make known My Mercy through My Holy Mother as *Co-Redemptrix*. Like the good thief, as he has come to be known, that many will embrace and return to be reconciled to Me and they will be with Me in Paradise one day soon. This is the eleventh hour of Mercy.[70] It is the only way to return. My Mother will help them as She has helped many, even you."

I love you Jesus, thank You, I thank Thee Master.

"Amen, Amen"

All evil is taking place all around and a great darkness befalls[71] ... Jesus' hour is at hand and He knows it.

"Mother!" *Soul to Soul He speaks.*

"I entrust all my Priests and all the faithful *Remnant* to You, take care of them, My hour is completing[72] but Yours has just begun."

She looks at Him and says:

"Let it be done unto Me according to Thy Will.[73] Here I am Your born slave. Amen, Amen, Amen." (*March 25th, 2016, Good Friday*)

---

[70] Mt 20, 1-16
[71] Mt 27,45
[72] John 17,1
[73] Luke 1,38

49. KNOW AND UNDERSTAND: WHEN DIVINE MERCY ENDS, THE FURY OF DIVINE JUSTICE WILL COME INTO BEING

"I Am who I Am, Eternal Father, known to you through My Beloved Son Jesus, Who pleases Me much[74] and Who reconciles you to Me. If you chose this path, I come with the Love of Heaven awaiting you that We may share in Eternal Glory.

Beloved children of Mine, know and understand I Am the Eternal Father, True God in the First Person, All Light, only revealing Myself."

Iveta beholds a Vision: And now Heaven opens... Ahhh! ... and all I see is the Bright Light and The Throne of God. Ahhh! ... Am I so worthy to see this? Ahhh! ...

"It is here I welcome you all My children. Go and bring the lost sheep![75] I call especially My chosen ones[76], beloved in the Vineyard[77] , to prepare all My children for these moments.

All present here, I thank you, I thank you with Fatherly Love and I desire with greatest desire that you pray for the fulfillment that This Daughter Who has pleased Me" *(He points now to The Blessed Mother through The Archangel Michael)* "be proclaimed *Mediatrix of all Grace, Co-Redemptrix* and *Advocate* for your sake, that She may dispense the Graces you are in need of for these moments.

Know and understand: When Divine Mercy ends[78], the fury of Divine Justice will come into being. Your prayers are of most importance to understand, to reconcile your brethren to Me.

---

[74] Mt 3,17

[75] Luke 15, 3-7

[76] The priests

[77] John 15

[78] Mt 25, 1-12 etc

69

I AM WHO I AM, Your Heavenly Father, made known to you by My Beloved Son Jesus. Amen." *(October 13th, 2016, Mt Batim, Goa, India)*

50. THE CONSECRATION TO MY IMMACULATE HEART: IT IS SIMPLE CHILDREN, SIMPLE!

Our Lady speaks:

My beloved children, I have come down once again this day to be with you and I desire with great desire to stay with you as you Consecrate yourselves, each one of you into My Immaculate Heart. There are many here who do not understand the Consecration to My Immaculate Heart: It is simple children, simple! Simply give Me your heart and tell Me to do all that God desires in you for which you were created, exchanging your will for the Divine Will and I will conform you in the Order and Grace of God and lead you to Holiness in which each one of you is called to be. *(October 14th, 2016, Mt Batim, Goa, India)*

51. ONLY PRAYER CAN EFFACE THIS TERRIBLE DISASTER

"Beloved children, children of God, I Who Am Jesus of Nazareth, Who laid down My Life for each one of you present here and to all those who will hear these Words and heed them, those who will embrace the Cross:

Now understand you are entering heavily moments of great sorrow, sorrow because man continues to offend their God, I Am He.

You are at the threshold of World War three, only prayer can efface this terrible disaster, for good and bad will perish in it.

To My beloved chosen sons, My Priests: I Am Beloved of The Father and you are beloved of Him through Me. If you only understand the Power that I have entrusted unto you, fear not, be bold, go out there and conquer Souls and your reward awaits you in Heaven!

The Great Apostasy now will come into being, the One World Government will come into being, fear not! My Mother, My Holy and Blessed Mother will take care of each one of you if you trust and entrust yourselves to Her Immaculate Heart and cover yourselves each day with Her Immaculate Mantle. Many of you will face *Martyrdom*, this must be the Blood that must be spilt to purify My Church, My Bride!

My Brides, the Nuns known as, I love you, stay obedient and know that I am with you, and lead all the little children to Me when they come to you. I am Jesus of Nazareth, the second Person of the Triune God, the Holy Trinity, here making My Word known to you and soon you will receive Me under the appearance of Bread and Wine, My True Flesh and True Blood, given to you to fortify you for these moments!

Now I desire to make known My desire: That you pray and petition your Holy Father, My beloved chosen son Peter, My Peter the Rock on which The Church today stands[79], His Holiness Pope Francis I in union with *Emeritus Pope* Benedict XVI, the hidden Pope, to proclaim My Blessed Mother as *Mediatrix of All Grace, Co-Redemptrix* and *Advocate*. It is then that Heaven will open and dispense the Graces necessary for all God's children to fortify you in these moments. I am Jesus of Nazareth The High Priest, True God and True Man. I love you all My brethren. Amen. Amen." *(October 14th, 2016, Mt Batim, Goa, India)*

---

[79] Mt 16,18

52. THE HOLY SPIRIT: YOU WILL FIND HIM NOWHERE EXCEPT IN SILENCE

Our Lady speaks:

"Beloved children now I desire to make known the message of God, the Holy Spirit, My Spouse. You will find Him nowhere except in silence. He is The Author of The Fountain of Grace and Love of God. You will receive Him through the Consecrated hands of My beloved chosen sons, My Priests, many of whom today are present here. They are healing instruments for your infirmities.

Understand through reconciliation begins the first healing, and then the anointing of their Holy Hands Consecrated to make Jesus present here, that you may be fortified with this Grace.

The Holy Spirit is the Author of these times, He will make all things known to you plainly. Know and understand He only desires your silence, there He will impart every knowledge, every wisdom and understanding that you desire and there you will understand good and evil.

Now beloved children prepare to receive the Holy Spirit, as I Bless another Image, a 'Medal' that has been entrusted to My beloved chosen son Reverend Father Conceição, Conceição in My Name, Immaculate Conception. I love him dearly and now I Bless The 'Medal'.

"IN NOMINE PATER ET FILIUS

ET SPIRITUS SANCTUS. AMEN."

This 'Medal' now will go throughout the World through him for Veneration. Amen." *(October 15th, 2016, Mt Batim, Goa, India)*

72

53. YOUR HOLY FATHER WILL ALWAYS BE WITH YOU, EVEN IN THE UNDERGROUND MOMENTS

Our Lady speaks:

"I desire with great desire that you pray for your Holy Father, My beloved chosen son, The Bishop of Rome, His Holiness Pope Francis I, also *Emeritus Pope* Benedict XVI, the hidden Pope. Much prayer is required, the enemy is rising but he will not be able to conquer till the hour of God is to be. By that the understanding is that your Holy Father will always be with you even in the underground moments of Holy Mother, the Catholic Church, this is all you need to know.

Be not afraid, be not anxious! Only entrust all into My Immaculate Heart and pray, pray, pray beloved children the Holy Rosary in your families! Come together in your communities. Come together on this Holy Mountain, for through it much can be bought and Satan will be kept afar!

Beloved children, know and understand now, you are entering a great heavy moment upon Earth. The fury of God is kindled, yet through your prayers I can buy this moment for more time for conversion of many of My children that are astray. It is upon you I lay this yoke to pray for all your brothers and sisters. Do not give up! There is hope always in God. I Love you dearly.

I am the *Mother Of God*, The *Mediatrix Of All Grace*, *Co-Redemptrix* and *Advocate* in Heaven, The *Immaculate Conception*, by Whose power I will crush Satan. Amen."
(October 15th, 2016, Mt Batim, Goa, India)

YR 2017: I COME TO INVITE YOU TO CO-REDEEM WITH ME, I WHO AM THE CO-REDEMPTRIX, UNITED TO "JESUS" THE REDEEMER

54. SOCIALISM HAS BECOME THE WAY OF LIFE

Our Lady speaks:

"Beloved daughter, little one of Mine and My Jesus, I desire with great desire this 1st Friday in Lent of the year two thousand and seventeen, the day being, and beginning second of the third month of the year two thousand and seventeen, the hour 11:00p.m., to end on the third day of the third month of the year two thousand and seventeen-11: 00p.m, that you suffer for the unborn and for the terrible holocaust of children being sacrificed[80].

For socialism[81] has become the way of life and this is leading to the terrible destruction of families and the Domestic Church by the evil one, Satan himself! Be on guard! Warn My children, beloved to Me, their Heavenly Mother, weeping for them!

Will you help Me little one Cleophas?" *(Ash Wednesday, March 1st, 2017)*

*

Our Blessed Mother speaks:

"My beloved daughter, little one of Mine and My Jesus, Cleophas. Once again, I come to invite You to co-redeem with Me. I who Am the *Co-Redemptrix*, united to Jesus the *Redeemer*.

This that I invite you to suffer as a Victim Soul is for the Universal Church for your reigning Peter, My beloved chosen

---

[80] Abortion

[81] Socialism may be understood here as an ideology that is willing to bring justice and happiness without God's grace.

son, the Bishop of Rome, His holiness Pope Francis I, in also the understanding for *Pope Emeritus* Benedict XVI, the hidden Pope, for the offences committed by the clergy and religious against the holy Virtue of Purity, against the new doctrine to change the Holy Virtue and Truths of the teachings of The Bride of Christ, the Catholic Church, made know to her and through her to all her children by Jesus Christ, through His Holy Spirit.

This you shall suffer from the hour of Divine Mercy on the 16th day of the third month of the year two thousand and seventeen to the hour of 12:00 a.m. of the eighteen day of the third month of the year two thousand and seventeen.

Know and understand this shall be the manner of suffering for this purpose and reparation of the offences committed by Priests and Religious Nuns of disobedience. And a great weight of anxiety has befallen upon your Holy Father today Pope Francis I, His Holiness, also anxious moments upon the hidden Pope. This is how My adversary is inflicting them.

This manner shall be for the following week and the one to follow that. Will you help Me?" *(Ash Wednesday, March 1ˢᵗ, 2017)*

55. TO ABORT A CHILD IS A TERRIBLE CRIME AGAINST THE AUTHOR OF LIFE

To abort a child is a terrible crime against the Author of Life. It is an insult to God that creature would murder creature, especially the mother would murder her own child out of fear of man and lack of Love for God. Even such God forgives if they would repent, yet the ransom must be made paid. God will desire an account from them. No one escapes the judgement of God.

Holy Mama, how much She suffers and now she speaks:

"As *Co-Redemptrix*, redeeming so many Souls that are lost in the terrible pursuit of Socialism to please mortals out of fear of man and to commit such an offence, lost in the desires of the gratification of the flesh, this crime is so terrible, terrible and increasing every day! If you only knew what sorrow has befallen upon mankind because of this sin and the wrath of God is kindled![82] It only awaits my resignation in the understanding that I no longer Myself can bear the suffering[83] of the cry of the innocent child, all now in My Body making up for this suffering to obtain from God the time so that Souls may repent. Not much longer can I endure this Myself and allow this sin to manifest itself to this degree.

Pray children pray, pray many Rosaries against this sin that continues in the highest degree to offend God, the Author of Life. Satan is snatching them and yet through this suffering of this little one of Mine, and very few other Souls that respond to my call to be victims Co-Redeeming with Me, I am able to ransom some of them, yet many are falling into the fire of Hell, for prayer is lacking! Yes, yes My beloved children, lacking!

I desire to thank all those who pray. Know you are of great importance and your prayer rises to calm God's wrath and bring down His Mercy even upon such creatures. I am able to open the hearts of many mothers who now repent for what they have already committed and today many will cease committing such a crime and let God be the Author and the Father of these children, who truly Is." *(Friday after Ash Wednesday, March 3rd, 2017)*

---

[82] Rom 2,5

[83] Rev 12,1

56. THE ANOINTING OF THE ANGEL ON THE FOREHEAD OF THE ELECT

Holy Mother speaks:

"These are those spoken of in scripture as the children of darkness.[84] I will make known to you, fear not, I am with you! To all those who have consecrated themselves to My Immaculate Heart and to the Sacred Heart of Jesus My Divine Son, We will come and make Our dwelling in you and help you against these forces.

The time is coming for the anointing of the Angel that will bestow the cross on the forehead of the Elect.[85] Stay faithful and fear not even if you have … to suffer death, your Crown awaits you in Heaven.

I Am the *Mother of God*, Your Heavenly Mother, suffering with you, Co-Redeeming with Jesus the Redeemer, My Divine Son Amen." *(Friday after Ash Wednesday, March 3rd, 2017)*

57. POPE FRANCIS' HEART IS ROOTED IN THE DIVINE SAVIOUR

Our Lady speaks:

"My beloved daughter, little one of Mine and My Jesus, Cleophas now co-redeeming with Me, the *Co-Redemptrix* united to Jesus My divine Son Jesus, the *Redeemer*, suffering for your Holy Father.

---

[84] Eph 5,8 and 1 Thes 5,5
[85] Rev 7,3 and Ezekiel 9, 4-6

It is with great desire I desire that you make known much prayer is needed for the Holy Father, My beloved son His Holiness the Bishop of Rome Pope Francis I in union with *Emeritus Pope* Benedict XVI the hidden Pope. The suffering this day will grant him the Grace of Fortitude against the assaults by the faithful who call themselves 'faithful' yet are disobedient to his Magisterium. He is a simple Pope. His heart is rooted in the Divine Saviour his Master, Jesus the *Redeemer* as a Merciful Saviour. He comes before you all, my beloved children in this manner, to prepare you before Divine Justice befalls you.

How much he loves you even to the point of death. If you only understand and accept that God's ways are not your ways! Be open to receiving his message of Love and Mercy as he prepares the flock for the terrible persecution that is going to befall all mankind!

I love you dearly, pray, pray, pray beloved children! Pray the Holy Rosary as often as you can and do not neglect this prayer of much importance now. I Am the *Mother of God*, Your Heavenly Mother who loves you dearly, the *Mediatrix of all Grace, Co-Redemptrix* now Redeeming with this little one of Mine and My Jesus for your world. Amen." *(First Thursday and Friday of Lent, March 9-10th, 2017)*

58. MY ADVERSARY HAS ENTERED THE CONVENTS

Jesus speaks:

"My Church, what has become of you? My Brides, you who are known as Nuns, who are faithful to Me in your virtue of obedience to this vocation which I have called you to, and your obedience to the virtue of purity as My Brides, your Virginal Purity!

Pray My beloved Brides and know that I love you. Pray for those who have abandoned Me and are seeking to be like what Mary of Magdala was.

They have subjected themselves even to greater crimes. They desire to practise abomination with one another, reducing themselves to such slavery to My adversary who has entered the convents where you dwell.

My Brides remain faithful to Me even though you see those who are causing havoc. Pray for them, do not be silent! Report such to your Spiritual Fathers and to the Bishop of that Diocese in which each one of you are. This crime must be exposed for they are leading many who come for consolation and counselling to such, and soon it will be a widespread epidemic among you, of this abomination, and you will be driven away by those who have supported you! And you who have abused Me in this manner, know that I still love you, yet this abomination will cost you.[86]

You have chained yourselves like you have chained Me now[87] and have given the end of the chain to My adversary! Yet My Holy and Blessed Mother through this little Soul prays for you that Your Soul will be saved.

Your bodies will be torn like those in the theatre, the amphitheatre where you were thrown to wild beasts in the past days. Now you are those, yet if you renounce this manner of abomination and claim Me as your God, I will rescue your Souls with the price of My Blood.

I Am Jesus of Nazareth who loves you, agonising for you in union with My Blessed Mother Co-Redeeming with me,

---

[86] Mt 18, 6-9

[87] Jesus is living His passion.

the *Redeemer*, She the *Co-Redemptrix* and this little one co-redeeming with Her for your Souls.

I love you! I love you My Brides. Amen. Amen." (*Third Friday of Lent, March 24th, 2017*)

59. CO-REDEMPTRIX AND ADVOCATE

"Divine Wisdom is greater than all the philosophers of this World. In this manner we must understand the role of Our Blessed Mother as *Mediatrix of all Grace, Co-Redemptrix* and *Advocate*.

Now We see Her when the Angel Gabriel came and announced to Her that She was to be Mother of God. It is only then, and before that She had no knowledge of what She was or what She was to be!

This *Eastern Gate*[88] was styled by God with All Grace to begin the Role of *Mediatrix of all Grace*. It is through Her, the Word of God that existed in the beginning[89] who debased Himself, entered and was conceived in Her Womb[90]. She now feeds Him all Grace to prepare Him for the Role of *Redeemer*, the Saviour of Mankind! In her Womb, the Saviour, the *Redeemer* God, willed to be for nine months. There She became now *Co-Redemptrix* beginning the Suffering Role and preparing the Divine Saviour with Love and Fortitude to go forth.

Then we see at the foot of the Cross as She becomes Our Mother. Jesus entrusts Her to Saint John, known as the

---

[88] Our Blessed Mother is the "Eastern Gate" through which the Word of God comes to us. See Ezekiel 43,4 and 47,2
[89] John 1, 1-2
[90] Luke 1, 31-42

Evangelist at the foot of the Cross[91], to take Her as the Mother, thereby making Her the Mother of all humanity! Here we understand the role of Her as an *Advocate* before Him.

Now at the Mountain of Ascension[92] where She stands and Jesus ascends to the Father, as the Father receives Him and bestows upon Him what was His from the beginning[93], taking His place now as King of Eternal Glory and Divine Judge[94]: Here now we see Her as the *Advocate* of all of us God's children who will intercede before the Divine Judge, a Solemn Role She plays and will play in the days ahead. Amen." ... *(Fourth Thursday of Lent, March 30th, 2017)*

60. SUCH A STENCH OF IMPURITY IS RISING DAILY!

Our Lady speaks.

"My beloved children see how much God loves you! Through this little one is God's Mercy revealed to you once again. How your Heavenly Mother is suffering, suffering for you with all My Love, to return to God!

Do not let these deceivers allow you to abandon your Heavenly inheritance[95]. Yes, this sin you have committed and to those who ponder on committing, I plead with you with a Motherly Heart to not believe these deceivers and promptings of Satan to commit this act of killing the innocent in your wombs. Do not give consent to such an

---

[91] John 19, 25-27
[92] Luke 24, 50-51 and Acts 1, 9-11
[93] John 17, 5
[94] Mt 25, 31
[95] Mt 5,12 and Mark 10,21

abomination and to paganism and yet, if you have done so, plead Mercy and return to the order of truth by confessing and repenting! And yes, My beloved children, you who have committed this crime will have to carry this cross all the days of your lives and yet I will help you carry it! I will carry it with you, such is this offence!

Know that for the cries of these children, the cries of the innocent, the wrath of God is kindled ... for such a stench of impurity that is rising daily!

Know and understand My beloved children and to all My faithful who pray for this terrible offence of this sin of impurity: The stench of such a crime both among the faithful and unfaithful, the faithful out of fear of men and the unfaithful because their conscience has become so dull that they do not understand what they are doing. As for the pagans who follow pagan gods, it has become a way of life!

O! how I cry to you to turn from such an offence against God the Creator. Here this little one is co-redeeming with Me, the *Co-Redemptrix* to the *Redeemer*, united, offering Ourselves to the *Redeemer*, before God Our Father Who loves you so much! Know this love by repenting!

This crime is extending among even the Religious and some of My beloved chosen sons have fallen into infidelity before God committing the sins of the flesh and giving into such an offence before God!

Repent children! Repent! Repent before it is too late![96] I Am Your Heavenly Mother who Loves you dearly, *Mediatrix of all Grace*, bestowed upon Me by My Divine Son the *Redeemer*, Grace and Truth itself, *Co-Redemptrix* united to the *Redeemer*,

---

[96] Mt 25, 1-13, etc

Advocate before the Advocate, and before God the Father, *Advocate* before God the Father, the Divine Judge. I Am your *Advocate* before the Judge Jesus, the Divine and Supreme Judge, who Judges on repentance of the heart!

I love you dearly, suffering and pleading for you, awaiting the moment to be proclaimed on Earth by your Holy Father today, Pope Francis I, and suffering greatly to restore you back to God in union with the hidden Pope, My beloved Chosen Son Emeritus Pope Benedict XVI. Amen." *(Fifth Friday of Lent, April 7ᵗʰ, 2017)*

61. IT IS CHILDREN THAT MY ADVERSARY IS SEEKING TO DESTROY, THE FUTURE OF YOUR WORLD

"Beloved children of God, I am God in the third Person of the Holy Trinity, known to you as The Holy Spirit. I am the Spouse of the *Immaculate Conception*. My Beloved Spouse mourns, Her Immaculate Heart is torn with grief for so many of Her children have abandoned Her and have contrived insults and mockery against Her and the thorns of ingratitude are pierced around Her Immaculate Heart!

It is the desire of God that you foster deeply to ransom these Souls back, which more and more are increasing in number!

Make known the devotion made known to you by The Second Person of the Holy Trinity known as The *Five First Saturdays* for reparation against the sins committed against the Immaculate Heart of Mary, the Mother of God. This devotion will bring the Fruit if you obey it, as it has been made known. The ransoming of so many children, lost in sin, children of the faithful - Catholic children - will also bring conversion of the non-Catholic, if you pray for them. It is of great importance today in your World where sin is devastating the family life and plunging into darkness more and more children. The Immaculate Heart of My Spouse bears the thorns of The Crown that was placed upon the Head of The Second Person of the Holy Trinity[97], Jesus True God, True Man, the *Redeemer* and She as *Co-Redemptrix* is enduring this suffering! Her pain is like a woman in labor,[98] but in silence and through Victim Souls known to you, as this little one is enduring with Her to make reparation for the suffering of The Immaculate Heart of Mary, the *Mother of God.*"

What pain!...

"This pain is the pain of a loving Mother Who weeps in silence for Her children! Some of whom, because of lack of prayer are no more, like the weeping of Rachel,[99] known to you before the birth and suffering of Jesus, True God and True Man: Now the *New Eve*[100] now weeps for Her children in union with your prayers of the *'First Five Saturdays'* which are of Great importance for your World.

Increase Adoration before Jesus! It will console the Immaculate Heart[101] in union with the Sacred Heart of Jesus and Souls will be brought back, especially that of children. It is children that My adversary is seeking to destroy, who are the future of your World. Amen, Amen, Amen." *(Wednesday of the Holy Week, April 12ᵗʰ, 2017)*

---

[97] John 19,2
[98] Rev 12,1 and John 16,21
[99] Biblical figure of the suffering of Our Lady
[100] Rom 5,12-15 and Irenaeus of Lyon Teachings
[101] Of Our Lady

62. THE FIRST FIVE SATURDAYS ON THE HOLY MOUNTAIN OF MOUNT BATIM

Our Lady speaks:

"Make known to My beloved chosen son, the Bishop of your Ancestral Land, His Grace Filipe Neri Ferrao. I thank him immensely through the pains of my Immaculate Heart in enduring this day for your World. He has brought me consolation by desiring and making known his desire to please Me, by Consecrating Goa to My Immaculate Heart as was the desire of My Immaculate Heart made known and spreading it to those he welcomes in union with him to make known their desire united to His: To Consecrate all over in the land of India, the Bishops and Priests, the laity in union with the Religious who will join on the day that marks what has come to be known as the Centenary of My Visitation in Fatima. It is a day of rejoicing; even I, who am the *Immaculate Conception* bearing these Thorns in My Immaculate Heart of ingratitude and insults and blasphemies that are against My Immaculate Conception, will rejoice in receiving this consolation! For God desires this!

Also make known to him little one of Mine and My Jesus Cleophas, to bring into being the devotion of the First Five Saturdays, as it has come to be known, on the Holy Mountain of Mount Batim Ganxim, My Visitation site, where I wait for My children each day to visit Me and through Me they will come to a deeper Love of My Divine Son Jesus, Who waits for them in the Holy Eucharist. I love him dearly and I thank him immensely and through him I thank all My beloved children, My chosen sons and My chosen daughters and all My beloved children who will join in the celebration for Consecrating their Diocese and themselves to My Immaculate Heart....

I Am the *Mother of God*, I Am the *Immaculate Conception*, Whose Immaculate Heart grieves for My children and is being pierced with the Crown of Thorns, the same Crown borne on the Sacred Head of My Divine Son Jesus , as *Co-Redemptrix*, Redeeming with the *Redeemer*, the *Mediatrix of all Grace* and *Advocate*, awaiting that moment to be proclaimed on Earth as I Am in Heaven. Amen." *(Holy Thursday, April 13th, 2017)*

63. TO CALM THE WRATH OF GOD WHICH IS KINDLED AGAINST YOUR WORLD

"My beloved children I speak through this exhausted little one of Mine, who is enduring the suffering of My Immaculate Heart in reparation for the countless Souls, to ransom them back to God through Me.

I desire with great desire to make known of the grave offences by My chosen sons and chosen daughters who have join the ranks, grieving My Immaculate Heart, of disobedience and offences against the Magisterium, against the Holy Father, your Holy Father today Pope Francis I who suffers so much! Pray for your Holy Father, I petition you My beloved children, My faithful, to pray for Him; to also pray for your hidden Pope Benedict XVI, who also suffers greatly for such insults. Your prayers and every bit of suffering and fasting is greatly desired by me as reparation against these insults and to calm the wrath of God which is kindled against your World. Pray, pray, pray many Rosaries! Offer many Holy Hours and raise many Holy Sacrifices!

I love you dearly, I Am your Heavenly Mother, the *Mother of God*, the *Mediatrix of all Grace, Co-Redemptrix* and *Advocate* in Heaven. I await your prayers on Earth and to be proclaimed that I may dispense these Graces upon you My beloved children to endure the wrath of God when it breaks forth. Amen." *(Holy Thursday, April 13th, 2017)*

64. RETURN TO ME BY YOUR CONSECRATION EACH MORNING TO MY IMMACULATE HEART

Our Lady speaks:

"My beloved children, do you yet not understand how God the Father willed it that My Immaculate heart would be the portal of Divine Mercy and the road that leads to Truth and Grace?

And to you My beloved chosen sons, My Priests and my beloved chosen daughters and Nuns, do you not realise We have very, very, very little daylight time! If you think your world now is in a chaos, you have not yet understood a greater chaos is moving in like a high wave to disrupt the faithful.

Foster devotion to My Immaculate Heart! It is of great importance! My Motherly Heart longs to gather My children who are estranged from Me and do not yet understand the way. Yes, there are other ways that lead to the Mercy of God but it is through strange ways and strange depths by which you will reach this and through many struggles, yet the way to go through My Immaculate Heart is easy. I have suffered for you and will suffer for you this night once again.

Many of you seek other ways and you cut the umbilical cord of My Motherly Grace! To you My beloved children, return to Me by your Consecration each morning to My Immaculate Heart. God has chosen this part for you, seek no other! I will lead you safely to Jesus Our Saviour, My Divine Son, Our *Redeemer* of Whom I Am *Co-Redemptrix* and He the *Advocate* before God Our Father, and I your *Advocate* before Him, the Divine Judge.

Understand this manner and you will be in peace though there will be a great turmoil around you. I have much to say through this little one of Mine.

Now beloved children examine your conscience and see where I Am in you. How then will you lead your non-Catholic brothers and sisters who are lost to this truth, the way, the only way! They must first see it in you. I am here awaiting your yes!

I love you dearly. I Am the Mother of God, your Heavenly Mother, the *Mediatrix of all Grace, Co-Redemptrix* and *Advocate* in Heaven, awaiting your prayers to bring it to fulfilment on Earth. I love you dearly, return to me! Amen." *(Holy Thursday, April 13th, 2017)*

65. YOU WILL REVEAL A GREAT UNDERSTANDING OF THE SUFFERING NECESSARY TO REDEEM SOULS LOST IN SIN

"Beloved daughter Cleophas, little one of Mine and My Jesus, it is your Heavenly Mother greatly pleased with you, now desiring your complete and total surrender. Your spiritual Fathers are praying for this too. Total surrender! Worry not about the things around you! Be not anxious!

Today you will begin after you return from the Holy Sacrifice in *remembrance of* that First Holy Sacrifice. You will co-redeem with me the *Co-Redemptrix* and I, the *Co-Redemptrix* with the *Redeemer*, My Divine Son Jesus. You will understand how valuable this moment is, and through you, you will reveal a great understanding of the suffering necessary to redeem Souls lost in sin and the conversion needed to bring those who have yet not the understanding of the True God Jesus, True God and True Man! Now you will walk with the Man-God, through Me the *Co-Redemptrix*, Who is the *Redeemer* and you will co-redeem with Me to understand the value of suffering. Will you help Me?"

Iveta: Yes, Holy Mother, I have anxious moments, and I busy myself with talk and noise because I'm afraid of this anxiousness. Yes, I'm ready, will you help me help, You?

Our Lady speaks:

"Beloved daughter rejoice! You are carrying a Cross and for that you were made. I Am here with you. You are not alone. Do you not understand, your love is so great to comfort My Immaculate Heart sorrowing for your World, for so many of your brothers and sisters are lost! You yourself see so many, and today you can help them by helping Me!

I love you and I accept your 'yes'. Now my beloved of the Beloved, Felix Xavier, will you also give your consent, your 'yes' to Me, to help Me by helping this little one undergo this suffering? "

Felix Xavier: Yes, Holy Mama

Holy Mama speaks:

"I welcome you into the Abode of My Immaculate Heart to also feel My Sorrow. How you Comfort My Immaculate Heart! If you only understand that this is the devotion most needed in your world. I thank you, Amen." *(April 13th, 2017)*

66. SATAN IS GOING TO MAKE AND WAGE WAR AGAINST ME, THAT IS MY CHILDREN

Our Lady speaks:

"Do you understand daughter, this what is forthcoming, this is what lies ahead in the days that will mark the increase of the birth pangs of persecution: They are close at hand to you, be not afraid; entrust all to My Immaculate Heart and take refuge into My Immaculate Heart! It is that hour that is about to befall where Satan is going to make and wage war against Me, that is My children, that is you - known also as the Church Militant. Some of you will march forth and will go to Martyrdom and some of you will lie in anguish as you make your way into My Refuge. Stay close to Me always! Here you are co-redeeming now, little one of mine and My Jesus, Cleophas, to understand this moment. Amen."

Now Holy Mama speaks:

"Be open and silent to the Voice of the Holy Spirit, My Spouse. He will make known where you are to stay and wait. Follow every direction and instruction as He leads you. It is no time to doubt! To those who will doubt, they will fall into the hands of My adversary and will die as Martyrs. At that moment it is an offering in co-redeeming with Me, the *Co-Redemptrix* in union with the *Redeemer*, Our Saviour!" ...

Now Holy Mama says

"See daughter" ... *She shows me how the soldiers are arresting those who follow Christianity, Catholics! They are asking them to denounce their Faith in Jesus. There are many that will do so out of fear!*

Our Lady Speaks:

"It is your suffering My daughter, My beloved one, now co-redeeming for them to take courage and not to denounce their Faith."

Iveta: I'm heavy, I'm so heavy. Holy Mama is holding Her Mantle around me and She is praying, while everybody else has fallen asleep. I look at Her and She smiles. She knows about this weight, that I also am about to sleep.

Holy Mother speaks:

"Daughter, keep awake with Me, pray daughter with Me."

*

"Are you still sleeping? Take your rest, My betrayer is close at hand."

.... *Then He withdraws and goes back to pray.*

Peter is not sure if he can handle this. The Lord is going to leave him in charge. He is almost in despair within himself. Did the Lord really mean I am to take care of His sheep, His lambs? "Look at me Lord", he's saying, "I'm a wretched sinner, I'm so weak", and the Lord hears him and speaks to his Soul.

"Take courage Peter, My strength in you is sufficient and it will not betray your role; you will do what I have asked of you. Take courage, this night I Am suffering for you and for those who will come after you in the line of succession till the last Peter before the desecration sacrilegious[102] who will sit on this throne of yours."

Peter is listening but he is confused. "What's wrong Lord, I'm sitting under a tree and in anguish and You talk about a throne."

The Lord speaks:

"You do not understand it now, but you will understand in a little while. Now pray, pray for the flesh is weak but the spirit is strong in you.[103]"

"Now do you see daughter,"

---

[102] Mark 13,14
[103] Mt 26,41

Our Holy mother speaks:

"This is the anguish, and now the suffering you are co-redeeming with Me for your Holy Father ....

Iveta: ... but I am so weak, how can I help? (Holy Thursday, April 13ᵗʰ, 2017)

67. ONLY A FEW PRIESTS AND NUNS WILL BE SPARED

"Are you still sleeping Peter? Get up, it is time! The Son of Man has been betrayed[104] into the hands of sinners. My betrayer is close, he is upon Us, can you hear?"

Iveta: ... What horrible sounds, they make sounds as though to drive away creatures ... what sounds ... clanging of feet, banging of swords, marching, mocking of the elders and the Pharisees and the others who come with them. They are carrying clubs, like the policeman in India do and the soldiers have swords and they come. Judas marches in front smiling away; he thinks he's doing a wonderful deed. He tells them now: "The one that I kiss[105] is the one you are seeking but be gentle with Him." ... and they just look at him with such a mocking look. The word gentle is not in their hearts, and he comes running. Peter, James and John are standing, they can hear everything, and they don't know whether they should run or stay within their hearts, but they take courage and they stay. It is the prayers of Our Holy Mother now strengthening them as it will strengthen us ... and Judas comes, and Judas Iscariot kisses The Lord on His cheek and the Lord says: "Friend[106] why has thou done

---

[104] Mark 13,14

[105] Mt 6,48

[106] Mt 26,50

93

this? You know it would have been better for you never to have been born[107] than to betray the Son of Man."

... and before you know it they have grabbed the Hands of the Lord and they chain Him, tying both His Hands behind His back.

Now Holy Mama speaks:

"Beloved daughter, what you see is how many of My Priests, My chosen sons beloved and dear to Me will be led away. Peter, James and John, some will be spared for a while and like John, some will be spared to go into the Refuge for the preservation of the Catholic Church, and many will die like Peter and James the death of a Martyr!"

Iveta: ... crying ... Holy Mama!

Holy Mama speaks:

"Take courage daughter, take courage!"

Holy Mama weeps ... Iveta is sobbing as Our Holy Mama sees Her Son being led away.

This is Soul to Soul, Mind to Mind, Heart to Heart of the vision of what Jesus and Our Holy Mama is going through. Now She says to me:

"Do you understand, you are Co-Redeeming with Me for the many that will die and be led in this manner. You are co-redeeming for many brothers and sisters who will betray each other, as it is written. Father against son, son against father, mother against daughter, daughter against

---

[107] Mt 6,24

94

mother-in-law, brother against brother[108]. They will put each other to death and think they are doing good. Amen.

Now daughter, Jesus will be led away as you have known in the past of what will take place. Now at this time you are co-redeeming in the suffering of silence, as they will place Him in that terrible prison cell, in the cellar with a terrible stench. Now many will plead and seek a place like that just to take a refuge from their plight.

Know and understand now: The fury of My adversary is kindled against My children, against My church! As My last visitation in Fatima[109] marks the closing of the hundredth year known as Centenary, you will understand what will unfold, all is in place!

To those who pay no heed, they will perish like the rest; the good and the bad!

I love you little one of Mine, now you will suffer in silent anguish and We will pray for all the chosen Sons and the Nuns who suffer now as only a few will be spared, as is the preordained Plan of God! Amen."

Iveta: Will I die this night. My body, my heart is suffering gravely! I am suffering, breathing…

Our Blessed Mama speaks:

"Yes daughter, you are suffering but you will not die, it is not time yet for you. Now let us now pray …"

Iveta[110]: … give me some Holy Water (April 13th, 2017, Holy Thursday)

---

[108] Luke 12,53

[109] October 13th, 2017

[110] To her husband Felix

68. THERE IS HOPE, EVEN FOR SUCH!

Holy Mama speaks:

"Do you see now you are Co-Redeeming with Me and united to the Redeemer?

Beloved daughter this is the stench of the sins of the flesh and the destruction of every human family who have embraced this form of life. Do you see the darkness in this cell! This is the darkness of the conscience! Today, with this suffering of yours, united to Mine and Our Divine Saviour, I as *Co-Redemptrix* to the Saviour, the *Redeemer*, and you as a little vessel co-redeeming will open so many hearts! You will break the darkness of these hearts! Their repentance will come, but the unit of the family will be broken apart!

Also know daughter that this co-redemptive suffering will envelope the families who are Consecrated to My Immaculate Heart to bring them protection they are in need of, against the world that condones such a lifestyle! Even the animals live a better form of life! There is no respect among creatures in family units; they curse each other, and they speak such foul words as though it is a talk that is normal. Only prayers can bring these Souls into repentance, for prayer will break the darkness of the conscience!

The prayer most efficacious is the Holy Rosary! It will dismantle the darkness of the mind and the heart, restoring the conscience back. These creatures that go about living this kind of a lifestyle, many are the faithful, have joined the pagans!

Know and understand they will be the ones, if you do not pray, who will march against you the faithful, to destroy you because you appear to them as a threat! Amen."

Our Blessed Mother speaks:

"My beloved children I speak to you to abandon this form of lifestyle. It will bring you no joy and no peace even though now you think you are in state of happiness - which only gives the lease to Satan, My adversary. In due time he will abandon you and leave you desolate, and your faith will be suicidal, for these sins only lead to a belief of 'no God' and that there is no life left, which is not true!

I plead with a Motherly Love to return! Here with Me today is your little sister Cleophas, co-redeeming, throwing up blood that you may return! All this because there is hope, there is hope even for such, for Our Jesus is suffering so much like He did in that first Good Friday! He continues suffering in your world to bring you back! Although He suffered once, if you repent, His mercy is for you!

I Am here as *Co-Redemptrix* interceding to help you! I await with tears, tears for your 'Yes' and 'help me Holy Mother' - that's all I wait to hear, and I will help you! I Am a Mother Who loves you! I do not look upon your wretchedness. I will clothe you with My Garment, My Immaculate Garment and help you return! Amen."

"See daughter, how important it is to pray. Many have abandoned prayer! Pray is so important! When you pray the Rosary, I am able to open the clogged arteries of the Soul. The Soul is the invisible heart of man. Without the Soul, the heart cannot function. Prayer is like brand-new blood. The Blood of Me, the *Immaculate Conception*, runs through their veins, their arteries and the Blood, the Precious Blood of Our Saviour, renews the Soul as a refreshment! Amen." (*Holy Thursday, April 13th, 2017*)

69. IT IS NECESSARY FOR ALL MY CHILDREN TO OFFER UP THEIR SUFFERING TO CO-REDEEM EACH DAY

Holy Mama speaks:

"Yes, daughter every little sacrifice, every little suffering is a great consolation to the Master, the *Redeemer*! Know now and understand, you are part of the Master's Body, just as I Am a big part of His Body. He is the Head and yet We are all part of His Body, so it is necessary for all My children to offer up their suffering to co-redeem each day of their lives, for such is the hour now! This is the prayer I taught the little children, the little Shepherd children in Fatima. You all must recite it too:

'O My Jesus I love thee, and I offer this suffering for the conversion of sinners and for all the offences and insults committed against the Immaculate Heart of Mary. Amen.'

Pray this prayer beloved children when you offer up your suffering to Jesus and to console My Immaculate Heart. This prayer will shower graces to bring conversion. And to you My beloved daughter, kiss the 'Medal.' Now I intercede as *Co-Redemptrix* to shower Grace for conversion before time. Do you understand now in union with this prayer, kiss the 'Medal.' I have made known through you its promises to all My beloved children who will wear it with fidelity. Amen."

*

Now Jesus speaks to My Soul:

"Little one of Mine and My Blessed Mother, Cleophas, you are co-redeeming this day through the *Co-Redemptrix*, I the *Redeemer*, do you understand? It is in this way the persecution that has begun all over will increase and escalate alarmingly! It is coming close, even in the country you live in. Many will be crucified unjustly! Make no defence[111], the Spirit of Mine and My Father's in Me will come and reside in each one of My children and speak through them. It is in this way they will co-redeem to save those who are the elect chosen for the times of *'the Underground Church'*, both Priests and Nuns, My Brides and My Faithful. Many of you must pay the price!

Now pray much! Pray, Pray, Pray in the manner taught by My Holy Mother, My Sorrowful Mother! How I wish to release Her of this anguish, but it was for this moment, now as *Co-Redemptrix*, that She will help you in your suffering to Co-Redeem many Souls of the faithful who have fallen prey to My adversary and of the non-Catholics who do not know Me yet as their God. They will come and even shed their blood and remain faithful to the teachings of Mine and My Holy Catholic Church, My Bride. Amen."

*

"Where is He, where is He?" says Holy Mama. "Come", says John makes and his way through the crowd and they come very close to the platform where Jesus was and will come again before He is led away to be crucified.

Mary of Magdala is screaming "Do not crucify Him! He has done no wrong! And there are many others like her … this is how they are Co-Redeeming."

Holy Mama turns to me and She speaks to my Soul:

"Daughter, little one of Mine, do you understand now, this is how it will be in the days ahead when My children will offer up their suffering in the persecuted moments We will undergo, to co-redeem for the purification needed for the Bride

---

[111] Luke 21,14

of Christ, the Catholic Church! What they have done to the Lord, they will do to the Priests! They are jeering at Me! They will jeer at the Nuns! Many will be put to death! Those who are consecrated to Me, to My Immaculate Heart will suffer, but will not be raped! It is those Who are not consecrated to My Immaculate Heart will suffer such, the awful stench of rape!" *(Holy Thursday, April 13th, 2017)*

70. KEEP VIGIL AND DO REPARATION FOR SUCH OFFENCES!

She is running. I can see Her through the eyes of my Soul. She has gone to the Praetorium to see Jesus, but they have led Him away into a room where they now put on His own garment and prepare Him for crucifixion. They mock Him and spit on Him and Jesus makes no protest. Holy Mama comes running. John nods to the guards to allow Her and motions with his hands "to let Her be, She is His Mother", he says.

She sees all His blood on the ground and His flesh. She takes off Her veil and wipes the Blood.

John and Our Blessed Mother are wiping all the stones as well as the pillar. Holy Mama is carrying His Flesh!

Now she speaks to My Soul:

"Little one of Mine and My Jesus Cleophas, this is how Jesus is betrayed by many! Pieces of His Sacred Flesh are thrown on the ground and trampled! The irreverence! And those who make sacrilegious Communion do this to the Master! Offer up many Holy Communions and raise many Holy Sacrifices on the Holy Mountain of Mount Batim for reparation for such offences! You yourself keep vigil, doing reparation for such offences! They will increase, they will break your Tabernacles and scatter Jesus' Sacred Flesh all over! They have already begun! It is at the hands of the faithful, who have fallen into the grasp of Satan that Jesus suffers in this manner!"

Iveta: … Holy Mama … I'm trembling mother!

Holy Mama: "Be not afraid I Am here."

Iveta: "Mother, how can you say that (crying). Look what they're doing to Jesus? "

Holy Mama: "Daughter "

She speaks to my Soul, but She is looking at the Lord. "Give thanks to God the Father. It is for the sins of Man, your sins and the sins of all your brothers and sisters that this suffering has befallen you. Now you are co-redeeming after repenting for yours and pray that many will come to do the same. In this way, We will win Souls for God! Amen."

Oh! … Oh! … crying … I have never seen Him like this Ahh …

Our Lady: "This is the understanding of Co-Redeeming; you are now feeling this from a close vision." *(Holy Thursday, April 13th, 2017)*

71. DO YOU SEE HOW VALUABLE SUFFERING IS?

Now she speaks Soul to Soul, Co-Redemptrix to Co-Redeemer.... I am just a little vessel. Now Holy Mama speaks to me, and through me to all others who are co-redeeming.

"My beloved children, do you see how valuable suffering is? You will see the fruits in due time. Worry not about being consoled or receiving consolation for your prayers or suffering. I speak to you all Victim Souls, worry now only of offering your suffering for conversion of sinners, especially those who are spreading heresies and schisms in the Church, the Catholic Church! It is a grave offence against the Holy Spirit, My Spouse.

Know and understand now: You will preach with your life, not your Words! The Words of the Gospel spoken in Scripture, in the Holy Book, the Holy Bible, as it is come to be known is alive in you, each one!

Do not fail to Consecrate yourselves to My Immaculate Heart. It is through My Immaculate Heart that you will enter into the Sacred Heart of Jesus, there according to the Will of God Our Father, to suffer His suffering in His Humanity as Man-God.

I love you all dearly. I thank you for your consolation in this moment. Amen."

*

Jesus speaks Soul to Soul to me:

"Little one of Mine, Co-Redeeming with My Blessed Mother the *Co-Redemptrix*, united to Me the *Redeemer*, how you console Me!"

Iveta: Me Lord, what have I to offer Ah! ... I exaggerate my suffering.

"No daughter you are wrong in that understanding and do not share My thoughts. You conceal more your suffering as is the role of My Holy Mother and it is right. It is called silent suffering, this way of offering yourself to redeem Souls!

Now as you enter with Me, it is Grace you will obtain for your Holy Father, My beloved Priest, My Peter! O how He suffers! How I would have loved to have released him from this moment, but for that He was born to carry this Cross. He is not alone. My Mother is Co-Redeeming as *Co-Redemptrix* with him and also My Peter, the hidden Pope known to you by their names: the reigning Pope, now the reigning Peter, Pope Francis I and the hidden Pope, the hidden Peter, Pope Benedict XVI.

Your suffering, little one of Mine though it seems so little to you, will buy back many Souls thereby comforting their hearts and strengthening them: Souls of Priests, Souls of Bishops, Souls of Cardinals, Souls of Nuns, My Brides who wish to abandon Me and choose another Jesus whom they proclaim by their infidelity to Me!

I Am Jesus of Nazareth, now taking My Cross for your sake and for the sake of the many, like on that First Good Friday. Amen. Amen." *(Holy Thursday, April 13ᵗʰ, 2017)*

72. SILENCE IS NEEDED TO LISTEN AT EVERY MOMENT TO MY SPOUSE THE HOLY SPIRIT

Soul to Soul, Heart to Heart, He speaks to His Mother:

"Mother, Mother help these children of mine. They see Me in this manner and do not understand it is for their sake that I am enduring this, and so are You! I love Thee Mother, Blessed art Thou among all Women, for thou has borne the Son of God. Holy art Thou among all Women for Thou has obeyed the Will of God, Co-Redeeming with me now as *Co-Redemptrix*! Amen. Amen."

Now Holy Mama looks at me and Speaks Soul to Soul while the crowd has stopped, as though.

"Little one of Mine and My Jesus, Cleophas, O beloved daughter, how much is your Love! You have obeyed the will of God. You have sacrificed so much! This is the Co-Redeeming power with Me: Your obedience and your fidelity! This now is the Grace that I will bestow upon your Holy Father who is in anguish for the many of God's children that do not obey, for the many faithful who are condemning him unjustly! Take courage, it is only prayer that is needed now and silence to listen at every moment to My Spouse, the Holy Spirit Who will speak to your Soul and rest in your hearts when you invite Him in!

I love you! I have already made known the manner of the Consecration for all Mothers for their children to My Immaculate Heart. Follow it and worry not! I, the Heavenly Mother will take care of them and protect them, and if you interfere as mothers, I will not go against your Will. You must surrender it to Me, so that I can do all as a loving Mother in kindness and gentleness to bring them back to God in loving Mercy. Amen."

*

Holy Mama takes me back to what we call the tenth station, where Jesus is stripped of His garments. This[112], She asks the Soldiers not to take ... She gives them as though Her second Mantle, not the One carrying the Flesh of Jesus, to cover His Sacred Private area.

Now She reveals Soul to Soul.

"Beloved daughter, do you understand this moment? Many of My children will suffer in this manner. Famine and war that are yet to come will bring this suffering. How I long to prevent it, only pray, pray My children, pray!"

Now She reveals, She takes me to Mount Batim Ganxim, this Holy Mountain, Her Visitation Site.

---

[112] Jesus garment covering His Sacred Private part.

"I desire with great desire that many Holy Sacrifices be raised for the many Souls that must suffer the consequence of sin: Wars and famine, pestilence, man-made wars and man-made devastating plagues.

I desire with great desire that My children bring forth processions to venerate Me, for the offences committed against My Immaculate Conception and My Immaculate Heart, grave offences, thereby rejecting God in the Second Person of the Most Holy Trinity present today with you in the Most Holy Eucharist!

This will console and bring reparation to console My Immaculate Heart and the Sacred Heart of Jesus. Amen." *(Good Friday, April 14ᵗʰ, 2017)*

73. THREE QUARTERS OF THE EARTH WILL VANISH!

"My beloved children, in this Holy Morning that is in remembrance of that First Holy Saturday, I come to implore you with the urgency to pray, beloved children!

Know and understand there are many of you who suffer various ailments, and your physicians know not want to do with you. It is that hour now that you may understand to Co-Redeem with Me, the *Co-Redemptrix*, as is this little one of Mine and My Jesus, your beloved sister Cleophas is doing this day and whenever I call her to do so.

Beloved children, the urgency I call you to is to pray! Take up your weapon which is the Holy Rosary. It is your means now to pray against what is kindled against you, the war of evil against evil, an uprising because of the greed of Man.

Prepare My children, prepare now! Should you not heed My Message to pray, pray, pray, in solidarity with your Priests, your Nuns, the Holy Rosary - this must be now the call of urgency to pray, for World War III is about to begin!

My Motherly Heart weeps for so many that will perish! Three quarters of the Earth will vanish and now what will remain in the quarter, will be what God will choose the *Remnant* from!

In this War, creature and creation will be devastated! I ask of you with the urgency of, the plead of My Motherly Heart! We have no more time but to prepare, prepare Souls, by living each day united to my Immaculate Heart. It is of vital importance for you to Concentrate yourselves to My Immaculate Heart and to prepare by fostering the devotion to My Immaculate Heart of *the First Five Saturdays* and as many as you can attend till that crucial moment when man will rise against man!

Humankind will no longer see as others see humankind, but as a threat to their greed! You have seen it in small doses, now is the big one. Only your prayers can avert this evil! Many of you who can fast and pray, foster to this moment of fasting and praying on the First Fridays and the First Saturdays!

I Am your Heavenly Mother praying this day with many of you who are praying and consoling My Immaculate Heart and the Sacred Heart of Jesus. Soon you will celebrate the Resurrection known to you as Holy Easter Sunday, but many of you will not see this day for the *war of evil against evil* has begun! You My children have become a threat for the evil one, and he has lured many of the faithful in his court and has given them the weapon to annihilate one another, as nation will annihilate nation, and many are walking this path of perdition![113]

---

[113] Mt 7,13

I Am here with you to walk this moment with you. I love you dearly. I Am the Mother of God, the Mother Who sorrows of Mercy for you, the *Mediator of all Grace, Co-Redemptrix* and *Advocate* awaiting this moment that I may dispense My Grace, but you do not pray My beloved children as I have made known! Only a handful are praying the three thousand Hail Marys and Holy Marys to bring its fulfilment! I Bless and thank you and I assure you of My Motherly protection! I love you all dearly, your *Advocate* in Heaven reminding you, interceding for you in your last hour of agony. Amen." *(Holy Saturday, April 15ᵗʰ, 2017)*

74. DO REPARATION BY FASTING AND PRAYING TO CONSOLE THE SACRED HEART OF OUR LORD

"Beloved children of Mine, how My Immaculate Heart desires to be loved by all Man! The Sacred Heart of Jesus is inflicted by ingratitude and abandoned by My faithful and by the lack of prayer by My faithful to console the Sacred Heart of Jesus, Our Lord and My Immaculate Heart!

Today I ask of you beloved children to do reparation by fasting and praying to console the Sacred Heart of Our Lord.

I ask of you, little one of Mine and My Jesus, Cleophas: Will you suffer until the hour of Divine Mercy to console the Sacred Heart of Jesus living with you in all the Tabernacles of the World and abandoned in so many Tabernacles?" *(First Friday, July 7ᵗʰ, 2017)*

75. HER FALLEN AWAY CHILDREN FROM THE FAITH

Archangel Saint Michael:

"I am Saint Michael the Archangel known to you, the one who stands in the Presence of God, here before you at the command of Our Most Holy and Blessed Mother, Whose Birthday we celebrate today in unison with the Catholic Church.

I come to ask of you little one of God, beloved daughter Cleophas of the Blessed Virgin Mary, our beloved sister to endure the suffering that will befall you that has already begun[114] until the hour of Divine Mercy this day, in reparation for all the offences and ingratitude that Our Blessed Mother receives from all of Her fallen away children from the faith. These are the offences the Immaculate is terribly offended with, and God who sees it, is about to chastise the World with a heavy chastisement that has already begun and escalating!" ... *He pauses, and He smiles.*

"Today beloved children endure a fast, you little one of the Blessed Mother and of the Lord Jesus, Cleophas, and you beloved of the Beloved, Felix Xavier, till the Hour of Divine Mercy. This fast will be offered up for your Holy Father. It is an immense weight befalling Him from all the false accusations among the Hierarchy!

I will be with you. I will not leave you! Invoke My Presence when you sense danger or interference! At the hour of Divine Mercy, Our Blessed Mother will come and receive the merits of this suffering and will take them to the Throne of God to ransom Souls and to buy time that you may prepare! Will you help Her?" *(Nativity of the Blessed Virgin Mary, September 8th, 2017)*

---

[114] Iveta was already in suffering.

76. HOW SORROWFUL IT WOULD BE WITHOUT THESE PRAYERS

Archangel Michael speaks.

"Beloved children of God, I Am Saint Michael the defender of God's elect Who stands in the Presence of God here before you, also the servant of Mary, always a Virgin, *Mother of God, Mediatrix of All Grace, Co-Redemptrix* and *Advocate* who awaits this proclamation, but is so in Heaven, interceding for your World.

She has come now before you to gather up this suffering as prayers to ransom Souls in the Universal Church and the Domestic Church. Oh! what a state the Catholic Church is in and yet your prayers and the prayers of all the faithful rise to ransom Souls for God. I am here before you, to give you the message of Our Blessed Mother ..."

Our Lady speaks.

"My beloved daughter, little one of Mine and My Jesus, Cleophas. O! how pleasing an odour you have become to offer all of yourself for the Catholic Church - both the Universal and the Domestic! Today your prayers and the prayers of My beloved of the Beloved, your husband Felix Xavier and those who prayed on the Holy Mountain of Mount Batim-Ganxim rise to ransom Souls from the Universal Church and the Domestic Church.

How sorrowful it would be without these prayers, for your shepherds have gone astray and are leading many of My children into perdition! It is only your prayers that will sustain and enable Me to bring these Souls back to God. If you only knew how valuable your prayers are and how valuable this suffering is! I thank you, My beloved of the Beloved, for giving your 'Yes' and consent even though you were reluctant in the understanding. It is not always for you to understand, it is only for you to surrender all to My Immaculate Heart. If it is not of God, I will crush it!

I am the *Immaculate Conception* and all that is entrusted into My Immaculate Heart that is not in the *order* of Grace and Truth, will be destroyed! Such is the power entrusted unto Me.

Today also is the birthday of this little one and it is most important that you understand when you come home from the Holy Sacrifice, to take your vows, your Baptismal vows. You will understand this in the days ahead. It is fitting to remember what God has done for you!

Little one of Mine and My Jesus, I thank you for responding to My request, even though you suffer the darkness of your doubt. Now there will be many moments known as the *dark night* of your Soul, beloved children. When you entrust all into My Immaculate Heart, no harm will come to you and even in these dark nights your walk will be as though you are walking in the Light, for the truth will always walk ahead of you as the Light of Jesus, My Divine Son.

I love you dearly, I Am the *Mother of God*, your Heavenly Mother together with all the Angels and Saints and the Most Holy Trinity dwelling in My Immaculate Heart. I wish to bestow a Blessing upon you and through you, little one of Mine, upon the Souls that you have prayed for and will pray for till the final hour of this day. Receive this Blessing "IN NOMINE PATER ET FILIUS ET SPIRITUS SANCTUS AMEN."

God the Father thanks you, God the Son thanks you, the Holy Spirit My Chaste Spouse thanks you, Saint Joseph My Chaste Spouse thanks you and all the Angels and Saints thank you, I thank you My beloved daughter, I Am always close at hand.

Be not anxious, be not troubled, I love you dearly! Amen."

*

This Message is for all those who gathered on Mount Batim-Ganxim (India)

"My beloved children, I thank you for remembering and commemorating this day. In remembrance of my first Visitation, you ascended this Mountain to pray and to thank God for Me, a Gift to you as your Heavenly Mother, always here waiting for you and to help you.

Only pray for your Shepherds. I desire with great desire that many Holy Sacrifices be raised upon this Mountain and you will see the fruit through which I will be able to rescue the most hardened sinners and also rescue those who do not believe in the faith of the Catholic teaching, yet they are my children! I love them dearly. I thank all those who are known as non-Catholics who come up on this Holy Mountain. I Am their Mother and love them and I will intercede for them too! I Bless you this day and I promise to be with you always.

She pauses with a deep pause and a sigh ...

"I thank all those who are unable to come in, yet have kept, both My chosen sons, the religious and the laity, and have prayed in remembrance of this day of My Visitation on this Holy Mountain. You will understand God's Salvific plan to your World in these days ahead.

Come beloved children, come in numbers, and bring forth Processions, reciting the Holy Rosary!

I love you dearly, I Am the *Mother of God*, Your Heavenly Mother, the *Mediatrix of all Grace, Co-Redemptrix* and *Advocate* in Heaven, it will come to be known as the last dogma, the fifth dogma[115] on Earth through your prayers! Amen." (*Anniversary of the first Visitation of Our Blessed Mother on Mount Batim, September 24th, 2017*)

77. YOUR WORLD HAS BECOME A WORLD OF HOLOCAUST

Archangel Michael bows in greeting before us and He speaks.

"Children of God you are like incense that is now incensing the throne of God and soothing the wrath of God in the understanding of buying Heaven time to ransom Souls from the slavery of sin.

I Am Saint Michael, who stands in the presence of God here now before you, little one of Mine and My Jesus. I speak on behalf of Our Holy Mother, whose servant I Am! To Me you are My beloved sister Cleophas. I bring the message She wishes to entrust through you to all Her beloved children. She is here to receive the merits of this suffering. It will continue till the hour of three (3pm), the Divine Mercy hour.

Now He speaks Her message.

---

[115] "Divine motherhood" proclaimed at the Council of Ephesus in 431, Our Blessed Mother being conceived "without any detriment to her virginity, which remained inviolate even after his birth" (Council of the Lateran, 649), Immaculate Conception (see Constitution "Ineffabilis Deus" of December 8, 1854), and Our Blessed Mother Assumption proclaimed by Pope Pius XII on November 1, 1950 on his Encyclical "Munificentissimus Deus". The fifth Dogma will proclaim who Our Blessed Mother is for us.

"My beloved daughter Cleophas, little one of Mine and My Jesus, how much you have loved with God's Love in you. How much is your suffering this day! I have been close to you, though at moments you were not granted to know that I Am here. It is such a suffering! Today I come before you, to thank you for your 'Yes' and your fidelity to suffer as a Victim Soul united to My Divine Son Jesus, Your Saviour, Your Redeemer, I as *Co-Redemptrix* Redeeming My children, through this suffering!

The children made known to you are those in the vocation of Holy Matrimonial Love, in marriages today. Catholic marriages in the Domestic Church, disintegrating in values! Today you have ransomed so many of these marriages by saving the children who were threatened to be aborted! Aborted for reasons of thinking as the world thinks, with insufficient values in Catholic Marriages!

Life is threatened and even used as holocausts, sacrifices to Satan! Today you must understand these children were to be aborted and you suffered the torments of the mind and the anxiety of these women, beloved daughters of Mine, who do not understand the value of Life and how precious it is in them! These are future Priests and Nuns that would have been killed this day!

Insufficient values because they feel unloved, unwanted, because they are given the understanding that there is abnormality in them, yet instead of turning to God they turn to the abomination of killing these children, known as abortion, as a quick means to do away with this child and they do not understand that they are offending God, Our Father who is the giver of this life!

Beloved children how I love you, turn to Me! I Am your Mother, your Heavenly Mother, even when you are in the distress of this manner, turn to Me! I will help you! Do not commit such an abomination for which you will be paying the price till the last breath on Earth. What reparation is needed!!"

Now She pauses and She weeps! She weeps … Oh Mother! … tears, tears of Blood rolling down Her Cheeks … such is the pain in Her … crying … and the anguish to save these children! …

"I thank you beloved children for choosing not to abort these children but to embrace them as a cross, a Joyful Cross … and Grace will be granted to you! To the Fathers of these children, the Earthly Fathers, you are only an instrument! Embrace this child in your life this day! God will give you all that you need. His Love is sufficient, and His Grace will help you in all the needs for these children. Do not give consent to such an abomination!! Your world has become a world of holocaust of such! Do not follow that counsel nor that evil path which only leads to Hell, where Satan waits for you!

I love you dearly, I thank you Amen."

She smiles at me …

"I Am the *Mother of God*, I Am your Heavenly Mother, the Mother of all God's children, the Mother of all humanity, interceding for you in your vocation of the Holy Matrimonial understanding in the Catholic Marriage, as *Co-Redemptrix, Mediatrix of all Grace*, to grant you the Graces you are lacking, and *Advocate* before the Divine Judge when you continue to offend Him in embracing the ways of the World, that you may turn from this path and embrace His yoke which is light and burden free! I Am here to guide you, your Heavenly Mother Who Loves you dearly! Amen."

Now Saint Michael repeats "Amen." He sees and I now see Souls that are ascending – Souls of these miscarriages to Heaven, because earlier this day I was granted the Grace to do a Spiritual Baptism by giving them names of the Saints, Our Holy Mother's name as Mary, Joseph, John, Magdala, Jacinta, Catherine, David, Jacob. Amen.

The Vision closes ... Suffering continues till the Divine Mercy hour 3:00 pm. (First Friday of October, October 6th, 2017))

YR 2018: ONLY SHE ALONE AS MEDIATRIX AND THE MOTHER OF GOD, THE WOMAN WHO IS CLOTHED IN THE SUN, WHO WILL CRUSH THE HEAD OF SATAN IN THE END CAN HIDE YOU AND RESCUE YOU

78. MANY ARE FALLING INTO DARKNESS BECAUSE THEY DO NOT HAVE THE UNDERSTANDING OF THESE MOMENTS!

Now I see Our Lady coming before the hour of Divine Mercy and She comes to receive this Suffering for the Holy Father and here now the Archangel Gabriel, my second Guardian Angel[116], brings the 'Message', Her Words to us:

"My beloved children, if you only understood how much you console Me and Our Lord by praying for the Holy Father, you would do it more frequently in these times as the persecution is increasing and the terrible stench of schism in the Catholic Church is spreading like wildfire, as humans would call it. And many are falling into this, without even realizing and discerning! Those who even claim discernment - have no discernment- for they are falling into gossip and into the trend of belonging and walking the path of perdition.[117] Pray beloved children, pray to remain obedient! Pray for their Souls, pray for their conversion!"

... then She pauses and looks at Me.

"I desire with great desire little one of Mine and My Jesus, Cleophas to thank you for subjecting yourself to this kind of obedience at a moment's notice, though I understand you did not understand the vision presented to you at the Holy Sacrifice of the Holy Father, yet you received its understanding as you presented it to your spouse My beloved of the Beloved Felix Xavier, whose discernment was clear for he was in prayer and I thank him immensely for praying for the Holy Father with such a fervent and diligent manner of praying, raising this prayer, the Holy Rosary and the Hail Marys, the three thousand Hail Marys.

---

[116] Archangel Gabriel was given to Iveta as a second Guardian Angel to help her in the suffering: Iveta can give the heavy suffering to him

[117] Mt 7,13

How wonderful an odour of incense and prayer rose for the Holy Father! And now united to this suffering, you will buy much strength, if you only understand how important it is for you to remain hidden and in prayer. You are often tempted of belonging and going out there to make the Word of God known. It will come to be, little ones of Mine. Only do it as I have asked!

I thank you, My beloved of the Beloved, once again for now diligently responding to My request to bring forth these Messages and putting them in order. It is of great importance for daylight time is shortening, darkness is increasing, and many are falling into darkness because they do not have the understanding of these moments! Teach them My beloved of the Beloved, how to understand My message already made known to them in the book that titles: *'The Mercy of God and the Call to Return to the Harbour of Truth.'*

Here they will understand to stay obedient and faithful to the Holy Magisterium and the head of the Catholic Church, His Holiness, My beloved Chosen Son - today Pope Francis I. He is suffering at the hands of the faithful, and much suffering - for all the false accusations and false charges that are rising against him, that he may distance the seat of Peter and prepare now for the one who will lead My children astray totally, the antipope! It is his love of power coming into being now.

Be careful to keep in prayer. Practice silence that you may hear the Spirit of God leading you and not the Spirit of this World and the father of lies[118] and deceit, the spirit of the antichrist!

I love you dearly, I am the *Mother of God*, Your Heavenly Mother, the *Mediatrix of all Grace, Co-Redemptrix* and *Advocate* in Heaven. Through your prayers it will come to be! Only pray beloved children, only pray!"

---

[118] John 8,44

Now She smiles and Her attire is like a Queen. She has a Crown on Her Head, which marks twelve Apostles with the crosses on it - The Crown of the Mediatrix of all Grace. Her Gown is flared out of Her external mantle and held by the Angels.

The Mantle embraces the Catholic Church. She is holding us all in it, the Universal Church. The Gown that is flared out are those who have Consecrated themselves this day to Her Immaculate Heart and are protected under Her Gown, protected! The Angels come and bring it around us and stand as Guards.

The Rosary is in Her right Hand and the Scapular of the Mediatrix of all Grace is in Her left hand, draped through Her Middle Finger and 'Jesus' is suspended in Her Immaculate Heart and the Chalice is holding the suspended 'Jesus' on top and underneath are the two keys of Peter.

She smiles and bows at us in conclusion of Her Final greeting.

Our Altar returns and now I see the Mediatrix of all Grace completely as She depicts herself in this vision. The Vision closes. (Friday after Ash Wednesday, February 16th, 2018))

79. TODAY THERE IS SUCH POVERTY OF FATHER DEPRIVATION!

St Michael speaks:

"Beloved children of God, I am St Michael who stands in the Presence of the Lord, Our God here before you at the command of Our Heavenly Mother, Who stands next to Me and desires that I bring forth these Words to you."

Iveta: I'm having difficulty in my heart.

"I am Her servant, beloved children of God. This hour, known as the hour of Divine Mercy, now as it closes for this continent, yet it is still the hour of Mercy through the intercession of Our Blessed Mother as *Mediatrix of all Grace, Co-Redemptrix* and *Advocate* Who held the Lifeless Body of Her Son, Our Saviour in Her Hands, now present before you in Her Immaculate Heart."

... and now the Words of Our Lady. She speaks:

"My beloved children, I thank you for keeping vigil in prayer with Me, this day known as Friday, the second Friday in Lent, the Holy Time of man's redemption in remembrance to understand what God gave for them, for you, for us!

I thank you, little one of Mine and My Jesus, for this day, enduring this suffering for the Domestic Church, that is the little church in each family. The head of the Domestic Church being the husband, the father.

Today there is such poverty of father deprivation, the lack of love of the father figure for his household! His responsibilities have shifted into the ways of the world leaving a dangerous poverty in his household. The abuse is so widespread! Violence controls the dominant nature of his authority, yet it is not the way of God! He is to rule his household as Priest, Prophet and King of his household, keeping his family with the knowledge of God, as Prophet. King, as having dominion over his wife, who is his Queen, and over his children with love not with malice and not with the whip of his tongue, and not with the whip of his hand to be used as a fist fight! It is breaking and tearing families apart today, for such a lack of Love!

I come to ask of this little one to suffer this day that I may ransom some of the homes that are torn in this kind of poverty and restore these families back to the order of Grace and Truth - Catholic families!

I come to ask of My beloved children, My sons beloved to Me to love their wives and their children with that Love that Jesus, My Divine Son shows for His church[119], a sacrificial love, and to be providers for their families, but mainly to be providers of keeping the Truth, the Life and the Way of the teachings of the Catholic Church!

His will be the continuation of the *Culture of Life* as it has come to be known, the ways of God, for the future generations! Deterioration in families, from lack of this, will lead to the culture of death and to the death of the family with a horrible stench!

My adversary is providing them tools of every kind to destroy the family and to be unfaithful husbands to their wives, thereby leading their wives even astray to infidelity to the Sacrament of Holy Matrimony, Matrimonial Love!

I come to beg you My sons, My beloved sons, head of the families and role models of your household. I come also to call foster fathers right now, widows who have remarried and foster fathers who have adopted children.

I thank you for taking up this role as father figure for these children who would be abandoned and I ask you to entrust all into My Immaculate Heart each day, your entire family! In this way I will help you. I also ask you to Consecrate your families to My Chaste Spouse on Earth, Saint Joseph Who was the Foster Father, the Father Figure of Jesus on Earth. He will help you raise your family to be inhabitants of the future Church in the *Culture of Life*.

I love you dearly. I Am deeply and gravely concerned of the worries that surround the families today. But I Am here as

---

[119] Eph 5,25

Your Mother, Your Heavenly Mother, to bring God's strength and Grace to each family, to strengthen you against the attacks of the adversary, My adversary, God's adversary, against His little Church, the Domestic Church. St Michael is here to defend you. (*St Michael nods a 'Yes' to Our Lady*)

You must recite His chaplet and invoke His Presence when you see the need arising.

I love you dearly, I Am the *Mother of God*, I Am Your Heavenly Mother, the Mother of all God's children, the *Mediatrix of all Grace, Co-Redemptrix* and *Advocate* interceding for you this day and each day when you invoke Me under this title for your needs before the Throne of God.

I await to be proclaimed on Earth that I may dispense the Graces necessary for you in this terrible, terrible, terrible time of persecution, against the Domestic Church. Through your prayers it will come to be on Earth! Continue praying for this intention known as the *Fifth Dogma*, diligently children! Amen." (*First Friday of Lent, Feb 23rd, 2018*)

80. THE WAY OF THE WORLD HAS BECOME THE DOCTRINE AND PRECEPT OF TODAY'S FAMILIES

St Michael Speaks:

"I Am Saint Michael Who stands in the Presence of God now here before you at the command of Our Blessed Mother, whose servant I Am, Mary Virgin.

This understanding I bring before you, stands as the understanding of Divine Justice. Should you obey you will reap rewards of Eternal Salvation. Should you disobey and walk in the ways of sorrow that offend God, you will reap for yourselves the sorrows of eternal damnation. This I speak to all God's children known as women, mothers."

Now He speaks (the words of Blessed Mother):

"My beloved children, little one of my Mine and My Jesus, Cleophas, beloved of Me and Jesus, Beloved of the Father, Felix Xavier, how pleasing you are in your reverence and response to come before Me to pray at this hour of Divine Mercy. It is prayer that is lacking in every home and for this My adversary is its cause and has entered through the front door to bring disharmony and disruption to families and to accuse mothers, who have thrown themselves to his ploy and plots, by entering into the world and its ways as being bread earners! This is not God's order; the bread earners are the head of the family! It has come to be and has brought disrespect to their spouse who in turn have become disturbed and do not know their roles and have brought violence into homes!

Today My beloved daughters, you who are known as mothers are clothing yourselves with immodesty - and lack innocence by which you are clothed with My Grace. Many of you even dishonour Me and do not understand that I Am your role model! By this, I do not come on my own, but the Father has appointed Me as your Model and Mother of all God's children.

If you draw from Me even now, you will bring harmony and you will learn patience - which you are in much need of- and forgiveness! When you embrace yourselves with unforgiveness you bring sorrow and you have led your children astray. This generation is now clothing itself with perverseness and terrible iniquity and are embracing the ways of the world, as modernism and socialism. This has become the doctrine and precept of today's families!

123

Today this little one suffers for Mothers who desire to return to the *order of Nazareth*. To them I will impart My Graces to restore them back to the order of family life. And even if they pray, their children which they fail to pray for and fail to entrust them by name into My Immaculate Heart, they I will protect against the lawlessness of today's terribly saturated doctrine of the father of lies[120] and the father of this world. Though it is his hour coming into being, yet know he has no power over the Father of Jesus[121] ... the Eternal Father who has appointed Me as the *Eternal Mother*.

Beloved children return to the *Harbour of Truth* and embrace God's Ways! To all you mothers: Do not succumb to the ways of the world, do not seek the things of this world! Be content with what you have and all that you need will be given to you. You will lack nothing if you seek first the Kingdom of God![122] All else will be entrusted to you that is needed for you to glorify God. Amen.

I Am the *Mother of God*, I Am the Mother of all mothers, I Am Your Heavenly Mother, the *Mediatrix of all Grace, Co-Redemptrix* and *Advocate* in Heaven interceding for you when you invoke Me under this title of Mine. I await to be proclaimed on Earth and through the prayers of My beloved children who faithfully pray for this intention of Mine, it will come to be on Earth!

I love you dearly, I am here to help you return to God and to the order of God's family. Amen." *(First Friday of Lent, March 9th, 2018)*

---

[120] John 8,44

[121] John 19,11

[122] Mt 6,33

81. IN MANY ORDERS, THE TEACHINGS OF THE ONE WORLD RELIGION HAS SEEPED INTO IT

Now Our Lady speaks:

"My beloved children, you always are a pleasing odour to Me when you pray. You console My Immaculate Heart; but you are often distracted about the things of this world and the concerns of the people, My beloved children, out in the world. You must pray for them! You must talk less about the things of this world and engross yourself in prayer. The Holy Rosary is of most importance! Do not recite empty prayers, like empty words before Me, for I cannot bring Graces down upon you. Only the Rosary is the most efficacious prayer needed for your World today!

You ask for the exchange of My Heart, yet your hearts are concerned with the affairs of your world and not about the Word of God. I thank you My beloved daughter for responding to My request. Even though heavy burdens are laid upon you, which is not God's way, help will come! You must be open to accept help and overlook faults in others, as God overlooks faults in you. Do not think you are more righteous than others!

Beloved daughter, today you suffer for the Universal Church, for all the Mother Superiors, the Superiors and the Postulants, the Novices who will enter to become Brides of Christ. Yet there are many who have entered already, who are not called by My Divine Son. They come to escape the world, they come because they have been betrayed by men. It would be better for them to remain out into the world and to practise to be virgins. In this calling, one is called in the Holy State of Virginity, preserved to be the Brides of Christ.

This Soul must understand as one who is called to pray for the world and not be concerned about the affairs of the world. Today in many Orders as they have come to be known, the teachings of the *one world religion* has seeped into it and infiltrated into the minds of even the elect, which are called to be Nuns, as Brides of Christ and has brought terrible confusion!

The practise of the new age movement has entered because many are seeking to follow various orders. It is well for them to follow the direction of the Founders and Foundresses. Here it is already outlined and made known to them what their duties are and in each Order. This will change when Russia is Consecrated to My Immaculate Heart in the thousand years of Peace, the era of Peace that I promised, in which I will make known on Holy Thursday, that is Me and My Jesus the *Redeemer* and I as *Co-Redemptrix* will bring to enlightenment what this era of Peace will hold, and how this Joy of the Living Gospel will be lived by the Religious and by the laity."…

…Now She pauses, and She weeps. She is seen kneeling, praying at the hour the Nuns must pray, individually before Jesus. They are missing in prayer, because they are away practising infidelity to God and abominations, while Our Holy Mother takes their place.

"As for those who do not belong to this calling, the adversary is mocking God in this calling. And these are those who seek to be married and who seek to become priests to Consecrate Jesus, it can never be so! That is reserved for the Sacrament of Holy Matrimony and are for those who are called in this vocation and for the continuity of the human race. And for the calling of the Priesthood and the following of the Divine Redeemer as the High Priest and the Consecration of The Holy Eucharist, these are for men - only called in this vocation to serve God, as in male."

Our Lady weeps and is now silent.

"How I love My children dearly. I desire to help those who are called in this vocation as Brides of Christ of My Divine Son Jesus, who are confused. If they will entrust all into My Immaculate Heart each morning, I will help them like I helped the pious Mary of Magdala who had fallen, to remain holy as a bride of Christ, who gave herself after repenting. It is I Who formed Her and brought Her to the Lord to accept to be a Virgin, a Consecrated Virgin and His Bride.

As for the Mother Superiors who have been called and nominated for these positions and the Superiors who teach and the Prioresses who teach the *order of Grace* and the order of this calling: Be on guard against lawlessness! You must spend much time in prayer. Entrust all into My Immaculate Heart! There are many among you who do not belong! You must be on guard against such within your walls. You are concerned about the affairs that are external; yet Satan has entered!

You must understand this moment of disturbance among you. You are looking for the robber[123] that might come from the external and yet he is within your own walls! When you see and when you hear of abominations among those who are within your Orders, bring them before your Spiritual Father, the Priest. They will come before you all, for you are their Spiritual Mothers; but you must bring them before the Spiritual Father to be delivered and exorcised even, and should not they desire to be delivered, you should treat them as one not called and release them, or else there will be great harm and disharmony within the Orders.

Do not solicit, as in advertising for such a calling! This calling is a calling, for God's Holy Spirit will guide them to you. You as superiors together with your Nuns who have been formed and novices must pray for this, for them to come to

---

[123] John 10,10

you! It is in this way you will be safe to know that those who are called, will come to you and peace will remain within the walls of the Holy Orders.

These are the times also, because of the lack of prayer many who have been called and have been tempted, have fallen into temptation and have not responded to the call; but are practising now to be consecrated virgins and yet have not embraced the calling to be Nuns. This Sacred calling is a calling that must be understood as a pillar that holds the world, without which the wrath of God, which is kindled and is overflowing, would have come long before this day. It is your prayer and the prayers of the faithful that are rising now! Prayer must be practised vigilantly! How I love you, how I pray for you!

I Am here as *Co-Redemptrix* and as *Mediatrix* to cover you with My Grace, Graces after Graces[124] that you are losing because of various concerns of this world. Yet you have to be concerned only of one affair and that is prayer. Pray, My beloved Brides of Christ of My Divine Son.

I clothe you with My Immaculate Garment and present you before My Divine Son, when that hour comes for you to be His Bride.

I love you dearly, I thank you for the many who have responded and remain faithful, uncompromising to the ways of the world. I Am She, the *Mother of God*, I Am the Mother of Nuns, I Am your Heavenly Mother who loves you dearly, the *Mediatrix of all Grace, Co-Redemptrix* and *Advocate* in Heaven.

Pray for your Holy Father today Pope Francis I, who is weighing heavy with this heavy cross in union with Pope Benedict XVI who is also weighing. Your prayer is needed

---

[124] John 1,16

for him too and for the intentions of My Immaculate Heart that I be proclaimed *Mediatrix of all Grace, Co-Redemptrix* and *Advocate*. It will come to be, should you pray for this intention! I love you dearly. Amen."

Saint Michael now smiles, bows at us. "I will protect you for you invoke Me. Continue in this manner diligently! Much is coming to past now. Do not grow lax, do not be concerned of the affairs of the world out there. You are called to the semi-monastic life, embrace it with joy! I Am here with you at the command of Our Blessed Mother, Saint Michael. Amen." *(Second Friday of Lent, March 16ᵗʰ, 2018)*

82. MANY OF THE SEMINARIANS HAVE COME FROM SATAN AS HIS PRIESTS!

St Michael Speaks.

"Beloved children of God, I come before you today at the request of Our Heavenly Mother Who is present here, Who has been praying with you, to make known Her desire. Her servant I Am! I Am Saint Michael Who stands in the Presence of God now here before you. How pleasing an odour you are to God as you observe this time to understand your redemption that Our Dear Saviour has won for us at the price of His Precious Blood[125] and His ignominious suffering to reconcile creature to Creator. Yet creatures have become hardened of heart and reject this price of Redemption!"

He pauses and now he speaks the message of Our Blessed Mother:

"I thank you for responding to My request to come and pray before Me and My Jesus at the hour of Divine Mercy."

---

[125] 1Pt 1,18-19

Today I come to make known the Sorrow of My Immaculate Heart. This sorrow entails My beloved Sons who have joined the synagogue of Satan[126] and who teach this doctrine in the Seminaries. The smoke of Satan has entered the Seminaries and many of the Seminarians have come not from the call of Jesus, the High Priest to follow in His Footsteps, but from Satan as his priests! Many of the professors who are priests themselves are teaching anti-god doctrine. They have abandoned the teachings of the Catholic Church to bring in what is called the new age movement, the one world religion, the changes as they call, needed for these times; these times in understanding not to stand for the truth as has been from the beginning of this Institution, known as the Seminary.

In obedience to the Holy Father today on the seat of Peter, the Bishop of Rome My beloved chosen son agonises for such horrifying crimes! His Holiness Pope Francis I in union with the hidden Pope Emeritus Pope Benedict XVI weeps for them too with Me! They are rising with the understanding to forsake celibacy, in the understanding what My Divine Son Jesus revealed as the High Priest to embrace that Priests should be married and that women can be ordained as Priests. It is not so! This is Satan's synagogue preparing for this *one world religion!*

Know and understand now these are those times coming into being. These seminaries will stand as though standing for the truth even in the times of persecution where My seminaries will be in the *Underground Church,* in places that no one would want to live in. Yet I will be with them and they will keep the order of the High Priest Jesus Christ and remain in obedience to the Seat of Peter, even when it will be infiltrated by the anti-pope and those who follow him. Amen."

She speaks now to all Her children:

---

[126] Rev 2,9: "those who say that they are Jews and are not."

"My beloved children, know and understand it will be time for you to leave your churches and to pray at home, when you hear the doctrine that will be preached against My *Immaculate Conception*, against the Divinity of Jesus present in the Holy Eucharist as True God and True Man. When this is defiled, walk away from these churches! These are the churches that will stay open as Satan's synagogues.

My Priests will come to those who I will send them to, and I will be with them. You are to pray as I have made known. This will take place when the one sitting on the Seat of Peter today, Pope Francis I will flee to the *Underground Church*. Yet my church will not be without Peter the Rock. You must only believe! Many of you where your churches are closed, will make Spiritual Communions. Jesus will come to be with you in this manner and in due time from moments, My Priests will come to give you the Holy Sacrifice and the Consecrated Eucharist.

Fear not I will make known this to you once again! Now close at hand, these moments are!

Pray, much prayer, beloved children as I have made known, that I be proclaimed *Mediatrix of all Grace, Co-Redemptrix* and *Advocate* on Earth to assist you and to be with you in these times and to dispense the Graces you will be in need of.

Fear not, even if Martyrdom is the call for you! Stay faithful to Jesus! He will not abandon you! He will receive you in Heaven should Martyrdom be your lot of suffering. Carry your crosses with fidelity and entrust all to My Immaculate Heart. I will assist you when you call on Me and I will intercede for you when you call on Me under the title of *Mediatrix of all Grace, Co-Redemptrix* and *Advocate* in Heaven. I wait to be proclaimed on Earth, by your prayers it will come to be! Amen." *(Third Thursday of Lent, March 22nd, 2018)*

83. THE GREATEST SIN RIGHT NOW IS ABORTION PARADING BEFORE THE LORD

Jesus casts himself upon a stone, a big rock, and there He kneels, and there is a light shining. It's the light of the Angel bringing him the Cup[127], but in anguish before Him are parading all the sins and sufferings he must undergo for us.

The greatest sin right now is abortion parading before the Lord ... and Euthanasia comes before him. Man plays God! This is the horrible stench of impurity ... now every sin is parading before God and Jesus Christ cries out to the Father:

"Father, if thou will let this Cup pass Me by"[128] ... and then he bows His head ... "But not as I will, but as thou will, if I must drink of it. "

Then He gets up and staggers and is sweating, it is a fear sweat, and He comes to his apostles and He finds them fast asleep. 'Peter', He calls out "Peter are you asleep?" There is no answer from Peter... "Take your rest" and He staggers back and falls upon the rock again. This time the Angel is closer to Him, just holding the Cup, and the Lord screams out again, "Father" with the same words "Let this cup pass me by" but He adds now here: "If I must drink of it, let not my will be done but thine", and He drops. Now His sweat is changing. It has a tone of Blood all over the face and it is dropping on the ground.

Jesus appears frightened and He comes and keeps coming like a drunkard, staggering!

---

[127] Mt 26,39

[128] Mt 26,39

132

"Are you still asleep" *He says to them* "The hour is at hand when I will be betrayed into the hands of sinners."[129] *Peter barely looks at the Lord, trying to open his eyes and he sees The Lord as though bleeding, but he cannot do anything. He is so weighed down and he falls back into sleep as he shakes James and John; but they cannot get up.* "The Lord, The Lord!" *he says,* "Look at the Lord, something is wrong with the Lord!"

He still doesn't understand the moment.

The Lord goes and falls on the rock again and now He is silent for a while. There is a silence; but the noise - of the guards, the soldiers - is drawing near. The soldiers are jeering and mocking and laughing as they march - a horrible sound of fear.

Now I see so many Guardian Angels of all those praying, and Jesus speaks to my Soul.

"Daughter "

Iveta: How can I help you Lord?

"Know that I have conquered this moment that will befall all My beloved children. This is how they will come when Martial law will be implemented everywhere in the world, on Earth. The first - will be those who are following a culture of death and have embraced Satan as their god. These are all the laws of the antichrist and laws of the antipope!

My Peter is in anguish, fear not! I Am with you My Peter! I will not abandon you! I promise that the gates of Hell shall not prevail against my Church[130]. This I speak now of my Church that I will hold fast as the Underground Church. Till that moment I will make known ... Amen, Amen." *(Holy Thursday and Good Friday, March 29th-30th, 2018)*

---

[129] Mt 26,45

[130] Mt 16,18

84. WHAT MUST I DO TO YOU?

Jesus speaks Soul to my Soul. He speaks to the priests.

"My Priest, my Beloved, I who Am the Beloved of My Father, prepare your sheep! Many of you will face this moment yourselves. Know that I am with you and have conquered it for you. Your Crown awaits you in Heaven. You will understand when I am lifted up[131] as I have made known to you. Stay united and close to my Blessed Mother who is Co-Redeeming with Me.

Your blood is the blood that is needed for my *Remnant* to go forth. Your blood is needed to purify My Bride the Catholic Church! Your blood is needed, united to Me to ransom Souls from the cruel slavery of the devil, My adversary Satan himself who has lured many of My Priests to follow him into his courtyard.

I am Jesus of Nazareth, The High Priest suffering this day as I did that first night, Jesus of Nazareth. Amen. Amen." *(Holy Thursday and Good Friday, March 29th-30th, 2018)*

*

Jesus' Face is so swollen, and His Eyes are puffed ... but He makes no protest! They tie a rope around His neck and hang Him up and then cut the rope immediately and he falls...

Iveta: Oh! Oh! Oh... Crying ...

This is a horrible torture ... They discuss among themselves whether to take Him now or wait for the soldiers because there may be people on the streets. Jesus is lying on the floor and they take the

---

[131] John 12,32

rope from around His neck and tie another one around His chest and lift Him up and throw Him down again. There is no light in the cellar except that of the lanterns.

Now the Lord to me, Soul to Soul:

"Little one of Mine"

Iveta: Yes Lord … crying…

"Thank you for waking up and you, My beloved of the Beloved. I Am He now suffering for all sins. Thank you for embracing My Mercy. Do you understand this suffering? This is what they do to those who have no voice!

These are the criminals, not in your prison cells but in your hospitals, who take the lives of the innocent, who take the lives now under the law of the death culture; known to you as Euthanasia, depriving you of suffering for My Justice, that is My Love! My Justice is not like the unfair Justice on Earth of those who Judge unjustly - acquitting the guilty and condemning the just!

My justice is for those who repent and embrace My Mercy." *… and now there is silence.* "I Am Jesus of Nazareth suffering this day."

Then Jesus shows me. "Many of my Brides, yes little one of Mine, Nuns" *He shows me* "have committed the offence of impurity against their vow of chastity and there are many Priests involved in such diabolic acts and they are committing this offence of putting this little baby to death under the law of abortion." *And Jesus says:*

"What must I do to you? Is not My Love sufficient that you would abandon Me for my enemies, but you allow Satan to enter you?

"Know that even now, if you repent and cling to My Blessed Mother, She will nurture you back, Who is Co-redeeming for you with Me."

... and then I see these many Angels, Guardian Angels. Now I also see Guardian Angels of Priests and Religious. By that I mean they are not like regular Angels, like little Angels. They have Archangels as their Guardian Angels - those who are called by God to this vocation of Priesthood and Religious.

They have all formed a ring around me and they are praying. Some are reading their office and offering it up. Some are reading the Holy Book, the Bible, the Word of God. Some are praying the Rosary, and some are just praising God like the Charismatics do. But they are praying, and they are praying now for the Religious and the Priests.

This suffering is mainly applied now at this hour for them.

And Jesus speaks again:

"Many of you will desert Me. You will abandon Me, like those who abandoned Me this night! Know that I have prayed for you. Repent and return to Me! Return by embracing the Love of My Blessed Mother who will nurture you back to Me. Many of you will deny Me. Fear not! Only repent and return to Me through my Blessed Mother who is Co-Redeeming with me."

When Jesus said that many of the Priests will deny Him, they are those who clothe themselves like the common man and do not wear a collar.

"But I love you My Priests. I Am dying this day to reconcile you to your humanity. My Divinity in you is sufficient; yet your humanity overtakes! Only repent! Walk away from the vices of the world that are laid as snares for you by My adversary through the Hierarchy. Satan himself lays traps, as snares!

I Am Jesus of Nazareth, the High Priest now suffering. I thank all of you who are praying in solidarity with this little one this night. The morning is coming when the night will turn to light and they will do this even in the light - what they have done to Me.

Fear not! I have conquered them. Stay faithful as you have been, remembering that your Crown awaits you in Heaven when I Am lifted.

I Am Jesus of Nazareth, True God and True Man, I love you all My beloved children Amen, Amen." *(Holy Thursday and Good Friday, March 29ᵗʰ - 30ᵗʰ, 2018 Good Friday)*

85. WHEN DARKNESS FALLS AND PERSECUTION ARISES

The crowd screams and shouts out aloud "We have no King but Caesar[132]! It is Barabbas we want released[133]!" ... and in the crowd are those faithful to Jesus and they scream "No He is innocent! Not that murderer over Jesus of Nazareth!"

So, Pilate is afraid of the crowd and he comes to Jesus and he says, "So you are a King[134]." And Jesus replies "You say so." Pilate says, "Have I delivered you to be condemned, it is your own people."

---

[132] John 19,15

[133] John 18,40

[134] John 18,37

Now Pilate is sitting there, while Jesus is in silence, wondering what to do, so he comes out and takes his seat, his seat of judgement, and Jesus speaks Soul to Soul.

"Little one of Mine, My beloved daughter Cleophas, you see, this is how it will be in the days ahead. My Mother has made known that daylight time is short. When darkness falls and persecution arises, they will condemn the just - that is you My faithful, My Priests and acquit the guilty! Lawless men will walk while the just will be condemned! They will bring false witness against you. You who pledge your alliance to me your God, suffering in remembrance of that first Good Friday, known to you.

I am your recompense, complete! Stay in My Light! Embrace My Blessed Mother. She will help you all through these moments. I love you. Jesus of Nazareth, True God and True Man, the High priest. Amen. Amen." *(Good Friday, March 30th, 2018 Good Friday)*

86. I ASK YOU TO EMBRACE THE SACRAMENT OF RECONCILIATION

Jesus speaks:

"Little one of Mine, Cleophas My beloved daughter, understand the hour is befalling upon all mankind because of the grave offences committed against God the Creator and the lack of repentance of sinful men! And you My faithful who I thank and love so much, many of you will be treated in this manner: They will put you into prison cells and scourge you! They will inflict great tortures upon your body. It is for this reason I ask you to embrace the Sacrament of Reconciliation and receive Me worthily that I may be fully in you, enduring all of this with you. I have already conquered this moment!

Worry not! Your Crown awaits you into all Eternity where you will rejoice when I Am lifted up. I am Jesus of Nazareth your *Redeemer*, asking you to embrace My Blessed Mother as Co-Redemptrix who will prepare you as She has prepared Me, Who will pray for you, Who prays now as She did that *first* night and the *first* Good Friday morning, True God and True Man. Amen. Amen." (*Good Friday, March 30ᵗʰ, 2018*)

87. YOU ARE LITTLE VESSELS OF REDEMPTION

I see countless Souls who are doing the 'stations of the Cross' at this hour united to us, offering it up. If they only knew they are offering it for conversion of so many of their loved ones! And Jesus is carrying His cross as He walks, the cross is hitting His Brow and it is pushing the Crown of Thorns deeper into His brow...

Iveta: Ah Ha!!!!! ... crying Ah!!! ... loud sobbing ... crying ... Blood is coming out of his Sacred Head ... crying ... and Jesus speaks Soul to my Soul:

"Little one of Mine, Cleophas."

Iveta: Yes, Lord I'm here. I don't know what I can do. Ah!!! ... now I see myself with Holy Mama, on Her right-side walking with Her, The Lord speaks: "Do you understand this moment?"

Iveta: No Lord I'm so ignorant ... crying how can I Ah!!! ... Sobbing ...

"I thank you for enduring this, with Me and My Blessed Mother. In this way you are little vessels of Redemption, I the *Redeemer*, My Mother the *Co-Redemptrix* and you are all Co-Redeeming with Her - those praying in this moment, honouring Me in this suffering with a great love for Me and My Sacred wounds, that I am enduring and will endure now till I Am lifted up. It is not over for you! It begins for you! Know that I have walked this path!" (*Good Friday, March 30ᵗʰ, 2018*)

88. MANY OF MY FAITHFUL HAVE LEFT ME FOR A RELIGION CALLED 'ONE WORLD RELIGION'

Iveta: I see the Vatican. There are people outside joking. And around and inside there is such a division. They are not with the Holy Father. A great percentage are not with the Holy Father!

"Do you understand what I'm showing you?"

Iveta: No Lord

"Do you see how they are divided, those that you see under the shadow of darkness are from My adversary. They once belonged to Me, but now they belong to the rank of the freemasons."

Iveta: No Lord Ahh!

"Yes, my daughter, this is how they have betrayed me - and among you are such too! Many of My faithful have left me for a religion called *'One World Religion'*. They believe in everything and they believe in nothing; because for them there is no God than the One True God Who created Heaven and Earth. I was present at that moment and I Am returning to Him when I am lifted up in remembrance of that First Friday - known as Good Friday to you now. Hold onto my Blessed Mother, She will not leave you! It is My greatest Love and even that you will understand it in a few moments. I emptied! Do not hold on to love of creatures, they will abandon you! The hour is coming when it is foretold in the Holy Book known to you as the Bible; you will be betrayed by those in your own household[135].

I am Jesus of Nazareth, True God and True Man, the High Priest. I love you Amen, Amen."

---

[135] Mt 10,36

*

Now He walks and He walks, and He is staggering as though going to fall and one of the soldiers from a distance grab a man coming down. His name is Simon, a Cyrenian[136]. But he says, "I have no dealings here, I'm just coming into town."

"Yes, but you look able, come I have a job for you." And he leaves everything as he is dragged to Jesus. Simon looks at Jesus and says: "What is all this, I carry this cross; but I've done no wrong."

"Not because of your wrong", they scream "Help Him!"

Simon says: "Did you hear what the crowd is crying out, that He is a King. He needs not my help." Then Jesus looks at him and Simon just changes and from his heart he says "Sorry, I'll help you." And carries the Cross with the Lord.

......Holy Mama in her Sorrowful Eyes, one tear here and there escaping, conceals all Her tears.

Iveta: Ah! ... crying ... Ah! ...

Holy Mama smiles at Simon in thanking him." You're his Mother?" Simon asks Soul to Soul and She nods ... crying ... "I'll help him." Ah!!! poor Woman ... and he thinks of his Mother ...

Jesus speak Soul to Soul:

"Little one of mine Cleophas."

Iveta: Yes, Lord here I am.

---

[136] Mt 27,32

"Do you see an understand? I desire My beloved children to embrace their elderly. Take care of them, do not put them into homes where they will kill them! Yes, many of My nuns run such homes, meaning operating them, taking care of these aged for you. How will you atone for your sins? It is by love and care of such!

I thank them, but the hour is coming that not even they can keep them alive, for as soon as a physician is required and they are to be hospitalised, they will be done away with, for they are a burden to the system of the antichrist. Their suffering is of great value if you only understand how many Souls they ransom! Some don't even know how to suffer; your Love is needed! You my faithful - visit such who have been abandoned by their loved ones; for such is the teaching of the ways of this World!

To you is given, little one of Mine Cleophas, My Beloved, to prepare for those yet to come, whom you will rescue. I will make them known. You only prepare with the help of my Blessed Mother and My Foster Father who will intercede from Heaven to obtain the necessary gifts and graces for this, his Namesake. The St Joseph Community Centre, known as to God as the St Joseph's Charity organisation. Organisation in the sense before Man, but before God it is simply your acts of Love and Mercy!

I am Jesus of Nazareth, True God and True Man, the High Priest. Yes, even the home for the Clergy must be understood in this order of preservation, in giving dignity to the aged. For God has created from the beginning a purpose for each creature and God will appoint the hour which has been written when I will come as a thief[137] and bid that Soul to come unto Me. Amen, Amen." (*Good Friday, March 30th, 2018*)

---

[137] Rev 16,15

89. ONE OF THE SEVEN BOWLS OF PLAGUE WILL BE THE DEVASTATING PLAGUE THAT WILL BEFALL YOU!

.........Now they are walking. As they walk, Veronica, as she has come to be known, in this moment pulls out her veil and runs towards Jesus. They try to pull her back but it's of no use. She seems to have a supernatural strength that not even the guards can keep her down.

"Let the mad woman go! Let's see what she's up to. We'll get her." *She runs to Jesus and the Lord looks at her with His disfigured face and she comes under the cross and she presses her veil on His Face to wipe it ...*

Iveta: crying ... What an act of Love?

They whip her but it does not seem to touch her. She is least concerned about all ... sobbing ... the suffering. She must endure ... crying ... She smiles and Jesus nods at her to say "What Love! "She grabs her veil and holds onto it and kisses it and she sees his Countenance on it. Jesus speaks to me Soul to Soul:

"Little one of Mine Cleophas."

Iveta: Yes, Lord Ah!!! ... crying ...

"Do you see this moment? Make known to My beloved children, it is in this way they must help My poor. They have been beaten and thrown on the roadside. Wash them and give them a dignified death. It is in this way you must profess your fidelity to Me.

... You see how many are addicted to drugs or have various kinds of vices. When you see them, show them Love - My Love, as I have made known to you. Clothe them and feed them and wipe their tears. Hear them cry! You will be able to ransom many Souls! Many are those beloved children in your own household! Do not forsake them! Simply love them as I have loved you. It is through your love they will understand My Mercy and return to Me.

I am Jesus of Nazareth, True God and True Man, the High Priest. Yes, My chosen sons, even among you, are those who have been addicted to various vices through temptations. Many carry burdens through bondages. You who have known My Love, show them fidelity by your Love for them and bring them out of their misery. Amen, Amen."

*

Soul to Soul Jesus speaks. Redeemer to Co-Redemptrix:

"Mother, Mother will you …" *Mama looks at me and She says:* "Yes speak no more My beloved Son, My Divine Son speak no more; I will help." *She looks at me to say again:*

"Do you see now, your suffering is ransoming such, giving them the grace to say no to this abomination of killing of the innocent under the rule of abortion."

Soul to Soul Jesus speaks to me again:

"Beloved daughter, little one of mine Cleophas and My Beloved Mother, My Blessed Mother Who is holding you at this moment and to all My beloved children, Priests, Nuns, and all my faithful who oppose this killing of the innocent, I thank you! I thank you! Your reward will be great in Heaven! Do not succumb to such evil. Yes, many of the nations have embraced it as a rule of life. No such rule is a rule of life, but a *rule of death*, eternal death!

I warn you, all you authorities and those in authority positions; you are condemning yourselves by embracing such a rule, as a rule of life.

This blood, you will pay the price for it, you and your household! One of the seven bowls of plague[138] will be the devastating plague that will befall you! You will not escape My wrath nor the cry of this innocent who comes before My Father.

It is well for you to repent and denounce such evil!

I Am Jesus of Nazareth, True God and True Man, the high Priest who is praying for such, the *Redeemer* with the *Co-Redemptrix* and united to the *Co-Redemptrix* all those united to this little one, as little vessels of co – redemption. Amen, Amen." (*Good Friday, March 30ᵗʰ, 2018*)

90. MANY DO NOT FOLLOW THE RULE OF THEIR FOUNDERS AND FOUNDRESSES!

Now Jesus speaks Soul to Soul:

"My beloved daughter little one of Mine, Cleophas and My Beloved Mother, My Blessed Mother. Do you understand the necessary means of bringing the understanding of the Constitution of Holy Orders dedicated to My Sacred Heart torn with grief and My Mothers Immaculate Heart pierced with thorns and swords?

My Priests who have said their 'yes' to Me and now embrace the ways of this World are leading My sheep and My little lambs astray. My Brides who have said their 'yes' to Me, who now denounce Me, who are not called for the vocation of Holy Matrimony, the Sacrament of Marriage are now entering to become brides of men! This is because they have not renounced their temptations but have embraced their temptations as a source of their happiness which will bring great misery to the Domestic

---

[138] Rev 15, 5-7

Church. Oh! they have already brought great sorrow to the Universal Church and there are many who are crying out to the Holy Father to allow them to be married, My Priests!

And even my Nuns want to become Priests! This must never be! This is not the Will of My Father who sent Me to Institute this manner of Sacredness of Holy Chastity. Many do not follow the rule of their Founders and Foundresses! They have devised their own rule and are following their own devices and have brought division! Many take the Rules of other Orders which is not the Rule of their Founders and Foundresses as they have been known. Those to whom My Spirit has dictated of how it ought to be, are confused of what to do! Many do not pray but follow the trend of belonging to socialism. Their vocation to pray is of utmost need now for humanity, for man to repent!

It is this prayer that is lacking, and the burden has fallen on My faithful who pray, and I thank them today. So many united to this little one of my Mine are praying and I Bless them all. I shall heed their prayer and I shall give ear to their cry of supplication. I shall facilitate their necessities according to the Will of Our Father. When I Am lifted up, I will pour My Spirit upon them[139]." (*Good Friday, March 30th, 2018*)

91. MY BELOVED PRIESTS: IF ONE OF YOU FALL AND DO NOT REPENT, MANY SHEEP FALL AND ABANDON THE FAITH!

Now they are stripping Jesus. They have thrown down His Cross … what pain, crying … The Blood has dried on his Garment on the inside to His Holy Wounds and as they strip of His Clothes, they pull the flesh and the Wounds become raw again. Holy Mama motions with pain and runs, and John and Mary Magdala hold Her back. The

---

[139] Acts 2,33

suffering of the Lord is painful and brutal; a brutality that you do not know ... crying ... no one could endure this suffering and live. They would die ... only in the power and love of God in the Lord Jesus! God Himself is so immense, it cannot be measured ... now here as Jesus stands and waits for them; they gather the nails and the hammer. Three soldiers on each side are chosen by the soldier giving the orders to do the nailing.

Jesus speaks Soul to Soul.

"My beloved daughter Cleophas, do you see what I Am about to undergo. Such is My Love for you and for all My children whom My Father has given Me. I will lose none of them. Will you help Me make My Love known to those who do not yet know of it, that they may repent and strip themselves of all that is holding them in bondage and hostage by my adversary - especially My Priests, that they will leave the ways of this world and embrace the ways of poverty and zeal for the Sacraments to be instituted upon My children who long to see such."

... and Jesus speaks to His Priests:

"My beloved Priests in whose Footsteps of Mine you follow, know and understand now, if one of you fall and do not repent, many sheep that have been entrusted to you fall and abandon the faith, ten thousand ... flee from the faith!

I have suffered this First Good Friday. Today this little one is enduring this suffering in remembrance of that first Good Friday united to Me and My Blessed Mother Who will suffer long after Mine is finished."

Now I see the Vatican, and Jesus is showing me how they will strip everything, just as "My Body has been stripped. They will strip when the desolate sacrilegious[140] takes the seat of Peter; but know that I Am your recompense, and My Peter will be with you always till the end of time! Some will know of him and some must believe that I will not leave you without My Peter.

Pray for the Holy Father my beloved who is suffering gravely and is often filled with a trembling fear of the events to unfold. Pray for My hidden Peter, My Peter today who sits on the seat of the first Peter; known to you as His Holiness Pope Francis I and my hidden Peter who prays and suffers and understands the moments that will soon befall the Church, the Catholic Church and how much more He must suffer, known to you as Emeritus Pope Benedict XVI, His Holiness, truly revealing the Holy state in which I call My Peters to serve Me, renouncing their humanity as their temptation.

Through your prayer beloved children, I call you to pray for them, they will hold as pillars of the Church, My Church.

I am Jesus of Nazareth, the High Priest who appoints with My Spirit the reigning Peter from the first to this day and will be till the end of time. Amen, Amen." (*Good Friday, March 30th, 2018*)

92. ONLY THE WOMAN WHO IS CLOTHED IN THE SUN CAN HIDE YOU AND RESCUE YOU!

The crowds are jeering and clapping, and Jesus reveals again:

"Know and understand My beloved children, I speak to you all through this little one of Mine, your beloved sister Cleophas. This is how they will jeer and clap at every effort that they are making and united to them are the faithful, who once were known as staunch Catholics, to denounce My Peter.

---

[140] Mark 13,14

148

Stay in fidelity to him, pay heed to his Words! He will reveal to you these times and you will understand when the hour comes to flee from the cities to the mountains[141] and those of My *Remnant*[142] into My refuge where My Mother waits for you[143]. She will carry all of you through these moments; those who will suffer Martyrdom and those who will go into the *Remnant*. Only She alone as *Mediatrix* and the *Mother of God*, the Woman who is clothed in the Sun[144], who will crush the head of Satan[145] in the end can hide you and rescue you!

I am Jesus of Nazareth, the High Priest. I have conquered this moment for you by My suffering Amen. Amen."

Now there is confusion. You see everybody, especially those coming into the city questioning and jeering. Peter is standing quite a way off and is watching Jesus. Some of the Apostles have fled, they are even leaving the country; but some are hiding and watching, and some are still in the upper room and will not open the door. At this moment in despair, I see Judas hanging and his blood falls to the ground[146].

Jesus speaks to Our Blessed Mother:

"Mother, Mother do not let My children who My father has given Me[147] fall into despair. Increase their hope and their fidelity in Me. Increase their love for Me as You have for Me Amen, Amen."

She nods and motions to Him not to speak.

---

[141] Luke 21,21

[142] Rev 12,17

[143] Rev 12,6

[144] Rev 12,1

[145] Gen 3,15

[146] Acts 1,18

[147] John 17,6

Now another area opens, and I see the 'United Nations' as it is called; it is believed to be a peace keeping understanding, but it is signing treaties to be allies with Russia in World War Three.

The vision closes and the document is rolled up. (Good Friday, March 30th, 2018)

93. MOTHER... FIRST YOU WILL PREPARE MY CHILDREN IN THESE TIMES OF GREAT PERSECUTION

'Mother behold thy Son[148]'. 'Son, behold thy Mother'
He drops ... crying ...

Soul to Soul, Redeemer to Co-Redemptrix:

"Mother I am leaving You behind. If I could spare you this moment I would; but for this You came into the World and brought forth Me in your Virginal Womb as the *Immaculate Conception* and the *Mother of God*. I Am He, will You be My *Advocate* for these that You may ransom them back to Me, Who is suffering and Who must suffer a little while longer?

Mother I wish that even when You come home to Me in Heaven, Body and Soul, Your role will be to prepare for My Second Coming but first you will prepare My children in these times of great persecution against My Church for this generation who otherwise would be cursed by My Father. But I have suffered this night and this day for them.

"I love thee."

Mama nods.

---

[148] John 19,25-27

"I love Thee too My Son."

"Amen, Amen." *Jesus says.*

There is silence ... Now His lips are parched; yet it is not what He will cry out for ...

"I thirst, I thirst![149]"

One of the guards sees Him and hears Him and he runs and dips the hyssop into the sour wine and brings it up to Jesus. Yet Jesus does not taste it. He smells it and turns away; it is for Souls He is thirsting!

Soul to Soul He speaks to me now:

"My beloved daughter suffering this moment with Me this day in remembrance of My first Good Friday known to you: I thirst for Souls! Stay united to My Blessed Mother who is Co-Redeeming as *Co-Redemptrix* and you with Her and with all My beloved children who are praying this moment. They are not praying for you but praying with you. They have formed a beautiful wreath to console my Mother's Immaculate Heart. I desire that they pray in this manner in the days ahead when they hear of persecution and wars, Earthquakes, and famines. All this must take place but through their prayers, yours through My Blessed Mother, many Souls will escape from the claws of Satan, My adversary!

I love you, I Am Jesus of Nazareth, True God and True Man, the High Priest suffering for My Priests and so must you ... known as the religious! Amen. Amen." (*Good Friday, March 30th, 2018*)

---

[149] John 19,28

94. I AM THE ONE THAT GOD HAS GIVEN ALL POWER, ALL GRACE

Now the scroll opens, and Archangel Gabriel holds it and stands below Our Blessed Mother. He speaks:

I hold now the scroll with the words of Our Holy Mother, the *Mother of God*, Our Heavenly Mother and She speaks:

"My beloved children here present before me, little one of Mine and My Jesus, Cleophas and My beloved of the Beloved Felix Xavier, her spouse I thank you for responding to my request, to suffer for your world that grieves my Immaculate Heart to bleeding moments and tears of blood that well up in my Immaculate Eyes, and fall through this suffering upon those who desire to come out of the grave demoralising standard that this nation Canada is plunging her children into, children who once belonged to God and now have embraced Satan as their ruler and king! Yet you my beloved children will not be harmed!

Do only as I have asked! Entrust all into my Immaculate Heart and of vital importance that you may know - like breathing is to you and your Souls – is specially the Consecration each morning to my Immaculate Heart.

Do not leave your homes without consecrating yourselves to My Immaculate heart! You and all your loved ones! All that I've entrusted to you must be placed back into my Immaculate Heart, all those who have come to mind by name, especially mothers bringing their children now, who will be exposed to such grave dangers! Only I can help! Truly only I can help! For God has empowered me and has bestowed upon me all grace, all power and all gifts!

The Heavenly Court of legions of Angels whose Prince is Saint Michael stands at My disposal to come before you when you call for help through My intercession.

I await the proclamation of the *fifth dogma*; where it will give Me power to protect all God's children Consecrated to Jesus through my Immaculate Heart.

Beloved children do not concern yourself with idle talk; prayer is important!"

... She is now raising the Rosary beads.

"It is the only weapon for your time and a prayer so powerful! If you understood its value, you would be reciting the Hail Mary and the Holy Mary continuously even when speaking to someone - listen, reciting the Hail Mary and Holy Mary, speaking very little!

Beloved children be not troubled, be not anxious! I am here with you. Only invoke My Presence! This Archangel who stands at My right, St Michael has the power to destroy any evil power that has been launched at you and will be launched at you. By launched, I mean, will be directed to harming but cannot do any harm, for God's shield stands around you and around those who invoke my Immaculate mantle. It is a shield where Satan cannot penetrate!

Know I am the the Woman Clothed in the Sun[150] and will crush the head of Satan![151]

My Immaculate Heart Will Triumph in the end and Russia will be consecrated to My Immaculate Heart and the era of peace will descend upon your world. Now you must go through these moments and I am the one that God has given all Power, all Grace, all Gifts to direct this moment and to protect God's children who will go through these moments,

---

[150] Rev 12,1
[151] Gen 3,15

through whom, the Remnant will be chosen! Your faith is vital! Know, you must pray for this Gift; specially my chosen Sons and the Brides of Christ, known as Nuns, the Religious, who must pray for this Gift!

I will come to receive this suffering in its fullness, little one of mine and My Jesus at the hour of Divine Mercy tomorrow, known as the first Friday.

I am the Mother of God, the *Mediatrix of All Grace, Co-Redemptrix* and *Advocate* in Heaven, awaiting to be proclaimed on Earth and it will come to be with your prayers.

I love you dearly. I thank you immensely for responding in this manner to be united to My Jesus and I Who Am Co-Redemptrix with the *Redeemer* Jesus, True God and True Man. Amen." *(First Thursday, September 6th, 2018)*

95. THERE ARE NOT MANY VICTIM SOULS

... so many deformed babies ... so much of damage is done with this drug ... Hail Mary & Holy Mary ... the legalizing of this drug is the worship of Satan and the sacrifice of the unborn ... Satanic behaviour ... Holy Mary ... protect us Holy Mama ... protect these children ... Hail Mary ... Holy Mary.

Many will be used as holocausts to Satanic worship, premature babies... Hail Mary ... Holy Mary ...

The legalising of this drug is a terrible implication for humankind ... it is Satan coming into power now ... Hail Mary ... Holy Mary ...

With it, all other drugs now will be coming into power as medicine to do away with so many children of God. They will be enslaved to this power of evil.

Holy Mama Speaks:

"My beloved children, know and understand this moment that is coming into being. It is the reign of Satan coming into being under the disguise of legalising this drug. Many of you will subject yourselves to it.

Know when you subject yourself to it, you will become Satan's advocate; you will rise against your own kindred and your own parents; and parents against their children, putting one another to death[152]. I warn you of this! I am the *Mother of God*, I am your Heavenly Mother. You leave me powerless when you choose Satan as your father and your mother and his advocates, the fallen angels to be your helpers. They will destroy you, limb by limb and use you as sacrifice to Satanic worship. This is the free will by which God has given you, now you must choose God or Satan as your God.

In the end My *Immaculate Heart Will Triumph,* as Satan will be destroyed and the era of peace will descend on your World. Know beloved children, God is always a winner.

It might appear that He is losing the battle, but He has given you free will to choose between Him and Satan who wants to be like God, but he is not! He has no power over God, only the power that God has given him for a time. Now you must realise you are entering an era of grave danger and darkness, when the Souls of humankind will be tainted, and on which will be written the laws of Satan, those who will choose Satan as their god, renouncing God!

Only through suffering like this little one of Mine and My Jesus, can such Souls be rescued but there are not many Victim Souls, not even My Priests want to be Victim Souls and I call

---

[152] Mark 13,12

them now to become Victim Souls, to rescue Souls! Do not be afraid of suffering, you have seen your Master in Whose footsteps My beloved chosen sons are called to follow. Know and understand, suffering will befall you even if you do not choose to be Victim Souls. Such is the hour at hand now!

Many of My churches will close down. By this, you may understand the Churches - the Catholic Church who honour Me as their Mother, The *Mother of God* and as the Mother of all humanity by which God chooses to ransom and rescue His Children! It is My hour of Power coming into being as the *Immaculate Conception* who will crush the head of Satan[153], but you must choose between Satan and God. It is then, I become Your Heavenly Mother, for all Power, all Grace has been entrusted unto Me to rescue My children now from the slavery of the enemy of God, Satan himself.

In the end, My Immaculate Heart will Triumph and the era of peace will descend upon Your World and the reign of The Immaculate Heart and The Sacred Heart of Jesus will flourish for a thousand years of Peace[154].

I Am the *Mother of God*, the *Mediatrix of all Grace, Co-Redemptrix* and *Advocate* in Heaven awaiting to be proclaimed under this title, through your prayers it will come to be, that I may rescue more Souls who are enslaving themselves to Satanic cults, embracing Satan as their god!

"Who is like unto God?

None but Thee! None but Thee, O God! O God, O God!

---

[153] Gen 3,15

[154] Rev 20,2

"None but Thee", cried out St Michael, who is your companion when you call on Him. He will help you to fight these forces of darkness. He is God's Mighty Angel, My servant as He calls Himself, servant of the *Immaculate Conception*, I am She.

I love you My Beloved children. I Am your Heavenly Mother.

I Am powerless when you do not invoke Me. I need your consent to embrace you and to rescue you from the slavery of the Satanic world and even Satan himself! He has no power over Me as the *Immaculate Conception*. I am She, your Heavenly Mother Who loves you dearly, the *Mother of God*, I remind you Amen." (*First Thursday*, September 6*th*, 2018)

YR 2019: I AM THE MEDIATOR BETWEEN YOU AND MY FATHER, BUT MY MOTHER IS THE MEDIATRIX BETWEEN YOU AND ME

96. ST. JOSEPH IS THE ONE TO INVOKE AND PRAY AT THE DYING MOMENT

Our Lady speaks:

"My beloved children, I thank thee immensely, specially this little one of Mine and My Jesus, for suffering for the brothers and sisters who are paying Divine Justice and for allowing Me to offer this suffering, to expiate the time they must serve in Purgatory. Do you understand, besides Me is Saint Joseph, My Chaste Spouse on Earth, now in Heaven. His Kingdom must be understood on Earth as 'silence'. He is the One to invoke and pray to, at the hour, at the final hour of one's transition from Earth into the Resurrection known as the dying moment, dying from Earth, rising into the Resurrection. Unto Him is given this special privilege, himself to bring Souls to Jesus, the Divine Saviour and to intercede for them at this moment. In the days ahead I will explain this understanding in the Kingdom of Saint Joseph. Amen.

Now beloved children I also desire with great desire to thank my beloved of the Beloved, Felix Xavier once again for assisting Me by helping this little one of Mine and My Jesus, Cleophas his spouse as she undergoes this suffering that will bear fruit, everlasting fruit to bring Souls back to God and into eternity with God.

I desire with great desire to make known that the next suffering, that will befall this little one of Mine and My Jesus, will be for the Universal and Domestic Church, for the great tempest that is rising for the sin of Sodom. She will suffer greatly but I will be with her through it all." ... *(First Friday of Lent, March 15ᵗʰ, 2019)*

97. THIS IS THE HUMAN THINKING THAT HAS EMBRACED TO BE LIKE GOD, THE DEMONIC WILL

Jesus motions with His hands to see... the soldiers being led by Judas. He comes marching straight to Jesus; but he has already told them that the One he kisses is the One they must arrest[155] to take to safety. Here the word schism comes forth.

Jesus speaks Soul to Soul:

"Beloved daughter of Mine, little one Cleophas: I the Master, thank you for immolating yourself in Me. Know and understand now: This kiss that Judas Iscariot will betray Me with, he thinks he is saving me from the Will of God that he does not understand. This is what you must understand - the 'schism in My Church' today!

These are those who will betray the Holy Father, My Peter, for they do not understand the Will of God. In this manner you will also understand that when I Am lifted up and breathe My last breath tomorrow in the understanding of that first Good Friday, you will see the curtain tearing[156] - this is the understanding of *the Great Schism*! There has never been one like this, nor will there ever be! This is the betrayal of My Peter, and by doing so they are betraying Me! This is the human thinking that has embraced to be like God - the demonic will - and yet they do not know! These are My faithful, once upon a time as the world would see them and speak of them. Today they betray the Catholic Church with a kiss like Judas. It would be well for them if they were never born[157]! Amen, Amen. "

---

[155] Mt 26,48

[156] Mt 27,51

[157] Mt 26,24

160

Judas comes marching and goes straight to Jesus and he kisses Him. And the Lord looks at him and says:

"With a kiss you betray me Judas[158]." *And Judas does not understand what Jesus is saying, he thinks he is saving Jesus from His madness of dying, and it is this very madness that is the Will of God and it is Judas who takes the Lord into this path that will lead into the Resurrection and Judas looks at Jesus now, as the soldiers come and arrest Him.*

And Jesus speaks Soul to Soul with Judas: "Why have you done this?"

Judas speaks to the Lord, Soul to Soul: "You said they were going to kill You and the Son of Man will be betrayed and will put to death and will rise on the third day. I don't want this to happen to You! You don't know what You are talking about. You must be experiencing some madness!"

And Judas looks at Jesus as though he is doing Him good, and Jesus speaks to Judas saying: "Judas, how I have loved you, even now", *and then it's like something breaks like a cord, like an umbilical cord from the Mother to the baby, and no longer can Jesus speak to Judas and no longer can Judas hear the Lord. And as they are walking out of the Garden of Olives, Judas looks at Jesus and they are beating Him, and Judas does not know what to do! He tries to stop them, but he can't.* "Go your way", *they tell him* "we have paid you."

... and the vision closes for me, and the suffering begins up on my body, the suffering of so many who will betray the Holy Father, the Catholic Church!

---

[158] Luke 22,48

... Many false witnesses are rising just like those that have said, "This is He Who said to destroy the temple and He would raise It up in three days[159]!"

They will march against the Holy Father not realising that they are spreading a devastating plague of lies and deceit, all in the name of 'Truth' and that the Holy Father is blaspheming God. They have already been drawn into the understanding and belief that he is the antichrist, and the hidden Pope is the antipope. Many are confused! They believe the hidden Pope, Pope Benedict XVI, Emeritus as a good Pope and could he be the 'antipope'?

Jesus speaks Soul to My Soul:

"How is it that the one you call 'good Pope', My hidden Pope, who is suffering so much for My Church, My Bride, who aids and stands by My Peter who is suffering great anxieties because of your false accusations - can this be so? Can the true Pope authenticate the false? It can never be! You are now bringing condemnation upon yourselves and upon your children who you are raising to live as true Catholics in the understanding of living the culture of Life, yet you have abandoned the fundamental, the Rock, that I have built My Church on[160], My Word stands[161]! It can never be nullified! 'You are Peter. Upon this Rock, I shall build My Church and the gates of Hell shall not prevail against you. I Am with you till the end of time.[162]' Do you not understand, you the faithful ones who love Me are betraying Me now with a kiss by betraying My Peter - The Schism!

---

[159] Mark 14,58

[160] Mt 16,18

[161] Mt 24,35

[162] Mt 28,20

I am Jesus of Nazareth, True God and True Man betrayed into the hands of sinners, suffering this night, for what is to come upon the whole world because of the Schism in the Catholic Church, My Bride. Amen, Amen."

The Vision closes for me.

... Holy Mama!

"Daughter I Am with you. Now you will take your rest till I will wake you up and walk with you to see what Our Loving Saviour, My Divine Son Jesus is enduring because of this Schism in the Church, the Catholic Church.

I am the *Mother of God*; I am Your Heavenly Mother carrying you through these moments. Amen." *(Holy Thursday, April 18ᵗʰ, 2019)*

98. THIS IS THE SCHISM, THE GREAT SCHISM!

They are kicking Jesus and taking Him. My body is experiencing this pain ... Ah! ... Lord ... I neither see nor hear, only feel the pain in my body ...

... Some of us, when they strike the Shepherds, will flee in nauseating cell like places. There will be no choice. Now you must understand this moment of false accusations and false charges will not come from those who do not believe. It is the spirit of pride, rebellious Souls full of conceit and jealousy that will kill brother against brother, mother against daughter, sister against sister, father against son.[163] They will think they are doing right, they will tolerate abominations and abominable people, but they will not tolerate those

---

[163] Luke 12,53

who believe in the reigning Pope, today His Holiness, Pope Francis I in union with Emeritus Pope Benedict XVI.

This is what the division is all about, the culture of death and yet they will think they are bringing in the culture of Life. In these, My Holy Spirit will not dwell! It is zeal for the law and the ordinances and precepts, yet no love! It is only love that will bring Mercy and Justice, but they will not embrace this Love! It is a false notion of love and self-righteousness by which they will march! They will drag you out of your own homes and beat you to death! They will even stone you in the belief that they are getting rid of all those who believe in the antichrist and the antipope, not yet on the Seat of Peter - but in belief that this is the one. What a horrible moment!

… They have taken Jesus back to Pilate from Herod.

"You see daughter", *Soul to Soul Jesus speaks:*

Now Holy Mama knows that I'm terrified. She puts Her Mantle around me, and now I can see and hear what She is going through at this very moment.

"You see how I was silent before Herod[164] and he did not stone Me but sent Me to Pilate back again, they will not even give you a chance to go before judges, they will make themselves judges and they will kill the innocent and acquit the guilty like you will see in a little while when Pilate will wash his hands[165] and condemn Me and set forth free, the guilty! Such is the coldness of heart, such is the lack of faith and it is not those who do not know Me; it is those who say they know Me, the faithful! This is the Schism, the *Great Schism!*

---

[164] Luke 23,9
[165] Mt 27,24

I Am Jesus of Nazareth, here suffering gravely for lukewarm Souls who have turned their gaze away from Me and My Father in Heaven! Amen. Amen." *(Holy Thursday, April 18th, 2019)*

99. YOU MUST COME TO HER AND THEN TO ME, IT IS THE WILL OF MY FATHER!

Jesus speaks Soul to Soul as He is led away:

"Little one of Mine, how I wish many would console Me like you do. If they only know how much I love them! They are worth much more than what they have lured themselves into. They have reduced themselves below the worth of animals! Even now if they would turn and embrace the cross I have designed for them in union with Me, they will rise!

Know daughter now, they will drag you off! I speak to the Church Militant in this manner. Many of you will be lacerated like this, beaten to denounce Me!" *... and here Oh Lord! ... Ah ... a Tear falls from Jesus full of Blood Ah! ... crying ... Ah! ... Lord I would gather that One and sprinkle it over the Souls that you want me to pray for ...* "If they only knew that denouncing Me would be eternal death, and yet they will embrace that out of fear of men!"

I Am Jesus of Nazareth, here suffering for each one of My children."

And now here He presents something quite different.

"I Am the Mediator between you and My Father, but My Mother is the Mediatrix - Mediatress between you and Me. Understand this manner: You must come to Her and then to

Me, it is the will of My Father! It is here you will understand the Consecration and the Love for My Blessed Mother that I have, that you must embrace, all you My beloved children like this little one and her spouse, My beloved of I, Who Am the Beloved of My Father, Jesus of Nazareth, Amen, Amen." *(Holy Thursday, April 18th, 2019)*

*

Jesus speaks Soul to Soul: "Little one of Mine Cleophas."

Iveta: 'Yes Lord'.

"Do you see, now you are carrying My Suffering united to My Blessed Mother. It is called the *'hidden suffering'*. This is how My *underground Church* will carry suffering. Many a time, they will be dragged out, members among them and they must bear witness to this and suffer! Do you see how they hail Me? This is the mockery of those who have joined the forces.

They have divided the Church's Militant and, in the hierarchy too, they have separated themselves, forming a 'new church'. There is no such thing as a 'new church', I Am not divided! I Am united to My Father and My Father to Me and My Bride[166], whose cross now your Holy Father, Blessed of Mine, My Pope, My Peter carries as was my instruction on that first day when I pronounced Peter, telling him that he would be the one to whom I would give the keys of My Church and upon him I would build My Church.[167]

---

[166] Eph 5,25
[167] Mt 16,18

Do you see how they mock Me? These are those who do not honour My Mother in what is called the 'Charismatic movement', after My Heart, yet not with Love! It is only a name, yet there are some who, truly in this charismatic movement, honour My Mother and have a devotion to Her in praising Me and hailing Her and worshipping Me and Consecrating themselves to Her Immaculate Heart to belong to Me. Her Immaculate Heart is Co-Redeeming with Me. Her Immaculate Heart will receive all the Graces bestowed upon Me by My Father and the Gifts that I have made known to you.

Now, when I expire and return to My Father and your Father,[168] She will be the One carrying you and My Church. In this manner, if you Consecrate yourselves to Her Immaculate Heart, your hearts will be circumcised of all evil.[169] She can cut through the thickest foreskin of evil that is choking your heart from receiving My Grace through Her and She will present you to Me; I Who Am the *Advocate* between Me and My Father and She between you and Me; I Who Am The Divine Judge in Heaven; She, My *Advocate* on Earth to bring you to Me and who will prepare you in spite of all your faults, even after I have died for you; yet you continue on the road of perdition![170]

Should you turn back and Consecrate yourselves to Her Immaculate Heart, you will understand that She will prepare you and even tip the scales by calling on Victim Souls like this little one of Mine, your beloved sister Cleophas, to suffer for you, who now is suffering for so many today who will turn and return through Her Immaculate Heart, and embracing

---

[168] John 20,17
[169] Dt 30,6 – Jer 4,4
[170] Mt 7,13

Her as their Mother, their Mediatrix - Mediatress and *Advocate*, Who will Co-redeem for them!

Jesus of Nazareth, Amen. Amen." *(Holy Thursday, April 18th, 2019)*

*

Jesus speaks now Soul to my Soul:

Do you see daughter: This is what they are doing with ropes in this widespread schism of My Church. How can you take the marrow from the bone? By separating themselves, they are taking out themselves and they are becoming like empty bones. The marrow exists in My Peter, the Life and Blood giving line of Sacramental Grace from My Catholic Church, My Bride.

They have begun such a mockery of Him in the hierarchy, they mock him at every moment. It doesn't matter what he says, their decision is made - like you hear the crowd, the Pharisees, the Sadducees, the Scribes and all the many that I healed and made well - they have even turned away their faces and have closed their ears, in seeing they did not want to see, in hearing they did not want to hear![171] I have spoken these words already that in seeing they are like those who cannot see, in hearing they are like those who cannot hear and in persevering they cannot perceive!

Do you understand the schism now? They have persevered diligently, they know all about Me, they know the ways, yet they do not understand Mercy and Love, and they have no Faith! Faith is born with Mercy and Love in each

---

[171] Mc 8,18

Soul. When you do not deprive the Soul of Love for God, in the littleness of humbling yourselves and not exploiting yourselves to play God and Love for one another, in Mercy that is forgiving, you will grow in faith and become rich in Love! It is then that Me and My Father will come to dwell in your Soul.[172] We will abide in you and you in Us! It is in this faith you will be born to a new life[173] with Me and My Father, and here My Mother will be with you. Through Her Immaculate Heart you will pass through this understanding and shed all that chokes you and blocks you of the True Faith and Love, embracing My Mercy!

Jesus of Nazareth, about to be condemned by so many … and Jesus sheds a tear Ah! … This is an understanding of lukewarm Souls that will not change. Amen, Amen. (Holy Thursday, April 18th, 2019)

100. THIS IS ABOUT THOSE WHO ARE CALLING FOR THE RESIGNATION OF MY PETER, TO DETHRONE HIM!

"Who do you want me to release, Barabbas (I cannot even pronounce his name, I'm shivering inside just watching the scene) or Jesus, King of the Jews. And they scream "We have no King but Caesar[174], release Barabbas!"

"I want no part of His Blood," says Pilate to them, "of this Innocent Man, I find no fault in Him. His blood be upon us and our children."[175]

---

[172] John 14,23
[173] John 3,3
[174] John 19,15
[175] Mt 27,25

Now Jesus speaks Soul to Soul:

"Do you understand this, little one of Mine, Cleophas?"

Iveta: "No Lord … crying I'm only a child, what is this?

Jesus speaks:

"This is about those who are calling for the resignation of My Peter, to dethrone him! These are those who call him the antichrist, the antipope! They do not even understand what they are saying. They want His Blood upon themselves, upon their children. They are walking the path of perdition[176] as My Mother made known. This is the deadly venom, as Russia was not Consecrated to Her Immaculate Heart in time, that has now entered the Elect and the faithful! You must understand and stay faithful, those who are Consecrated genuinely to My Mother's Immaculate Heart, My Blessed Mother, who suffers so much for your world now!

Jesus of Nazareth Amen. Amen." *(Holy Thursday, April 18th, 2019)*

101. ALL THE IRREVERENCES UNDER WHICH JESUS IS RECEIVED

Jesus makes no protest. Like a Lamb led to the slaughterhouse in silence, not even a bleat![177] Now Jesus is brought forth, and as they prepare Him to receive His Cross, the Cross is being brought out.

Holy Mama is at the back again. By back again, I mean that I had seen this vision in the years gone by in which She was

---

[176] Mt 7,13
[177] Is 53,7

gathering, wiping His Blood on Her Garment and Pilate's wife comes down and gives Her towels and looks at Her and says "Your Son?" .... Ah! ...And Holy Mama motions Her not to weep for Him but for her children, herself and for women and their children and She continues wiping. She picks up all His Flesh and puts It in a little bag that She makes from a fold in Her Garment and tucks it away in Her Belt to hold this Flesh.

Now Holy Mama speaks to Me.

"Little one of Mine and My Jesus, Cleophas, suffering this day for so many Souls, you do not understand what I have done. This is what happens to many sacrilegious communions under all irreverences with which Jesus is received, Fragments falling on the ground, Jesus left abandoned by those who do not wish to receive Him, left in the pews and thrown down in disbelief! This is how I send My Angels to gather Them, as you once did.[178] You were as Angels to undergo the reparation you must do, the reparation needed of prayers for such offences! Now this offence is widespread, and the condemnation[179] will befall as persecution! Here also understand this is the evil that I had predicted that Russia would spread its errors and laxity would be born in disbelief of the True Presence of Jesus in the Holy Eucharist as True flesh and True Blood!

Mary of Nazareth, Co-Redeeming with the *Mediator* as *Mediatrix* - Mediatress. Amen" (*Holy Thursday, April 18th, 2019*)

---

[178] It often happened that Felix and Iveta would find in some churches pieces of the Holy Eucharist thrown down in disbelief and would pick them up with great reverence.

[179] 1Cor 11,29

102. THE UNDERGROUND CHURCH IS PREPARED FOR THE FAITHFUL REMNANT

Holy Mama is held by Mary of Magdala and St John the Apostle. There are many women behind Her. It is like a little group of the faithful, amidst the crowd that is crying "Crucify Him!", and Jesus embraces the cross with open arms. They lay it on His right shoulder.

Jesus speaks Soul to Soul to Me: "Little one of Mine Cleophas, do you understand now?"

Iveta: No Lord, I understand that I must carry My Cross, for I do not understand anymore."

"Yes, in fidelity you must carry your cross,[180] and that's what My Blessed Mother will lay upon your shoulder in moments of your exile on Earth, to be united to Me. Now know and understand, the *underground church* is prepared for the faithful *Remnant*[181] who remain faithful, and not for those who have embraced the path of schism, the widespread evil of the once faithful who embraced My Cross - that is received the Sacramental Grace of the Church - and now betray! For they are playing equality with God and exploiting God's ways, to be brought down in a human and demonic way of thinking, by acclaiming that they are building a 'new church'. And this I will allow, yet your faith now will be tested against such, and not the unbelievers, to remain faithful to My Peter, the reigning Pope today, the true Pope after My Heart, My Sacred Heart and the hidden Pope. This you must understand of the antipope, of how he will take his place!

And the prayers of the hidden Pope are for you, the Church Militant now, as one will rise to build a 'new church' and he

---

[180] Mt 16,24

[181] Rev 12,17

172

will be the antichrist! Let not fear rule you, knowing all this! Only embrace My ways by Consecrating yourselves to My Mother's Immaculate Heart. Her Blessed Heart will reign and Triumph over all My adversaries in these times!

And of the most importance is the proclamation of the *Fifth Dogma*, as it has come to be known, that She be proclaimed *Mediatrix of all Grace, Co-Redemptrix* and *Advocate* to dispense the necessary Graces upon My Remnant, My true Remnant, not the 'new church' - there is no such thing! Yes, Heaven and Earth will pass away, but My Words will not pass,[182] not even the smallest dot![183]

I am Jesus of Nazareth suffering now for the *Great Schism* in the Church, carrying this Cross, praying that many will renounce this falsehood and return to the Truth. I am He in My Catholic Church, still standing on the Solid Rock I have built it on[184], and will stand! Amen. Amen! Now rest daughter, your body is tired." *(Good Friday, April 19th, 2019)*

103. TAKE COURAGE, I HAVE ALREADY WALKED THIS PATH!

Now Jesus speaks Soul to Soul to me:

"You My *Remnant*, the Church Militant as we have come to be known: Remain faithful! Remain faithful! What they have done to Me to this hour and at the hour that will lead to My Resurrection, they will do to you! But take courage, I have already walked this path, you only need to follow Me! And now you must understand to all you Holy Orders and those

---

[182] Mt 24,35
[183] Mt 5,18
[184] Mt 16,18

who remain faithful to Me: Among you are those who will do the same, what they have done to Me, they will do to you, I have already made known.

This is the great chastisement, the catastrophe of the loss of mankind's conscience that will lead to the reign of the antichrist and the antipope, yet I am with you through it all.

In the *underground Church* you will minister, and you will bring forth the fruit of the New Earth and the New Heavens[185], the New Order, the *Order of My Sacred Heart and The Immaculate Heart of My Mother,* for My Priests and for My Brides. You will understand that now in these times you will learn the part of amalgamating and I will be with you through it all, and so will be My Peter. Jesus of Nazareth, Amen, Amen."

Jesus speaks Soul to Soul as He is nearing the top:

"All the many papers that are spreading wicked lies of My Peter are destroying the minds of the innocent, their children and they will increase in their deceitfulness for I will permit such and they will grow stout in their pride while the consciences will grow dull at each moment and that with each lie they will not know the truth when it stands in their face. This is the Great Schism, like it there never was! I have made all this known plainly. This is worse for the Souls of the children of God who have chosen to walk the path of perdition, worse than the effects of World War Three, should it come into being!

Jesus of Nazareth, True God, True Man, now ready to be Crucified, Amen. Amen." *(Good Friday, April 19th, 2019)*

---

[185] Rev 21,1

104. THIS HOLY CHURCH BE REBUILT AND CONSECRATED TO ME UNDER THE TITLE OF 'MARY, MOTHER OF THE CHURCH, OUR LADY OF MOUNT GANXIM – BATIM'

Our Lady speaks:

"My beloved children, My beloved chosen sons, My beloved chosen daughters, how pleasing an odour you are to me! You have gathered in such large numbers. If you only understood this moment! You are the force that will go forth in these hours of darkness against the culture of death to build the *culture of life* as God intended it from the beginning.

I desire with great desire to thank you immensely and to you all who have been faithful to Me from the first moment I descended upon this Holy Mountain and claimed it for God: You will understand this day! Be patient with your heavenly Mother, for I have much to disclose to you.

This I speak now to the Shepherd of this Diocese, My beloved chosen son, the Archbishop, his Grace Archbishop Filipe Neri Ferrao. I thank you immensely for welcoming Me, though I knew you would not be present here and to the Diocese known as the sister Diocese of Goa, in Heaven, His Grace Bishop Alwyn Barreto: I am aware of your presence needed elsewhere, yet it is the duty of your heavenly Mother to welcome you and to make you aware of Her presence that will descend upon this Holy Mountain. Without your permission, it would not be possible. I thank you immensely and now I desire with great desire to place a yoke upon your shoulder.

This yoke: I desire with great desire that this Holy Church, once a full and living Tabernacle of God, bringing Souls back to God, that lies in a state of semi ruins, be rebuilt and

175

consecrated to Me under the title of 'Mary, Mother of the Church, Our Lady of Mount Ganxim – Batim'.

I promise you, My beloved chosen sons: I will not leave this burden upon your shoulders, I ask all my beloved children now present here and all those who are watching this moment through electronic devices made possible, to carry this yoke as Simon of Cyrene did. With your help, this Church will be rebuilt, and you will understand this meaning in the days ahead."

Now, She pauses and She speaks again:

"My beloved children, I now as your heavenly Mother warn you of a great evil that is tearing the internal forum of the Catholic Church under the disguise of living the Orthodox nature of the Catholic Church, yet dismantling themselves from the Holy Father, the head of the Catholic Church. How then will you see beloved children? This I speak to My faithful and My chosen sons and daughters also involved in this movement called *(Iveta: I cannot pronounce that word Mother)* schism *(Iveta: I am not sure)*. Do not worry, continue, you will understand. *(Iveta: Ok.)*

I assure that this reigning Pope is neither the anti-Pope nor the anti-Christ. He is coming soon and will sit on the throne of Peter as a desolate sacrilege[186]. His reign must come to be so that the power and glory of God will come to be known. Yet fear not, I am with you! I will walk with you, I will run[187] with you and I will carry you to skip these moments of darkness! Only Entrust all into My Immaculate Heart! Amen.

Now, I desire with great desire that you pray for your Holy Father, My beloved chosen son, His Holiness Pope Francis I in union with Emeritus Pope Benedict XVI, the hidden Pope who

---

[186] Mark 13,14
[187] Rev 12,6

prays for your world. I am aware that you have prayed for them. Continue in this manner! It pleases Me much and many blessings will you receive for generations to come. Amen."

Then, She pauses and She addresses the other[188]:

"Now I desire with great desire to make known the well, that contained the Holy water to bring forth prodigies and healings, first spiritual and then physical, must be re-blessed by My beloved chosen sons present here for the waters were tampered. God neither deceives nor can He be deceived! Know and understand, this well is dedicated to St John the Baptist. Such is the conversion of sinners that will come to drink of this water. And the Custodian is St Michael, yet unless God issues an order, he cannot do anything, except watch in suffering, as I do." (*25ᵗʰ Anniversary of Our Lady's First Visitation, Batim, Goa, India, September 24ᵗʰ, 2019*)

105. "DO YOU UNDERSTAND THE CHURCH INTO MY IMMACULATE HEART?"

Now, She pauses and She speaks again.

"My beloved chosen sons, upon you rests the weight of this terrible darkness. Yet fear not! Know and understand the power entrusted by God to you! You stand in the highest rank of man. Your office is of a higher office. Do not compromise! Only know that you have the power to exorcise all these children out of the spirits of darkness and bring them into the spirit of light. Know and understand also that you must take the sacramental Grace awarded to you and entrusted unto you by Jesus My Divine Son the high Priest, in whose footsteps you

---

[188] The other evil

follow, to carry this Mission and to lead the Church in union with the Holy Father. Remain faithful to Him!

And you, upon you My beloved chosen daughters, the brides of Christ, rests a very heavy weight to bring into being and to teach the children of the Domestic Church, to lead them to understand the Will of God into the understanding of the culture of life against all that is being preached to them by the culture of death. You will understand these moments. Amen."

Iveta: "Now, She seems to go back."

Our Lady: "Do you understand the Church into My Immaculate Heart?"

Iveta: "No Mother, how can I? I am only a child."

"I will protect the Church. I am the Mother of this Holy Church entrusted by God to all humanity. And at this very moment, I place another yoke on the shoulder of the Shepherd of this Diocese. When this Church is rebuilt, I desire with great desire that it be entrusted into the custody of the order known as the Carmelite order. The understanding is this, is simple: The *Mediatrix of all Grace* Scapular has its origin in the Carmelite Scapular, that is My Garment.

I beg of you now My beloved chosen sons and daughters to take a deeper love to come upon this Mountain and administer the pastoral care needed for the sheep that will come who are in distress and need your help. Will you help Me?

I love you dearly. I am your heavenly Mother. I will help you. Amen."

"I desire now with great desire to thank all My beloved children present here to understand that you have walked in fidelity for a quarter of a century with Me, and yet there is much to accomplish, and it will be so, for God never fails in His promise of love and His promise to bring love to all man. As the Mother of all mankind, of all humanity, I love you all and I thank you immensely!

I am the *Mother of God*, always present, reminding all Mothers once again who are failing, to consecrate their children by name every morning, to entrust them into My Immaculate Heart. I will take care of them. Only know that I can do so in these days. I love you dearly. I am the *Mother of God, the Mediatrix of all Grace, Co-Redemptrix* and *Advocate* in Heaven, awaiting to be proclaimed on Earth. Amen."

Iveta: "Now She rises, yet She leaves the miracle of the sun behind, so many can bear witness."

St Michael, the Archangel, defend us in this day of battle, be our safeguard against the wickedness and snares of the devil. May God rebuke him, we humbly pray and do thou, O prince of the heavenly host by the power of God, cast into Hell, Satan and all the evil spirits who wander through this world seeking the ruins of Souls, Amen.

In the name of the Father, and of the Son and of the Holy Spirit, Amen." (25th *Anniversary of Our Lady's First Visitation, Batim, Goa, India, September 24th, 2019)*

YR 2020: WHEN SHE IS PROCLAIMED, I WILL OPEN THE FLOOD GATES OF HEAVEN THAT ALL MY BELOVED CHILDREN WILL BE ABLE TO UNDERGO THIS SUFFERING OF THE PERSECUTION OF MY CHURCH

106. A MORE DEVASTATING PLAGUE WILL BEFALL UPON GOA TO PURIFY IT

Our Lady speaks:

"My beloved children, I thank you immensely for coming before Me this day at this hour, the hour when you would choose to rest and yes little one of mine and my Jesus, Cleophas, upon you rests a very heavy weight, the weight of sin that is manifesting itself all over ...

The Vatican in My Immaculate Heart as I have made known to you in My Visitation at Mount Ganxim, Batim is to be understood in this manner: There is a widespread epidemic ... *"... not that word again mother schism, schism ..."* Go on daughter it is alright, they will understand, ... that is rising at a rapid pace to overthrow the Holy Father. Prayer, much prayer is required to sustain him in these hours, it is of vital understanding. Yes, I am much pleased yet perplexed, with many wondering why they have to pray in this manner. It is as though they do not see, nor understand these moments, that many are praying at this very hour. And here before Me are they, through their Guardian Angels with candles lit, praying for the Holy Father. It pleases Me much!

Now I desire with great desire to make known the understanding, 'Batim lies in the shadow Fatima'. What you are now seeing as a disturbance[189], for Jesus said, 'The poor will always be with you, but I will not'[190]. You must understand this now: That the smoke of Satan has entered even among the hierarchy. Prayer is needed! You must stand diligently in prayer and in unified love for Me! You are seeing what I was praying for, that Goa would be Consecrated to My Immaculate Heart as I had made known. Yet it was not so, and now it is suffering

---

[189] What happened on Mount Batim
[190] John 12,8

the errors of Russia. Yes, even on my Holy grounds! Know and understand prayer is needed! The Holy Sacrifice must be raised! Processions must come forth! This will break the force that will cause great upheaval in the land God has chosen to manifest His Glory, God's Salvific Plan for your world. This must be understood in this manner: The Eucharistic Age!"

She pauses and tears roll …

"My beloved children I desire with great desire to make known to you: Should the Holy Sacrifice not be raised as I have asked, not just on the First Saturday but many Holy Sacrifices, to atone for the offences committed against the Sacred Heart of Jesus and My Immaculate Heart, the plague[191] that once God plagued the mountain of Ganxim-Batim and the surrounding villages, a more devastating plague will befall upon Goa to purify it; and yet God's plan will come forth! That this may not be, I ask you to be diligent in your prayer before Me. I am there waiting for you. Fear not! Be not troubled! Be not anxious! No harm will come to you, only through pray We can overturn evil! The prayer I desire with great desire is the Holy Rosary. It will bind the forces of darkness. Yes, even in your families, you must pray many Rosaries! Amen." *(Feast of Mary Mother of God, January 1ˢᵗ, 2020)*

107. THIS SUFFERING WAS TO FORTIFY HIM AS THE REIGNING POPE

"My Beloved children, I thank you immensely for responding generously to my request in every area. Yet there is one thing that distracts you. They are the duties of your calling.[192] They seem to be overwhelming and you are handling

---

[191] A bubonic plague that happened around the Year 1750

[192] The administrative work related to the Saint Joseph Community Centre at Foymont.

more than you should. It is well for you to now pray over these areas together and come to an understanding, till you allow help to come. And serve in this Vineyard of Mine for the Lord. You, my beloved of the Beloved, I thank you for all that you are responding to. And My Promise stands, I Am with you through it all! Even in your tired moments, you are able to do more than a well person would do. Know and understand: It is my Grace interceding at all times, yet do not be distracted! Of most vital now is what I will make known through these sufferings, this little one of Mine and My Jesus, your wife whom you have given so freely to suffer, to ransom Souls back. And in it you suffer with her too, I have made known that."

"Now I desire with great desire to make known, the suffering that she endured on Ash Wednesday, as it has come to be known, which begins the holy time of your redemption for all humanity. If they will only embrace and repent, this redemption is theirs through the Mercy of My Divine Son Jesus, the *Redeemer* and I, the *Co-Redemptrix*. And though these many little vessels, which are so very few, known as Victim Souls - as little vessels co-redeeming with Me, and I Who am the *Co-Redemptrix*, Co-Redeeming with the *Redeemer*. It is an understanding in what was said to fulfill what is lacking in the Sufferings of Jesus the *Redeemer*.[193] Yet one would say, how could this be? It was Willed by God that you carry some of the sufferings. Amen.

Now My beloved of the Beloved. Yes, you would say: 'Mother You got distracted'. No, it is on a purpose that I spoke in this manner. Here is the understanding of the suffering endured for the Holy Father. This suffering as I had made known, is the suffering for the terrible outrageousness, sacrilegiousness and indifference of the faithful, both in the Universal and Domestic Church, for the evil of Schism

---

[193] Col 1,24

that will tear the Church and will bring it to ruins, as in the understanding of its purification, which will mark the days of the Underground Church. The suffering endured by this little one was for the Holy Father, the reigning Pope today who has become … *(Iveta: I can't pronounce that word … I can't see clearly as I have weight on my right eye and am trying to read with my left eye. I'll come back later, if God lets me … another word for hatred … he has become …)* one that is hated by the faithful in the misunderstanding of what he says, how he lives and what he does, and yet he is Jesus and walks in the footsteps of the Lord, he is the Vicar of Christ Jesus.

This suffering was to fortify him, to console him and to give him the grace to move with love and fidelity to his calling as the reigning Pope." *(Friday after Ash Wednesday, February 28th, 2020)*

108. VERY SOON THE HOLY SPIRIT WILL BE TAKEN AWAY FROM YOU AND YOUR OWN SPIRIT WILL APPEAR AS THOUGH IT IS THE HOLY SPIRIT!

Now She pauses and speaks again. Now She speaks:

I see: So many, so many all over as though on the Globe, in the World - little pockets and by that I mean they were once under Our Lady's Immaculate Mantle and they were under Her protection, now there is like a semi-Mantle, the Mantle is torn[194]. These are those who have distanced themselves from the Holy Father, and now I see big convention centres everywhere and radio stations. They seem to be well to do people who have formed forces against the Holy Father. This I speak of the laity and what would be considered the future seminarians coming from these groups.

---

[194] John 19,24

Today Our Lady is ransoming the many who attend conventions and who do not understand which way to go, but seeing and hearing them, they are planning on embracing that route which would lead to perdition for them. Today in this suffering, Our Lady will be ransoming these Souls, giving them the Grace to discern further and to know and understand their truth. Their truth being, that this Holy Father is not the valid Pope; he is either the antipope or the antichrist. They themselves are not sure who he is!

Now the vision closes, and Our Lady is weeping. And She speaks. And as She speaks, the Tears that fall on Her White garment turn to Blood stains on Her Garment; yet on Her Cheeks they roll down as transparent Tears - like water, like our tears! But when they fall on her Garment, they are like Blood!

Now She speaks:

"My beloved children, how sorrowful a moment it has become to see so many of you consecrated to My Immaculate Heart - now tearing My Immaculate Heart and sorrowing It! And I weep! I weep for you to return to the harbour of Truth, the Catholic Church, to the Holy Father, today My beloved chosen Son, the Bishop of Rome, your Holy Father Pope Francis I. How heavy a Cross he carries, and I am with him to console him! How often he feels he cannot go on, and yet it is Me interceding as *Mediatrix of all Grace,* giving him all the strength to carry it through.

Know and understand: This path that you are taking, those who have already chosen it, should you not return - you are walking the part of perdition[195] - you and your children! There is no other way! You do not understand the ways of God! You have made God in your own image and likeness.[196] And it is

---

[195] Mt 7,13
[196] Gen 1,27

for this reason you consider yourselves above the law of God and you are spreading this terrible evil of Schism!"

Iveta: Here is that word again. I think I got it right, Yes? Mama nods her Head. Thank You Mama.

"Do you not believe Me daughter?"

Iveta: I believe Mother, help me in my disbelief. I looked at my husband to see if I had it right, instead of believing Mama.

"These now will come to be known as 'schismatics'. How you sorrow My Immaculate Heart! My beloved children you have come to be known as 'schismatics' and you are now leading others along this path of perdition. Very soon the Holy Spirit will be taken away from you and your own spirit will appear as though it is the Holy Spirit! Be on guard against such lawlessness that has come out of pride! Do not consider yourselves above the law! For God spared you and your children, to bring forth the beauty of being faithful to the teachings of the Catholic Church, yet not in a discriminatory understanding, as segregating yourselves and separating yourselves from the Truth, as being holier than you are! Only God is Holy and only God declares who is holy through the Catholic Church!

Beloved children, I long for you to return! Amen.

Know and understand now, little one of Mine and My Jesus: You will endure this for the twenty-four-hour period, in its understanding of suffering. Today this is for the Domestic Church, the following day it will rotate to the Universal Church. I will make known in its suffering for whom it is, you will be tormented for. For in this way, the Souls that you will ransom, if they do not choose - those who are following the path as 'schismatics', in this *schism* - they will give up the Faith completely and become advocates to Satan. It is for this reason now, My adversary will torment you! But I Am with you through it all, just as they did to Jesus in Gethsemane.

I love you dearly. I thank you, My beloved of the Beloved, for all that you are doing and, yes, for obtaining and working on it. When it is completed you will understand its meaning. Do not worry about the monetary means. All will be taken care of. Only do as I have made known!

I thank you immensely. I Am the Mother of God. I love you dearly, the *Mediatrix of all Grace, Co-Redemptrix* and *Advocate* in Heaven awaiting to be proclaimed on Earth. Amen. Your heavenly Mother who loves you dearly. Amen." *(Friday after Ash Wednesday, February 20ᵗʰ, 2020)*

109. THESE ARE THE FIRST BIRTH PANGS OF THE GREAT APOSTASY

Our Lady bows in greetings and speaks:

"My beloved children, I thank you immensely for praying, praying the Holy Rosary before Me and petitioning Me in these times of crises. Little one of Mine and My Jesus, I thank you immensely for offering yourself as a victim in Union with Me, the *Co-Redemptrix*. And we are united, you as co-redeeming as a victim, united to Me as *Co-Redemptrix*! And we are united and dwell in the *Redeemer*, to complete what Jesus made known was lacking[197]; yet nothing is lacking little one of Mine and My Jesus. It was in this way we participate in the Holy Sacrifice. Today this Holy Sacrifice has been suspended all over[198]. Yet, My beloved chosen sons are raising

---

[197] Col 1,24

[198] Because the Churches were closed during the Spring lockdown due to the Covid-19 epidemic

it in the manner to be understood as, the *underground Church*, of those in silence.

I thank you also, My beloved of the Beloved, for allowing your spouse to give herself in this manner. Be not troubled! Be not anxious! I have made known to you of all this is coming into being and all that I have made known, is coming to pass. Yes, it is true, these are the first birth pangs of the Great Apostasy. Many will fall away, who are known as borderline Catholics! They do not know which way to go. Pray for them! They too are My children! My Heart is sorrowing!

Know and understand that the suffering this little one is enduring this day is for the other Lung of the Catholic Church, known at the Eastern Rite and their Patriarchs. Know and understand they are in disharmony behind the scenes with the Holy Father, desiring to overthrow him. And many are embracing this Schism and are becoming Schismatics. It is the power of pride, Spiritual pride - most dangerous to the Soul! Today I will rescue those who are undecided and those who are of both Rites, of the Latin and the Eastern, who do not know which way to turn. I will come to receive this suffering in the early hours of the first day at the end of this day, twelve a.m. of the first day.

*

"I Love you dearly! I Am the Mother of God, the *Mediatrix of all Grace, Co-Redemptrix* and *Advocate* in Heaven interceding for your world. For those who invoke Me under this title, make known about the 'Medal' that has been entrusted to all My children who possess it: To kiss it continuously when they are in doubt. In this way, they invoke My intercession.

Make known also that they should form little cenacles and come up to pray the Rosary on My Holy Mountain, the Mount known as Mount Ganxim-Batim. If the Church doors are closed, they may form little cenacle rings and sit and pray before My Statue of Our Lady, *Mediatrix of all Grace, Co-Redemptrix* and *Advocate.* I will not abandon you beloved children! Do not fear this, this is a moment of great consolation! The consolation, you now have the power to intercede for Souls to bring them back to God. This is a moment of your faith in action, only believe! Your faith is that 'now' - that will move in the order of Grace and Truth, Jesus dwelling in you! Yes, make many Spiritual Communions! I will make known this manner too! There are many forms of Spiritual communions, yet it is simple. Only invite Jesus into your heart! Amen.

I Love you all dearly, I thank you immensely! I Am your Heavenly Mother interceding for you and through your prayers it will come to pass that I will be proclaimed on Earth as *Mediatrix of all Grace, Co-Redemptrix* and *Advocate* and Heaven will open the floodgates of Grace that will flow for you, to combat these moments. Amen." *(Friday after Ash Wednesday February 28th, 2020)*

110. YOU MUST TAKE FORTH THE MEDICINE THAT HAS A TWOFOLD UNDERSTANDING

"My beloved children, how I thank thee for responding in this crisis through prayer. Those that are now lukewarm are now igniting those who are in prayer, who fear men to rise and they see the evil behind it all, that is my adversary!

Rise, beloved children, rise with Me reciting the Holy Rosary! And We will make a speedy end to this evil that God has allowed for you to understand: The first birth pangs of the Great Apostasy.

Pray for your Holy Father! Pray for your Bishops! Pray for your Cardinals! Pray for your Priests! Pray for your Religious, who have grown indifferent and instead of leading you to prayer, they themselves have closed the doors out of fear for this virus. But I Am with you who have called on Me and am even with those who have not yet called on Me and am with those who pray for them. I thank you beloved children! It is in this way: Now these are the works of Mercy[199] that you are embracing - loving even your enemies and praying for them[200], praying for the Salvation of their Souls! Amen."

Now She pauses and She speaks.

"My beloved children, little one of Mine and My Jesus, Cleophas, My beloved of the Beloved Felix Xavier, I Love you. I Love you and I thank you immensely for responding to pray with Me, to keep vigil. Jesus will not abandon you, nor will I! It is now you must begin the mission!

… Know and understand now you must take forth the medicine that has a twofold understanding that I made known to you. Medicine that was used in ancient times for coughs like yours *(Iveta began coughing suddenly)* and viruses in times of epidemic.

The first understanding is a Spiritual understanding. The Blessed Salt and the Holy Water must be blessed with the prayers of the Church to ward off and to deliver one - of evil spirits. The second, is God's Fruit given as medicine: the onion - red in nature, has a tinge one would call mauve,

---

[199] Mt 25, 35-36

[200] Mt 5,44

a deep mauve (purple) - and honey. These must go forth now to combat this terrible anxiety! ... Know and understand the proportions are in this manner:

Blessed salt is a pinch as you would call, or a dab of it, or a few grains. The Holy water is a tablespoon, or a dash of it as a good dose. The honey, in proportion with the onion. The onion - small proportion is five tablespoons, medium is seven and large is twelve. This must be put together and kept overnight. In its preparation the 'I Believe', the act of Faith, the Catholic faith must be recited. In its conclusion, it must be brought to a boil, one boil, during which the 'I Believe', the 'Our Father', the three 'Hail Mary's', the 'Glory be' and the 'Hail Holy Queen', the profession of the Catholic Faith and the prayers of the Catholic Faith must be recited. This must be taken three times in the day of twenty-four hours. However, if one experiences a heavy breathlessness it must be given immediately - one tablespoon, children a quarter teaspoon. Know and understand now, this is all Mother Nature, of whom I Am The Queen that you may know!

I Love you dearly, I am the Mother of God, the *Mediatrix of all Grace, Co-Redemptrix* and *Advocate,* now at the same time asking you to petition the Holy Father to entrust all humanity to Me. I Am the *Mother of all Humanity.* In this crisis it must be understood that only I can help!

I Am your Heavenly Mother Who Loves you dearly. I thank all My beloved children for praying through the intercession of My Title, *Mediatrix of all Grace, Co-Redemptrix* and *Advocate.* The *Mother of God,* I Am She. Amen."

The vision closes. Our Altar returns. Our Holy Mother rises. The Archangels go behind us, and all the other Angels ascend with Her, except three circles of Angels who encircle us in these premises - this Mountain Foymont.

... Archangel Raphael holds the Scales this time, and in it, the medicine is in one end of it on My right, and on the other end are those who believe. They are like incense coals and it reads: 'To those who believe, it will bring forth the fruit of healing. To those who do not believe, it will bring condemnation, for they mock the Divine Spirit in Its Holy Wisdom and Understanding'. *Archangel Gabriel ascends. Amen. (Solemnity of the Annunciation of Our Lord March 25ᵗʰ, 2020)*

111. ENTRUST TO HIM THIS SYRUP THAT I HAVE MADE KNOWN

Iveta in Suffering for the Universal Church. She sees in a Vision:

... Our Lady of Grace, but Her Hands are waist high and there is a chain connecting them. She is crying!

The vision changes.

Now She is Our Lady Mediatrix of all Grace, Co-Redemptrix *and* Advocate *with the Rosary hanging from Her right middle finger and The Scapular in Her left hand. She is wearing an all-white Garment with the Sun behind Her pulsating and emanating gold rays on Her Garment and all around her as in the image of Our Lady of Guadalupe. Jesus is in Her Immaculate Heart in the Monstrance, that is like a Chalice. The two keys of Peter are below It. 'Jesus' is suspended in Her Immaculate Heart and Blood is dripping from the Eucharist into the Chalice, that is the Monstrance. Now again I see that chain, that was around Her hands and rays are emanating from Her hands, but they cannot come down to Earth. They are only emanating and coming down upon those who invoke Her under the title of* 'Mediatrix of all Grace: Mother of God, Mediatrix of all Grace, Co-Redemptrix and Advocate.'

Those who invoke Her under this title of Grace, whatever they ask of her and whatever She desires to reveal to them, is penetrating such Souls and such situations. But all throughout the World, these rays cannot descend. Our Blessed Mother is on a cloud, and under the cloud is this same chain that was seen around Her Hands earlier as She came as Our Lady of Grace, with Her Hands at waist level. This chain forms a circle around and below the cloud. This chain will be broken when She is proclaimed Mediatrix of all Grace, Co-Redemptrix *and* Advocate, *the* fifth *and* final Dogma, *which will permit Her to open the floodgates of Heaven for Grace to penetrate all Her children, to give them strength and all that is necessary, the Gifts of The Holy Spirit, to fortify Her children to go forth in these times of the persecution of the Catholic Church. And it reads below the 'Catholic Church', 'Christians' and it reads below 'Christians', 'All God's children, yet to know Him. Amen'.*

The Vision closes but Our Lady is still here ...

I was praying Thirty-three 'I Believes', meditating on the thirty-three years of our Lord on Earth and as I reached the seventeenth one ... We prayed 'The Angelus' together (1:00 PM) ... and the 'Our Father' in union with His Holiness Pope Francis I.

Now I see Our Lady Mediatrix of all Grace *behind Our Holy Father who is kneeling before 'Jesus' in The Blessed Sacrament, in Adoration[201]. The* Mediatrix of all Grace Medal, *if I am not wrong, is in His right pocket and Our Lady as* Mediatrix of all Grace, Co-Redemptrix *and* Advocate *is behind Him. Now He rises and picks up 'Jesus' in the Blessed Sacrament in the Monstrance and He turns around. Our Lady is behind Him, as he Initiates the Blessing that he is to give us. 'Open your arms and receive it', these are His words. Now join your hands as He pronounces the last words ...* "In the Name of the Father and of The Son and of The Holy

---

[201] On that day, Pope Francis led a "extraordinary moment of prayer" on the Sagrato of St Peter's Basilica in Rome. See: http://www.vatican.va/content/francesco/en/homilies/2020/documents/papa-francesco_20200327_omelia-epidemia.html

Spirit. Amen." "IN NOMINE PATRE ET FILIUS ET SPIRITU SANCTUS AMEN"

He turns around and places Jesus on the Altar and recites the last prayers.

Our Holy Mother turns around to us (as the Vision of the Holy Father closes) as Mediatrix of all Grace, *with 'Jesus' in Her Immaculate Heart, and She speaks.*

"My beloved children, I thank you immensely for keeping this moment with the Holy Father, your Holy Father, today the reigning Pope, Pope Francis I His Holiness. You are under his protection and prayer. He has invoked Me today to help[202]. Also, entrust to him this syrup that I have made known and let it go forth! It is an answer to his prayer, pleading to Me for all God's children and make known to him, that I still desire he proclaim the *Fifth Dogma*. This is not the desire of Me, the *Mother of God*, but of God Himself, Who he invoked today under the first title 'Our Father'.

I Love Him dearly. I am with him through it all. I shall protect him till that hour. I am His Heavenly Mother. He is My beloved chosen Son for these times in union with Emeritus Pope Benedict XVI, the praying Pope for your World. I love them dearly. Amen." (*Fourth Friday of Lent, March 27th, 2020*)

---

[202] "Dear brothers and sisters, from this place that tells of Peter's rock-solid faith, I would like this evening to entrust all of you to the Lord, through the intercession of Mary, Health of the People and Star of the stormy Sea." Pope Francis, March 27th, 2020.

112. THIS VIRUS IS OF A CHEMICAL WARFARE

"My beloved children, how pleasing an odour you are to Me and to the Divine Trinity. Know and understand, how I love you! How you please Me immensely by praying in this manner and keeping in solidarity with the Holy Father. Today this little one of Mine and My Jesus, Cleophas, suffers for the Universal Church known as the Latin Rite. These are the Holy Orders she suffers for, the Holy Orders that are denouncing the Holy Father and have become schismatics in this war of good and evil; evil known as the schism!

Know and understand: These are those today who have not united in prayer with the Holy Father, for they are in disbelief of him and go about doing what is evil in the sight of God, disobedience in its first degree! They have also the Eastern Rite by welcoming them to join them, and there are many also of the Eastern Rite who desire to follow them! And today as the Holy Father asked all Christians of every denomination to unite with Him, they have not united with Him and have brought great sorrow upon Your World![203]

Know and understand the Holy Father is very alone in this war, yet he does know. But make it known to him that I Am with him, that the whole multitude of Angels in Heaven are with him, that The Holy Trinity dwells in him! He is the Power of God in these hours of great darkness, especially in this first birth pangs of the Great Apostasy. His prayer today is to keep the Church unified and to keep the faithful in the faith of the knowledge of Jesus Christ in the Catholic Church. His Blessing is to ward off the evil of this virus known as the Coronavirus / Covid-19 and know and understand this manner of prayer has kept the faithful intact!

---

[203] http://www.vatican.va/content/francesco/en/angelus/2020/documents/papa-francesco_angelus_20200322.html

However, those who are lukewarm, and undecided will be attacked by this virus. ... Those who call on help, asking for your help you must give them the syrup without giving them the knowledge of what is in it. To this syrup, you will add what is called Maple syrup. You will add in dosage of five and seven and twelve tablespoons; you will understand this later. Yes, My beloved of the Beloved, you desire it to be in its proper text. It is well for Doctor ..., My beloved son, right now to make this dosage. Yet this is the basis of it: In the morning on an empty stomach before eating or drinking anything you shall take one teaspoon to one tablespoon, for little children it will be a drop or quarter teaspoon, and then one hour before your meal in the afternoon and in the evening again the same dosage. Know and understand however, in serious cases where they are attacked, in that moment of breathing, it is well to give them this dosage and even rub this as a balm on their chest and back[204].

Why must it be in this manner? For God has given medicine of Nature and man has chosen chemical warfare and this virus is of a chemical warfare. I Am the *Queen of Nature* and as the *Queen of Nature*, I fight this virus with Nature's Medicine that God has given for mankind! Know and understand there are serious consequences of disobedience against God!

I love you dearly, I will come to receive this suffering at the hour of 12.00 a.m., the ending of this day and the beginning of the next day.

This suffering is very serious! Now you will understand the word 'amalgamation' of Holy Orders which will no longer be Holy Orders, for the smoke of Satan has consumed them.

---

[204] The understanding of the Spiritual and Natural Medicine is given in the appendix section of this book.

Know and understand, I will make known another area in the days ahead. I love you dearly and I thank all My beloved children who prayed in solidarity with the Holy Father today when I joined him in raising this petition as the *Mediatrix of all Grace, Co-Redemptrix* and *Advocate, the Mother of God* before God and for those also who did not know, but continued to pray, they will receive the Graces and the protection of the intentions of your Holy Father.

As for those who rejected Him, still pray for them as your enemies[205], that their hearts will be open in time. I love you all dearly, I am sorrowing with great sorrow for the loss of Souls who have no one to pray for them! Amen." *(Fourth Friday of Lent, March 27ᵗʰ, 2020)*

113. THIS INFLICTION OF THIS VIRUS IS NOT TO BRING DEATH, BUT FOR THE GLORY OF GOD THROUGH THIS MEDICINE

"My beloved children be not anxious be not troubled! You are full of anxiety, yet know and understand, God will not leave you. The Bridegroom will be with you, I will be with you! You only need to invoke us and know that we will not abandon you.

Yes, it is sorrowful to see the manner in which the Church is now, and My Priests responding with laxity of understanding that Jesus is with them, yet they pick and choose who they want to see! It is sorrowful that they do not understand that all are brothers and sisters of theirs. It is well for them to take precautions, but it is not well for them to choose who they want to see and who they do not want to see, this shows lack of faith! Pray that they increase in faith. I commend many of My Priests now who do not fear men but

---

[205] Mt 5,44

fear God yet obey the authorities without denying God His proper place, and knowing that Jesus is True God and True Man and without Jesus, this battle cannot be won[206]! Yet I Love them dearly and I ask My beloved children, laying another yoke upon them, to pray for their Priests, their Bishops and their Religious. Amen."

"Know and understand this suffering now is quite heavy upon you. By the word 'quite', I mean it is a very heavy suffering; yet it is a quiet one, very painful! You are suffering for the Domestic Church, the Latin Rite and intermixed marriages with the Eastern Rite, that are embracing the schism in this sin. They are like those who are breaking away from the Holy Mother the Catholic Church, breaking away the umbilical cord with no head, it is to be understood! They are walking without the upper parts of the body, the head, the lungs, the upper limbs and soon they will throw themselves into a fury of confusion! And many will even subject themselves to suicide like Judas when they find that they have betrayed the Church of God whom they desire and follow with fidelity and have followed with fidelity for all these years! It is pride, Spiritual pride that has entered them thinking that they are above others.

Know and understand, this suffering that this little one of Mine and My Jesus, their beloved sister Cleophas is enduring, will ransom those, who desire to turn back at this point, who are also in confusion. You know many of them and there are some that know you, but you do not know 'them'. I will come to receive this suffering at the end of this day and the beginning of the next at twelve a.m."

Know and understand, in the following week known as the Holy Week, you will endure this suffering for the Domestic

---

[206] John 15,5

and Universal Church, each day. The suffering will release itself after Divine Mercy hour, and then begin again the following day at the end of the previous day at twelve a.m.

In each day I will import a small Word of its understanding, that is for the Domestic and Universal Church of both Lungs, the Eastern and the Latin. The Eastern is in a more severe devastation of understanding the Holy Father, the reigning Pope. They believe in what he says, yet they do not want to be under him! Again, you see Spiritual Pride! That must go! Amen.

She pauses and She speaks again:

Know and understand, many will be inflicted with this; this infliction of this Virus is not to bring death, the first death upon them, but for the glory of God[207] through this medicine. I will make known to you how you must bring it before them.

I Love you dearly, I thank you immensely! I Am the *Mother of God*, the *Mediatrix of all Grace, Co-Redemptrix* and *Advocate*, awaiting to be proclaimed on Earth. It is through this title of Mine, I will be able to help My children, Consecrated into My Immaculate Heart who have come to understand Me as their Refuge and through Me to Jesus in whom dwells the fullness of the Divinity[208] of the Divine Triune God, the Plenitude of God. Amen.

I love you dearly, I love you dearly, Amen." *(Fifth Friday of Lent April 3rd, 2020)*

---

[207] John 11,4
[208] Col 2,9

114. THEY DO NOT UNDERSTAND WHAT THEY ARE DOING

"My beloved children, I thank you immensely for continuing to keep Me company in this most sorrowful time, sorrowful for those who will not embrace the Cross and those who inflict others with the venom of Satan. I thank you immensely, I Love you dearly! I thank you, little one of Mine and My Jesus, for suffering this day for the Universal Church, for the Eastern and the Latin Rite.

Know and understand today you are suffering for this sin, which is tearing the Church apart. The internal forum of the Church is being torn by those who follow these leaders who are preaching against the Holy Father, the reigning Pope. They are those who are practicing the sin of Sodom and since the Holy Father will not give authorization for them to do as they please in the Eastern and the Latin Rite, the Priests and the Religious, they are marching against Him, using electronic devices to spread the venom of Satan, proclaiming Him as antichrist and antipope. They do not understand what they are doing!

Today little one of Mine and My Jesus Cleophas, you are suffering for those who they are enticing to follow them in this way. I will snatch these Souls from their claws. As for them, you are praying that they will see themselves as God sees them and that they turn away - they have destroyed their temples, that is their bodies - the temple of God; yet their Souls still awaits judgement. That they may not be judged for Eternal Damnation, this suffering I will use for those who repent and do not want to follow this path of perdition[209].

---

[209] Mt 7,13

You bore this suffering beginning with the right foot, the Wound of Jesus, the hidden Wound of Jesus on your right foot, then shooting its venom to the hip bone of the left hip, where their venom is dismantling the Priests in the Latin rite and the Religious in the Latin Rite to think like them. It then shot into the umbilical cord, where you experienced serious pain in your naval area, as though the umbilical cord was being pulled, as in those aborting children. You also now will experience the pain as when Jesus was thrown on the Cross, having been stripped of all His Garments except the one, My Mantle that was draped around His Sacred Part. I will receive this suffering at the hour of three p.m., the hour of Divine Mercy. It is the Mercy of God We are pleading for, before Divine Justice befalls! Amen."

She pauses and She speaks:

"I thank all My beloved children for uniting with this little one of Mine and My Jesus, Cleophas, your beloved sister! Remain in solidarity with Me! I have made known that I will answer your prayers. In this way We will march against the forces of darkness as you pray the Holy Rosary. It is in your power now to rise as Church Militant to protect the Universal Church against the destruction that Satan is planning of its closures. Yet you have little more daylight time, before the next *birth pangs* of the *Great Apostasy*. You will soon be experiencing renewal and return! Do not forget what My adversary can do! Keep vigilant and do what I have asked!

I Love you dearly, I Am the *Mother of God, Co-Redemptrix* and *Advocate* in Heaven, it will come to be proclaimed on Earth through your prayers. I Love you all dearly Amen." *(Tuesday of the Holy Week, April 7ᵗʰ, 2020)*

115. THEY DESIRE TO FOLLOW GOD, BUT HAVE MADE THEIR OWN IMAGE OF GOD

Holy Mama is here already. Jesus is in Her Immaculate Heart. We have no Altar but where Our Lady of Guadalupe's Tilma is, there She is all in White, with the Rosary in her right Hand and the Mediatrix *of all* Grace *Scapular in Her left Hand. Tears are rolling down Her eyes, yet She smiles and bows in greetings. The Archangels are prostrated in front of Her, St Michael in front in the middle, Archangel Gabriel on Her right and Archangel Raphael on Her left. Our Guardian Angels are prostrated in front of Her, behind Saint Michael, and She speaks:*

"My beloved children, what a tempest is weighing upon the whole world, yet if only people pray, God would quickly lift this dark shadow that is befalling all mankind in this war of good and evil. Know and understand now, I thank you immensely for praying and I thank all My beloved children who have taken up the Rosary, even those who never did so have begun to pray! Yet, there are many who used to pray, that do not pray! Pray for them, that they may return to this order of prayer.

Know and understand now: I thank you, My beloved daughter little one of Mine and My Jesus, Cleophas for carrying this Cross of the Domestic Church today. You are suffering for those who desire to follow God but have made their own image of God. These are those who home school their children, not all of them, but many are denouncing the words of the Holy Father making light of him and believing that he is the antipope. The horror of this moment is that they are installing this in their children.

Today you are enduring this suffering to rescue these little ones from the slavery of their own parents in the pursuit of teaching them right. To follow the Catholic faith, they are dismissing the understanding of the authority of the Vicar of Christ, Peter the Rock, My beloved chosen son, suffering for your World, His Holiness today the reigning Pope, Pope Francis I, the successor of Peter, the first Pope, walking in the shoes of the Fisherman.[210]

Know and understand that it is the Domestic Church, in the Latin Rite and the Eastern Rite, that have fallen prey to this kind of thinking. How I long to rescue them! I delight in their zeal to keep the Catholic faith, yet the yeast of their thinking is that they are the elite! And only God chooses those He wants to ransom to go into the time for the future Church, known as the *Remnant*. You do not choose to become the *Remnant*, not even I can tell you that you are the *Remnant*. Only God in the First Person, will mark the Cross of the Second person on the forehead of those He has chosen to do so. By *Remnant* it must also be understood, they also will suffer death, the first step in the times that lie ahead, known as the persecution.

I thank you immensely. I thank all My beloved children. I thank you, My beloved of the Beloved, for allowing your spouse to undergo this suffering. I understand it is hard to see her as though wasting away. I Am with her through it all. I will carry her through these moments, and I will bless all those who bless her and pray for her. And all those who curse her that she blesses, God will render a judgement upon them. I thank you immensely, I Love you dearly. Amen."

She pauses and She speaks:

"I will come to receive this suffering after the hour of Divine Mercy. It will lift from your body. I understand daughter it is heavy from head to toe. Your body is enduring it, especially the head that's weighing you down, for it is the suffering of the intellect to think they are wiser than God.

---

[210] Mt 4, 18-19

Know and understand: You will begin the next suffering in the same manner, yet it will be lifted at the hour of noon after the Angelus, to prepare you for the impending suffering of the Triduum, that you will rest in this manner. It will be a heavy suffering yet know I will carry you through this moment. You will endure it with Me. You will endure it as Co-redeeming with I, the *Co-Redemptrix* united to the *Redeemer* and all the little children, My beloved children little ones of Mine, who desire to pray and unite themselves to you, to offering every little sacrifice of theirs for the intention of My Immaculate Heart to console Me and to console Jesus, little vessels Co-redeeming with you, I will Bless them as they bless you!

I am the *Mother of God*, your Heavenly Mother sorrowing for so many walking the path of perdition[211], yet I will rescue those, through this suffering - many, many, daughter, you will have the privilege of seeing them, when this is lifted! Pray for your Holy Father now. His suffering begins in this Triduum. Amen."

Our Altar returns. The Archangels prostrate praying with us. Holy Mama rises. I see Her no more.

Archangel Michael rises and goes to the foot of the Mountain again. He also now is seen at the entrance of Batim with His Spear pierced to the ground. (Wednesday of the Holy Week, April 8th, 2020)

116. THIS SUFFERING TODAY IS FOR WHAT HAS COME TO BE KNOWN AS THE JEWISH ROOTS OF JESUS

Our Lady speaks:

"I thank you beloved children of mine for loving Me and for consoling Me, for keeping with Me in prayer, a daily Vigil,

---

[211] Mt 7,13

a constant prayer of your duty of the moment of your calling, and the duty that has been placed upon your shoulders as a yoke, the Cross of Jesus, as you carry in a deeper manner now. I thank you My little one of Mine and My Jesus, My beloved daughter Cleophas, for suffering in this manner.

This suffering today that you are enduring is for what has come to be known as the *Jewish Roots of Jesus and Mine*, the Jews who still do not believe and are deaf to the truth, they are like an infection in the ear of the Holy Father. Today your suffering is for their conversion. They are part of this schism, but this you may understand: Though they show their union with the Holy Father they are not with Him, and they would be very happy to know that He is overthrown! They would desire a Patriarch instead to take his place and to conceal their lie. They would love to disdain the Holy Father's teachings, that is the teachings of Jesus Whom they do not believe in, though they have seen and read all that was foretold and till today read about Him! This, the suffering you are enduring is in the mind. They are wise thinkers and rule by human thinking. Even the Word of God is put into action in human Wisdom and lacks Divine understanding in this literal sense, in some instances. I will come to receive this suffering at the hour of twelve, known as the hour of Angelus this day, noon time.

Your suffering for the Triduum will begin at nine p.m this day. Do not be distracted! You are much distracted, little one of Mine and My Jesus. Only Pray!

I love you dearly. I thank you immensely. I Am with you through it all. I thank all My beloved children who are co-redeeming united to your suffering, who is Co-Redeeming with Me as *Co-Redemptrix*, united to the *Redeemer* Jesus Christ Our Saviour. I thank you My beloved of the Beloved, Felix Xavier for your response and your fidelity to Me. I love you immensely! Know now, that you will be in deep communion in this suffering with your spouse, as she undergoes the immensity of the suffering. This is for the Holy Father and all the areas that are beating upon Him. It is like a consolation and a cloak around Him, a cloak of comfort, a cloak of fidelity, a cloak of fortitude, a cloak of hope, a cloak of total Faith! I Love Him dearly and I will be with you all through this suffering, for I too will be enduring it.

I Am the *Mother of God*, the *Mediatrix of all Grace, Co-Redemptrix* and *Advocate* in Heaven, awaiting to be proclaimed on Earth, it will come to be through your prayers, beloved children Amen." *(Holy Thursday, April 9th, 2020)*

117. YOU WILL ALSO PRAY FOR THOSE GONE BEFORE IN THIS TERRIBLE PLAGUE KNOWN AS PANDEMIC

Now She pauses … and She speaks:

"During this suffering you will also pray for those gone before in this terrible plague known as pandemic, known by its diabolic name as Covid-19/Coronavirus. These are the diabolic names under which one can break its power! 'One' means: Either by the laity or by My chosen Sons, the Priests, that is giving deliverance. Today as baptized Catholics, you have that power to do so! Deliver one another from this terrible weight! However, the medicine is needed, it will come to be! … It is truth now that will conquer this evil.

I Love you all dearly, I Am the Mother of God, I Am the *Queen of Nature* and as *Mediatrix of all Grace* in Heaven, interceding to obtain the Graces necessary at this time. Amen." *(Holy Thursday, April 9th, 2020)*

118. THROUGH THIS PANDEMIC, I HAVE RANSOMED MANY WHO HAVE PLEADED MERCY IN THEIR LAST MOMENTS!

Jesus speaks Soul to Soul to me:

"Many of you, My Priests will suffer this manner of torture. And you My Peter, will suffer the mockery to denounce Me before the one known as the antipope sits on your seat to bring about the desolate sacrilege[212]. You have just endured My loneliness, My isolation of how My people, My children have abandoned Me for the ways of the world and do not desire to turn back.

Yet through this plague, known as the pandemic, I have ransomed many who have pleaded Mercy in their last moments! It would not have been so, had they not turned their back to Me. This is the isolation you are suffering for My Peter, My beloved Peter. Upon you rests the weight of the Church and to you My hidden Peter, your prayers are victorious. I Love you both! In this way you will carry My church in these times. It is also now under the Domestic Church; the Universal Church will hide. The church must go underground, that is My *Remnant*. It is not those who choose to be the *Remnant*, it is those I have chosen to be the *Remnant*. Yet all will try to go underground and in the *second birth pangs* and the *third birth pangs* of the *Apostasy* - the *Great Apostasy*, many will suffer Martyrdom for there will be many amidst them like Judas, betrayal of every kind!

Jesus of Nazareth suffering for this suffering of these schismatics of both Rites which you carry, My Peter, both Lungs! Amen. Amen."

Jesus speak Soul to Soul to me:

---

[212] Mark 13,14

"Little one of Mine Cleophas, beloved daughter of My Blessed Mother, you are carrying now the agony to comfort My Peter on Earth, who carries the Cross of the Church today, My Cross! Make known to him that I Love him. He knows so, yet it is a comfort when he hears it from another source who Loves Me, a source who loves Her Church, a source who carries her Church in suffering, for the Church. Make known to him I have said "When I come will there be any Faith?[213]" This suffering is to fortify his faith against the assaults of My enemies, against the assaults of My Church while evildoers go on in their evil ways, yet My Church is forced to shut Her doors by the authorities, some of whom are part of this schism and some of those who belong to the anti-world, that is the antichrist and antipope!

Those who belong to Me are praying and working hard, hard to find a solution to open My doors, the doors of My Bride, the Catholic Church. I Love you My Peter, you who sit today on the throne of Peter, known as Pope Francis I.

Jesus of Nazareth suffering for you in your world Amen, Amen."

Now once again He speaks Soul to Soul:

"My beloved children, beloved of Me and My Father, beloved of My Mother, you who are co-redeeming with this little one who is Co-Redeeming with My Mother, the *Co-Redemptrix*, Redeeming with Me, to bring Souls back to Me, I thank you! Continue in this manner, you are a pleasing odour to God Our Father! I assure you that one day you will be with Me in Heaven.

Jesus of Nazareth, dying for love of you, laying down His Life, Your Saviour, Your *Redeemer*. Amen. Amen."

---

[213] Luke 18,8

*

Soul to Soul to Our Blessed Mother:

"Mother, carry my Peter, stir within him with a hunger to thirst for Souls. Many Souls are running away today, this very day on Earth from the Catholic Church in disbelief of My Presence, they do not understand this moment! Mother, ransom them back through this little one suffering for Me, Holy Mother."

Our Blessed Mother:

"Let it be done unto Me as you have willed[214]. Your Mother, Mary of Nazareth, Your born Slave. My God, I Love you. Amen."

Soul to Soul Jesus speaks to Me:

"Little one of Mine, Cleophas, beloved daughter of My Blessed Mother, I thank you for thirsting for Souls in this manner to suffer with Me this day. Make known of My desire for more Souls to embrace My Cross as Victim Souls. There are very few right now desiring to suffer, but there are many this day in this epidemic as it has come to be known – pandemic, Corona Virus, a plague! Many are victims and are enduring it, pleading for Mercy for themselves, for their families to know Me! They are My Saints who are washing themselves in My Blood.

Jesus of Nazareth, the High Priest, Your God, Your *Redeemer*. Amen. Amen." *(Good Friday, April 10ᵗʰ, 2020)*

---

[214] Luke 1,38

119. KNOW AND UNDERSTAND THESE ORDERS THAT ARE INFESTED WITH THIS EVIL HAVE A GREATER VIRUS THAN THE CORONA VIRUS

Jesus speaks Soul to Soul with his Blessed Mother:

"Mother carry My Peter! Wipe his Face and make known to my beloved children to carry him in their prayers and their suffering, wiping his face like Veronica wiped Mine. Amen, Amen."

She nods, "Yes My Beloved Divine Son. Amen."

The Seventh Station, Jesus falls the Second Time. "Mother" *Soul to Soul He speaks to His Mother:* "Mother help My Peter when He is in doubt and anguish for the sins that are committed against the Magisterium and by those who pledge their fidelity to the Magisterium."

She nods "Do not speak My Son", *She says, through that suffering countenance, while they are kicking at Him and trying to revive Him to get up, pulling at His cross! We are like Simon of Cyrene carrying the Cross of Jesus. We too like Simon shall fall with Jesus there.*

"Mother," *Jesus speaks Soul to Soul to His Blessed Mother:* "Carry My children!"

"My beloved children obey your Mother, My Blessed Mother Who will make known plainly to you, suffering this day for your world, Jesus of Nazareth the High Priest. Amen, Amen."

Our Lady responds "Let it be done unto Me as you have said[215]. Amen."

We move to the Eight Station.

Jesus speaks to the Women of Jerusalem[216]. He tells them not to weep for Him but for themselves and for their children. They are weeping now for themselves and pleading Mercy for themselves and for their children who are undergoing this suffering, as Jesus begins God-Man annihilation of Nations. This is of a very small dose to open the hearts of hardened sinners to repent. It seems cruel, but in proportion to the offences committed against God, every second, every day, it is so very little!

Jesus speaks Soul to Soul to His Blessed Mother:

"Mother carry My children, carry My Peter. I Am Jesus of Nazareth, the High Priest agonising for the closure of My Churches. Amen, Amen."

Our Lady responds: "Let it be done unto Me as You have willed[217]. Amen."

The Ninth Station: Jesus falls the third time.

What a fall, "Mother," *through this anguish, He speaks to Our Lady, Soul to Soul:*

"Mother, unto You will be entrusted all humanity and the hearts of all mankind when I Am pierced. Carry My Peter, carry my children! Now carry My Priests, my Brides who are growing weary. They are amidst those who are committing the

---

[215] Luke 1,38
[216] Luke 23,27-31
[217] Luke 1,38

211

offence as being schismatics spreading this heresy, this heresy like never it was, nor will ever be and all in the name of doing right and living as though Orthodox Catholics.

I Am Jesus of Nazareth agonising for My children, I Am entrusting all into the Immaculate Heart of My Holy Mother, Your Refuge and through that Refuge you will come to know the Refuge of My Sacred Heart to be led to the Eternal Father. I warn you through My Blessed Mother, the road is narrow[218], follow it! Mother teach them to do so! Jesus of Nazareth the High Priest, agonising for My Priests who have grown anxious in trying to save themselves and have forgotten to feed My Lambs for the future, and My Sheep[219]! Amen, Amen."

Our Lady responds, "Let it be done unto Me as you have willed[220]."

The Tenth Station. Here, as we call it the tenth station. Jesus is walking up and is coming to the place where He will be Crucified. They have arrived at the top of the mountain. There are two thieves on either side of Jesus. They are thrown first down already stripped and, in the Presence, as Jesus watches them being crucified, nailed to the Cross, they are screaming and swearing every evil foul word and Jesus is listening to them. Their crosses are taken now and placed into the holes ... raised and placed, agony in them and the swearing goes on.

Jesus speaks Soul to Soul to His Blessed Mother Who is standing at a distance. They are held back by the guards.

"Mother carry My Peter, they will swear and curse at him in this manner, let him not grow weary! Carry My Priests who

---

[218] Mt 7,13
[219] John 21,15-18
[220] Luke 1,38

they will swear and curse at too! These are those spreading the heresy of the schism in My Church."

Now He speaks Soul to my Soul: "As they strip Me, they will strip My Church that you are suffering for, little one of Mine, Cleophas, beloved of My Blessed Mother. Yet I have made known, I will be with you till the end of time[221]!"

Soul to Soul, the High Priest: "Mother watch over My little ones like this little one of Mine and protect them from fear and anxiety, protect them from the enemy that will come to despoil them in making them think that their suffering is useless[222]! Jesus of Nazareth the High Priest. Amen, Amen."

"Let it be done unto Me according to Thy Word[223]. My Son, My God I love you, Mary of Nazareth. Amen."

Now they are stripping Him. Oh! My God Oh! My God! Ah! ... am I worth so much Oh! Ah!!! that You would endure so much for us Jesus. I Love Thee Ah! ... everything that you will of me, let it be done unto Me, not as I but as Thou Will it for me. They strip Him and He is shivering with pain. As they are stripping His Loin, Holy Mama comes and gives them Her Mantle to wrap around His Loin. The centurion has compassion on Her and gives Her Mantle to the guards to wrap it around Him, covering His Sacred Part of Purity. Sacred and Pure!

Holy Jesus speaks Soul to Soul to me at this time as they are taking Him and throw Him on the wood of the Cross. Ahh! ... He makes no protest except a slight sigh, a very long sigh.

---

[221] Mt 28,20

[222] Isaiah 49,4

[223] Luke 1,38

"Little one of Mine Cleophas, know and understand, I thank You for suffering for My Peter united to Me through My Blessed Mother. You are suffering for those who desire to strip themselves of the Virtue of Purity. In their Priesthood, I have called this for! It must be the Priesthood of Purity! The desire to defile themselves with women, defile themselves with an abomination of exchanging the Holy Act for an abomination with men, men with men, women with women, such horror, defiling the temple of God in themselves! You are suffering now to ransom them to wake up and plead My Mercy! Those who have defiled themselves in this abomination, also embracing the Schism, have become Schismatics. Yet there will be a few who will repent, and their Souls will be saved; yet their bodies must be destroyed. They will receive, if they hold on to their fidelity after they have repented, they will receive a new body in the Resurrection!

My Peter, Francis I, Pope as you are called, how grave is your suffering for such offences in the Clergy, in the Religious!

Know and understand these Orders that are infested with this evil have a greater Virus than the 'Corona Virus', the first birth pangs of the Great Apostasy. They will close down the churches and there will come a time of what I have made known to this little one of Mine in the 'Secrets', you will understand its meaning, it will all come quickly like when a mother is in labour to bring forth a child, the birth pangs do not cease, but they come one after the other! When this is lifted, just as a mother has a little breathing time, be ready for the next!

I Love you My Peter, My Blessed Mother will carry you through these moments. Jesus of Nazareth, the High Priest, the One Whose Spirit rests upon you and in you and yet your humanity has not been taken away! And it is for that reason that you need My Blessed Mother and as She consoles Me now to strengthen Me, She will do so with you too! Amen. Amen."

Soul to Soul He speaks to His Blessed Mother:

"Mother carry My Peter in his humanity[224]. In his Divinity he is strong, for I Am with him in his humanity. He needs Your help! Jesus of Nazareth. Amen. Amen."

"Let it be done unto Me as You Will[225], Mary of Nazareth Your born Slave. Amen." *(Good Friday, April 10th, 2020)*

120. WHEN SHE IS PROCLAIMED, I WILL OPEN THE FLOOD GATES OF HEAVEN

Jesus speaks Soul to Soul to Me:

"Little one of Mine Cleophas, obey Thy Mother in all things big and small. Beloved of Mine, spouse of this little one, I Who Am Beloved of The Father obey My Mother in all things big and small, Felix Xavier."

It's as though He takes a breath in His painful lungs and He speaks Soul to Soul:

"Make known to My Peter, My Pope as He has come to be known Pope Francis I and My hidden Peter known as Emeritus Pope Benedict XVI, the praying Peter to proclaim My Mother as *Mediatrix of all Grace, Co-Redemptrix* and *Advocate*. She has this title already in Heaven interceding for those who invoke Her under this title on Earth. I have

---

[224] See above: "the One whose Spirit rests upon You." A divine gift has been given to the successor of Peter.
[225] Luke 1,38

bestowed this upon Her on Earth. When She is proclaimed, I will open the Flood Gates of Heaven that all My beloved children will be able to undergo this suffering of the persecution of My Church, which must come to be as it is written in Scripture. Scripture must be fulfilled[226]!

Jesus of Nazareth The High Priest Amen. Amen."

Our Holy Mama speaks to Jesus Soul to Soul:

"Let it be done unto Me as You have Willed[227]. I Am Your Mother, Your Born Slave, now uniting today all of My Suffering. I Love you! Amen."

Now there is silence, silence in the Heart of Jesus. It is as though He is giving it all to His Father and as though He is taking an account of all the work He has to complete for His Father in Heaven. Peter is watching from a distance and weeping, yet he will not come near, he is still frightened!

Jesus speaks Soul to My Soul:

"You see how Peter is at a distance, he is afraid of the authorities. He is afraid that he will be beaten. Today you are experiencing that fear too! In obedience to the authorities My Churches are closed, and I Am agonising this day for those who lack the understanding of My Divine Presence with them in the Holy Eucharist. I can make all things well! Pray, pray for an increase of Faith beginning with My Peter, today your Pope Francis I, pray for my Priests! I Bless those who have courageously taken upon themselves to open the Church for prayer, and to those who even have courageously understood

---

[226] Mark 14,49
[227] Luke 1,38

My Presence and are feeding My Lambs and My Sheep[228] who come to pray, I Bless them! These are those who are working to become future Saints, amidst you to this day!

I Am Jesus of Nazareth Man-God, God-Man, True God and True Man, the High Priest. Amen. Amen." (*Good Friday, April 10th, 2020*)

121. AT THE RESURRECTION MASS OF THE HOLY FATHER, THEY WILL RISE

… Holy Mama is here. She is dressed in a Navy-blue Mantle, like She was dressed at the Crucifixion with two Mantles. Her internal Mantle is white. Her Hands are like in the Mediatrix of all Grace, Co-Redemptrix *and* Advocate *Medal.*

The Archangels are prostrated and there are Rings of Angels all around Her. Above Her are the Heavenly choirs of Angels and below are the Earthly Angels. Now the Heavenly choir of Angels descend below Her as though Heaven has emptied all the Angels. They[229] will rise at the Resurrection Mass of the Easter Vigil to a Blessed and Holy Resurrection day!

Now there are many other Angels below, Angels who are praying, and they are now also forming a ring. These[230] are of those dying and have died from this terrible plague whose bodies are cremated in a large manner, some have been cremated in a large pit. The suffering today will be for them to rise into the Resurrection, when Jesus rises, in each of the different stages[231]! Now they are like candles lit and their Guardian Angels are holding their candles.

---

[228] John 21, 15-17

[229] Those whose Guardian Angels have just been mentioned.

[230] idem

[231] See section: 'The Thesis of Purgatory'.

At the Resurrection Mass of the Holy Father, they will rise and be given a new Body[232] in Heaven and will go into the three different stages according to their repentance at the last hour of their agony. The Mercy of God for them also will tilt the scales from all those who have been praying and pleading Mercy for them. Our Lady too tilts the scales to bring them in. There will be none in the third stage and the last level, that is closest to Hell, but one cannot cross into Hell[233], it is only an understanding! This all is in Heaven for their purification! Our Lady tilts the scales, as I said, as their Advocate throughout our intercession. Now as I undergo this suffering, the suffering in the different stages, which is a lamentation and agony of their suffering with the mercy of God, they repent through this agony.

I see more Guardian Angels coming. These are of those who have not been accounted for and yet have died also, unmourned, unloved! This marks the understanding that these Souls would otherwise have been Earthbound. In this special Resurrection Mass now, God lifts them up, many of them; many, not all! When I say 'not all', the understanding now is where She is showing me that the Holy sacrifice was raised by their families and their friends and Priests praying for these Souls, individual Souls by name, the general now goes to our Lord's resurrection, that is the Holy Mass celebrated by the Holy Father and all the Priests, Bishops, Cardinals that will raise the Holy Sacrifice.

Now there is very little prayer coming for me, for many have thought that it is all over, they were not aware that I need prayer too, so I must endure this suffering as raw! (Holy Saturday, April 11th, 2020)

---

[232] Not the glorified body, but they are clothed with a heavenly body, looking like Angels. See no. 137.

[233] Luke 16,26

122. THE JUSTICE OF GOD MUST DESCEND

Our Lady smiles. She bows in greeting. She is standing on a little cloud, and She speaks:

"My beloved children, how I thank you for responding to My request to pray on this day on this Holy Mountain, Mount Foymont. This Visitation is that of the one I was to come on the Twenty fifth day of the Twelfth Month of the year two thousand and nineteen (25th December 2019). I answer it today. It would have been on the Holy Mountain of Mount Ganxim, Batim.

Know and understand the reason why it is now here. Its journey begins at the root where the first Visitation of Me, made known to this little one of Mine and My Jesus, Cleophas, made known in this little house, a hospital once, now a little house in which I presented Myself to her. She knew nothing of Me and today I now open it to the World. Here the world will understand its moment.

I as *Mediatrix of all Grace*, *Co-Redemptrix* and *Advocate*, this title has been bestowed upon Me by God Our Father, God the Son, My Divine Son Jesus, Our Saviour and God the Holy Spirit.

I desire with great desire to make known in this *Visitation* of Mine the hour you are at - yet it is not complete - the *first birth pang* of the *Great Apostasy*. How it sorrows My Immaculate Heart to see so many of My children already lost in pursuit of another god! They have abandoned the True God!

Know and understand you must now prepare for the second birth pang. This will be a severe one for you, if you do not prepare! You must understand the *barter system*. You must understand to be self-sufficient, that you may not fall prey to the adversary, who will give you everything freely, yet it will cost you the price of your Soul!

Beloved children, know and understand I am here to make known to you this moment where I welcome you into My Immaculate Heart. There, I place you into the Sacred Heart of Our Divine Saviour Jesus, secure! And no one will take you or snatch you from Me, if only you are faithful to your Consecration to Me in the early hours of each morning of each new day.

And you, all you mothers, I invoke you once again to entrust all your children by name to My Immaculate Heart. Many of you are failing and have become anxious! It is not necessary for you to ponder. You can do nothing! I can do all things, for God has entrusted this moment to Me, as *Our Lady of Salvation!* Amen."

She pauses and She speaks:

"Beloved children it is here today you will understand God's Salvific Plan of being self-sufficient and yet also meeting the needs of those who have less through the *Saint Joseph's Charity* known to the world as the *Saint Joseph's Community Centre at Foymont*. It must go to the five Continents of the World. There it must bear fruit to preserve the *Remnant* for the future Church.

To those who cannot understand this moment, I pray you to be faithful to the Gospel and your fidelity to the Holy Magisterium of the Holy Catholic Church, the Holy Father. Here you will understand beloved children, to even be ready to lay down your life for the Truth; the Truth, as in Jesus Who will come to dwell in you and give you the strength to endure this moment like He has done to all the Saints and Martyrs. Amen.

Today I condescend on this Mountain to mark the understanding as *'Our Lady Mediatrix of all Grace, Co-Redemptrix* and *Advocate, The Mother of God'*. I Am She on this Holy Feast day dedicated to Me as *'Our Lady of Mount Carmel.'* It bears a link and you will understand it through the Scapular, which is My Mantle of love for all My children, My Garment, which will clothe you and protect you against the forces of darkness which seek to snatch your Souls!"

She seems to be walking all around. She's covering the whole Mountain with Her Garment … There She is … Our Lady of Mount Carmel … Now She comes.

"I thank you immensely for responding to My request to pray at this hour! Come all My beloved children who have joined in this moment of prayer which has been made known to you, to pray with this little one of Mine and My Jesus, Cleophas, your beloved sister. Amen.

Know and understand now, that I prepare you for the second birth pang of the *Great Apostasy*. It will be a sorrowful moment, yet it must come to be for the Justice of God must descend, that those who have been faithful may be preserved in Faith, and their fidelity for the *Remnant*, for the future Church, the Bride of Christ. Amen."

She pauses and She speaks again:

"I thank My beloved chosen son your Spiritual Father who has raised the Holy Sacrifice this day for this moment. I will be with him always! I thank him for embracing you and carrying you at this moment. He is united even at this hour praying with you … Amen.

Now I desire with great desire to make known: That the Peace of Jesus will descend upon you and in your hearts, to all those who have prayed even on the Holy Mountain of Ganxim-Batim, though it sorrows My Immaculate Heart to see the state in which it is. Know and understand it is a great suffering for My children to carry that cross and the Shepherds who have not heeded My request have brought much sorrow. Yet I love them! Only pray for them! Amen.

Know and understand, now I call on all the Shepherds in this time where My children are suffering and starving from the light of Jesus, they must return to the Sacraments! You must open your hearts to them. You must open the doors to them and lay down your lives for the sheep that have been entrusted unto you. It is you that the Lord will demand an account of the lost sheep[234] that go astray!

I am with you! Take courage, no harm will come to you! I have even made known to you the simple remedy known as the 'Spiritual and Natural Remedy' … I am with you all beloved children! I Love you dearly!

I Am the *Mother of God, the Mediatrix of all Grace, Co-Redemptrix* and *Advocate* in Heaven. I await, to be proclaimed on Earth! I thank you for your prayers and for petitioning the Holy Father and also praying for Him!"

… look at those clouds dancing, they all are encircling around Her … Here She is right up. Thank you, Mama!

---

[234] Mt 18,10-14

"Pray, Pray beloved children for your Holy Father. He is in need of your prayers! The Cross is weighing heavy on his shoulders, both the Eastern and the Latin Rites, for many in the hierarchy have embraced contamination, and the smoke of Satan has entered to sorrow the Holy Father and disagree with him on the Truth, and bring in the vision of the adversary, God's adversary!

I love you dearly, I Am your Heavenly Mother. Now receive the Blessing of Peace that Jesus has entrusted unto Me, the Most Holy Trinity dwelleth in me: "IN NOMINE PATER ET FILIUS ET SPIRITUS SANCTUS AMEN."

The Peace of Jesus ... give it to others! Amen." *(Feast of Our Lady of Mount Carmel, July 16ᵗʰ ,2020)*

123. BECOME LIKE THIS LITTLE INFANT JESUS IN MY ARMS

Our Lady speaks:

"Know and understand: The medicine I have made known, you must take it to protect yourselves against this demonic spirit of the "Corona virus" known as "Covid-19". Should you not, you will have to endure its suffering.

Be aware you will now soon enter the *second birth pang* coming into being. This little one of Mine and My Jesus has pleaded to give you time, so that the Churches may be open, and you may receive the Body and Blood of the *Redeemer* to undergo these moments.

I have interceded for this intention, for you, but do not *(Iveta: heavy is my heart Mother)*, do not overlook this time that I am giving you! Heed My request, make known to others even those not of the Faith. You must now prepare and give it to them should they desire it. Amen.

I Love you dearly. I am the *Mother of God, the Mediatrix of All Grace, Co-Redemptrix* and *Advocate*, awaiting to be proclaimed on Earth. Amen."

Our Lady speaks to me: "Now little one of Mine and My Jesus, I will come at the Hour of Divine Mercy to receive this suffering for the intention I have made known to you, for which you are suffering."

... Now, She points to the Little Infant Jesus, and She is showing me the cup that is overflowing with the suffering of so many Souls who have abandoned the Church, and the Little Infant Jesus whose face is fearful, yet in the arms of His Holy Mother, turns to look at Her, and He lifts up His little left Hand and He touches Her Chin and receives Consolation of strength.

Our Lady speaks: "Become like this little Infant Jesus in My arms. Amen." (*Anniversary of the first Visitation of Our Blessed Mother on Mount Batim, September 24th, 2020*)

124. THE THIRTY-THREE-DAY CONSECRATION

Our Lady speaks:

"... Make Known to My Beloved Children again, it is of great importance for them to embrace what has come to be known as 'the Spiritual and Natural Remedy', the syrup that I had made known. It seems so foolish in the eyes of the wise, yet it is the Power of God and the Grace in it - the Sacramental, that will destroy the power of evil that no other can do so. It is a battle between good and evil.

You are coming to the threshold of the *second birth pang*. I will make known in the days ahead how you must prepare. ...."

She pauses and speaks:

"My beloved of the Beloved, I thank you immensely for working, on what is called, the second book *"The Suffering and the Thesis of Purgatory'*. It is important for you to diligently finish it. I will give you Grace.

Know and understand, My beloved children need to know the direction they must take. It is what your Spiritual Father once, now with Me in Heaven, called 'affirmation'. They will need this affirmation!

Much will be unfolding. I thank you immensely for doing all that I have asked of you. I will help you. Continue in this manner and teach others to do the same.

Ask of them to do what has come to be known, the "Thirty-Three-day Consecration", and My Divine Spirit will direct them of My beloved Saint Louis Marie Grignon de Montfort. I thank you immensely!"

Iveta was in suffering for the people that have abandoned their Faith, in this first birth pang *of the* Great Apostasy *known as the pandemic and they desire to return to God. They have witnessed their loved ones perish, now their hearts desire to return to God and their Catholic Faith! This suffering will give them the Grace to return to the Catholic faith. (First Thursday, First Friday of November, November 5th and 6th, 2020)*

125. HOW SATAN IS PLOTTING NOW TO BRING AS IF THE HOLY TRINITY

Saint Michael speaks:

I come today at Her request to make known the intention of this intense suffering …

This suffering is befalling upon you for what has come to be known as the *'vaccine of diabolic nature'*[235]. The 'diabolic' is man playing God. Men who have become accomplices with Satan's plan to destroy God's elect! Catholics and Christians will perish under this vision of Satan as Martyrs and inherit an Eternal Crown forever - like the Saints gone before you. This suffering is for this vaccine and to be understood for those who will embrace it under the pressure of wanting to belong in the world and not understanding the Salvation of their Souls[236], for they will not heed the warnings already made known and being made known now! This suffering will buy *(back)* these Souls who have the intention to embrace the vaccine and thereby becoming Satan's advocates.

Know and understand: The Blessed Mother, Our Holy Mother, Mary a Virgin always, will come to receive it[237] at the

---

[235] This message does NOT condemn vaccination against Covid-19 but offers a disapproval of a *very specific type of vaccine* amongst the many vaccines that were tested at the time, namely, the vaccine that uses cell lines from aborted foetuses in its research and production process. This message offers elements of spiritual discernment. Please see the moral and doctrinal discernment that is given in the 'Note on the morality of using some anti-Covid-19 vaccines' from the Congregation for the Doctrine of the Faith of 21 December 2020 as well as the Message of 8th January 2021 in this book.

[236] The message of January 1st, 2021 also tells us about the negative effect of this vaccine on health itself.

[237] Iveta's Suffering.

last hour of this day which marks the entrance also of a new day, the First Saturday, tomorrow, the day being the 5ᵗʰ day of the 12ᵗʰ month of the year Two Thousand and Twenty. I am here as you invoke me to protect you."

… And now St. Michael shows me how the adversary is watching all over …

… and I will destroy and confuse his vision for you and for God's plan … and he is showing me now how Satan is plotting now to bring as if the Holy Trinity - the anti-God "trinity". And yet it is the same spirit of Satan in the World: To confuse Catholics and the teachings, the magisterium of the Holy Catholic Church, Catholicism! Amen.

"I am Saint Michael here with you this day as Our Blessed Mother will hold you in moments … The nausea that you will experience is the nausea that pregnant women experience, and it is at this stage that the children are aborted to take the tissues necessary for this vaccine[238]. These tissues are in contradiction to the Medicine made known by your Blessed Mother, the *Spiritual and Natural Remedy*, as it has come to be known, containing - what will destroy evil and the evil intent in the Temple of God, the human body - that is Holy Water and Blessed Salt with the prayers and power of the Catholic Church, in the personified Christ, His priest obedient to His Bishop and obedient to the Holy Father. Amen."

The vision closes, and I see no more, only the words:

"Saint Michael who stands in the Presence of God, here before you this day, and with you. Amen." (*First Friday of December, December 4ᵗʰ, 2020*)

---

[238] This is in reference only to the Vaccine that uses cell lines from aborted fetuses in their research and production process. See footnotes 235 and 236.

126. YOU WILL COME UNDER HIS KINGSHIP AND DWELL IN HIS SACRED HEART

Our Lady is dressed in a deep blue, sky blue garment, and yet as Our Lady Mediatrix of all Grace, Co-Redemptrix and Advocate, She has the pearl white Rosary in Her right hand, and the Scapular in Her left hand. She has Jesus suspended in Her Immaculate Heart. In the Monstrance is the Holy Eucharist. The two Keys of Peter are below the Monstrance. Her internal garment is white. There are stars all over Her external blue garment. Under Her feet is the moon She is standing on. The serpent is under Her foot, Her right heel. Our Lady bows in greetings, and She smiles at us. And She speaks:

"My beloved children, I thank you for preparing yourself for Me by reciting the Holy Rosary which pleases Me much and brings much consolation to my Sorrowful and Immaculate Heart which is in agony and pierced by so many arrows of ingratitude and even lashes to deny Me as the *Mother of God*, I am She, for God has willed it so for your sake and for this perverse generation; yet my children, I come to warn you against what has come to be known as 'the vaccine'[239].

There are many vaccines being prepared, yet this one which holds the 'tissue'[240] of the foetus of an unborn child, aborted for this reason, is a horrible and outrageous offence against God! This is done by Satan himself who desires to play God and be "god" in your world!

Be aware now he is mocking the Holy Trinity by coming in three persons[241]: the antichrist, the antipope and his spirit,

---

[239] This is in reference only to the Vaccine that uses cell lines from aborted fetuses in their research and production process. See footnotes 235 and 236.

[240] This message seems to be related to the use of a cell line, generated from fetal human kidney cells, extracted from the remains of a voluntary aborted fetus.

[241] See Rev 13,1-17.

playing as though the Divine Holy Spirit, by sending out false prophets and false messengers to torment the mind of God's elect, even … and yes, he is using the Word of God, the Holy Bible, which he has disfigured for his purpose[242].

I come to warn you, My Beloved Children, through this little one of Mine and My Jesus, Cleophas, who suffers for this cause this day, at My request, made known through the Prince of the Heavenly Hosts, Saint Michael, who will defend you against these forces when you call on Him and even send out the Heavenly Army to guard you, whose Commander He is, for God has appointed Him such!

I come now to warn you, as a mother would warn her children: You are in great danger should you ponder on accepting this form of belonging to Satan, once you have accepted it and received it[243], you will come under the power of his rule, rejecting God yet as though doing everything for God. You will do this by first rejecting the Holy Father, the reigning Pope Francis I, My Beloved Chosen Son, who is suffering many offences against Him and His papacy. You will come under Satan's rule to reject the Holy Magisterium of the Holy Catholic Church, and even be the persecutors of God's elect! Many of you all will be of the same household[244], some will choose God, and some will choose Satan, under the antichrist and the antipope, Satan's spirit of the World.

Know and understand I long to gather you. When you choose to reject this form of evil that is placed before you,

---

[242] See Luke 4,1-13.

[243] This is in reference only to the Vaccine that uses cell lines from aborted fetuses in their research and production process. See footnotes 235 and 236.

[244] See Luke 12, 52-53

you are making the choice of following the Eternal Promise with Jesus My Divine Son, the true and only Christ, Jesus Christ, your King of Eternal Glory. You will come under His Kingship and dwell in His Sacred Heart. You will come under the Queenship of The Immaculate Heart, and dwell in My Immaculate Heart, as you are now doing – to those who have embraced to respond to praying the Thirty-Three days Consecration to my Immaculate Heart, preparing yourselves for the Birthday of Our Lord Jesus. This birthday will be a unique one. By that you will understand when it approaches. Many will rejoice and many will weep! Amen.

… Now, I desire with great desire that you return to the Sacrament of Reconciliation, Confession, and receive Jesus in the Holy Eucharist, for the days are coming when, once more, they will deny you by closing the churches.

I am your Heavenly Mother. I will not abandon you! Stay faithful to your Consecration to Me, as now many of you are responding to My request. My Spouse, the Holy Spirit, will direct you. Be attentive to Him by being silent. And follow the direction He makes known to you, even though it seems so far! God knows best. Rid yourself of the world and all its pleasures, come into the conformity of simplicity and moderation and preparation for the *barter system*. The *barter system* is a way of love for one another and sharing when one has less of one item with the other, or even simply sharing with those who have none of such - that is necessary to sustain the basic bodily needs. God will provide, worry not! Only worry as in a joyful worry of sustaining your spirit and dwelling in My Immaculate Heart, and through Me into the Sacred Heart of Jesus.

You will understand what I mean by these words of Mine in the days ahead. I love you dearly, I thank you immensely!

I am your Heavenly Mother, awaiting to be proclaimed on Earth as *Mediatrix of all Grace, Co-Redemptrix* and *Advocate*, I am She in Heaven, that I may bring God's gift and all that is necessary for you to undergo these moments of persecution. It is known as the persecution of the Christians, yet the highest level of persecution will be that of the Catholic Church.

I love all My beloved children of all faiths, Christian faiths. I am still their Heavenly Mother. They have yet to understand My love for them. Amen. (*First Friday of December, December 4ᵗʰ, 2020*)

127. SATAN HAS MADE HIMSELF THE 'CREATOR'

Our Lady speaks:

Now, little one of Mine and My Jesus, I will receive this suffering, and this will be for those who have stood to be ignorant about the understanding of the vaccine[245], and will impart this Grace upon them, giving them the chance to choose where they were already decided in their thinking.

I will also rescue many of those women, my beloved daughters, who have subjected themselves in this mass understanding of aborting their babies and becoming the slaves of Satan! I will rescue them from this slavery by imparting upon them the Grace to know that this is evil, and through the Heavenly Hosts, with its Commander Saint Michael, I will bring them under the protection they are in need of, and hide them from him[246], and recover them to be Children of God.

---

[245] This is in reference only to the Vaccine that uses cell lines from aborted fetuses in their research and production process. See footnotes 235 and 236.
[246] Satan.

Know and understand, the most devastating method used now to abort children is what has come to be known as the 'laser technology', where those women, My beloved daughters, have been lured. Catholic women have been lured into understanding that their bodies will not be disfigured, and yet they will be sterile and no longer be able to have children, for which they were created.

There are other methods and Satan, the adversary is luring all into believing that it is the manner in which they can be happy and have children. Children are God's continuity for the humankind. Children who God is the author of, will be the Children *of Light* and those who Satan, using God's creation, has made himself the 'creator' - what does not belong to him to bring forth – will be the children *of darkness*[247].

Be aware of this, beloved children! Many of you whose wombs the Lord has closed for a time -understand there is a reason - do not seek such methods and become Satan's advocates! I come to warn you against this, and those who have embraced such will easily choose the Satanic world and deny God the right[248], who created them. All this for false happiness!

I now thank you for allowing Me to bring forth this word, little one of Mine and My Jesus, for cooperating with the Divine Spirit, even though you are much troubled and much anxious, for you do not give all to Me quickly. Only entrust all into My Immaculate Heart, and My Divine Spouse will guide you. I love you dearly, I thank you immensely, little one of Mine and My Jesus, Cleophas. Amen. (*First Friday of December, December 4th, 2020*)

---

[247] This is regarding Human cloning.
[248] ... of being the Creator.

YR 2021: ONLY TRUST IN GOD THROUGH ME!

128. IT WILL DESTROY YOUR LIFE AND EVEN YOUR HEALTH

Our Lady speaks:

"Little one of mine and My Jesus, … yes, it is next Friday you will endure this suffering, once again for "the" vaccine[249]. You will understand its necessity, especially for the faithful that they may understand what has come to be known as the vaccine containing the aborted foetus[250]. God will demand a life for a life. It is not to restore their life but to destroy their life that Satan has put this *(vaccine)* forth.

Yes, there are other vaccines being developed. Wait for them, should you desire a vaccine. Know and understand the simplicity of My medicine known as the *Spiritual and Natural Remedy* in the simplest form to understand how to fight this battle. And those who will embrace this vaccine[251] knowing its content, will enter to be demonic advocates! Know and understand such demonic advocates need to be exorcised when they turn from evil and turn to God. Today in your world, you are lacking priests who will take on this mission to exorcise the demon from many who are possessed by him already.

I warn you, do not embrace such a demonic power! It is not about restoring your life; it will destroy your life and even your health!

---

[249] This is in reference only to the Vaccine that uses cell lines from aborted fetuses in their research and production process. See footnotes 235 and 236.

[250] This message seems to be related to the use of a cell line, generated from fetal human kidney cells, extracted from the remains of a voluntary aborted fetus.

[251] This is in reference only to the Vaccine that uses cell lines from aborted fetuses in their research and production process. See footnotes 235 and 236.

Turn to God, turn to Me. Am I not your Mother who loves you? I am here to help you, and I will help you as the Mother of God, as your Heavenly Mother and *Mediatrix of all Grace, Co-Redemptrix* and *Advocate* in Heaven. When you invoke me under this title, I am able to restore you both spiritually and temporarily. Only trust in God through Me! I will take you safely into the Heart of God, My Divine Son Jesus where all rest, and into the bosom of your Heavenly Father whose Love Jesus is in your World. And you are in need of Him in the Holy Eucharist. I thank you immensely! Amen. (*Solemnity of Mary Mother of God, January 1ˢᵗ, 2021*)

129. SUFFERING FOR THE HIERARCHY WHO ARE RENDERING DECISIONS NOT IN THE ORDER OF GOD

Saint Michael steps forward and He speaks:

"I am Saint Michael, who stands in the Presence of God, appointed to protect God's elect, here before you, little one of Jesus and our Blessed Mother, Cleophas, our beloved sister - and you beloved of The Beloved, Felix Xavier, our brother - today suffering for your world especially for the Catholic Church, for the Hierarchy who are rendering decisions not in the order of God - who are rendering decisions in the understanding of the vaccine containing the aborted foetus of an unborn child, made in the image and likeness of God, aborted like in the days of the killing of children in the land of Mexico[252] - today preparing to worship Satan, yes, the faithful, even in the Hierarchy! This form of diabolic war will bring the Catholic Church to ruin - that is the structure! Yet the Church will stand, in the Domestic understanding of the *Underground*

---

[252] See the Apparition of Guadalupe, Mexico.

Church. Know and understand, this is in preparation to overthrow the Holy Father, His hour is coming!

This vaccine is to prepare - even the faithful who will embrace it will no longer be faithful but will pledge their fidelity to Satan and will join the movement thinking they are faithful to the Catholic Church - the anti-christ movement, to overthrow the Holy Father and to allow the anti-pope to sit on the throne of Peter.

You are entering the threshold of the *second birth pang* and this vaccine will bring laxity and infidelity, even among the Religious and the Priests. Many will fall away, and as though form their own Orders from the Orders they are serving. Many Orders will close down! This is what now is intended in the second birth pang."

… He pauses … and He speaks:

"Be not afraid, be not troubled, only make known - with total trust and full confidence in our God who is God - what has been made known to you and stand tall. This is the hour now you are preparing for and keep your fidelity by your Consecration in the morning, and your fidelity to the medicine that has been made known to you as *the Spiritual and Natural remedy*, of taking it three times a day. It is like to be made known now as a Tonic that will strengthen you against these forces. Amen". *(2ⁿᵈ Friday of the month, January 8ᵗʰ, 2021)*

130. POWER WILL BE GIVEN TO THE ADVERSARY TO TORMENT ALL THOSE IN THE CITIES

Saint Michael speaks:

"Know and understand now, beloved children, you must make known to the children, your beloved brethren who live in the cities, that this is the hour now that they must come away from the cities, for power will be given to the adversary to torment all those in the cities. Many will fall away, and many will die as Martyrs, and those who will heed this call, will not only save their bodies but their Souls.

Know and understand you are entering very, very, very heavy moments, yet I am with you, Saint Michael, with all the choirs of Angels. Make known the recitation of my Chaplet, and you will understand its meaning. Amen."

... He pauses, then He speaks again:

"The Holy Mother will come at the conclusion hour of this day to receive this suffering which you are enduring in a tranquil state and yet you will feel the immensity of the weakness of your body throughout this week. That is to be understood, the consequences in which it will lead to the state of one's body, when one takes the vaccine[253] – 'one' referring to the Soul of the faithful. And this will bring deterioration of the body and will subject them to the Laws of the *death culture* known as Euthanasia, for their bodies will no longer be able to function in a normal state. And the law implemented will now be used against them. These are even babies, youngsters - *that I am seeing ... now a vision is being presented* - all kinds, it is not just the elderly ... even the strong who want to save their bodies will lose it in this manner.

The vision closes and Saint Michael continues to speak, after pausing.

... I love you dearly, I come on behalf of the Mother of Our God, who is here before you, and who has commanded Me on Her behalf. I will protect you, only invoke Me!

---

[253] This is in reference only to the Vaccine that uses cell lines from aborted fetuses in their research and production process. See footnotes 235 and 236.

I am Saint Michael, Servant of Mary, always a Virgin, *Mediatrix of all Grace, Co-Redemptrix and Advocate* in Heaven awaiting to be proclaimed on Earth. Pray, pray, pray for your Holy Father, much prayer! Amen."

The vision again reveals Saint Michael holding the baby as He rises, the little aborted baby and the scales of Justice.

"The Justice of God will stand against all those in the understanding of ... A life for a Life! Amen."

The vision closes, I see Saint Michael no more, our Altar returns. I see Our Blessed Mother no more, but Her Presence is here. Amen. (2nd Friday of the month, January 8th, 2021)

131. HUMAN CLONING WILL BECOME THE TREND OF THE NEW MAN, THE NEW WORLD

... Saint Michael is present here ... This time He comes with the sword in His right Hand, and the sword is over His Head ready to strike, and He has the chain in His left hand, ready to bind, and He takes His position up, in front of Me toward my left-hand side, closer to you my husband, but above you.

Mama comes: She has been here all along, but only now presents Herself. She is dressed in a navy-blue garment, with an internal white garment. Her Hands are joined with the Rosary draped around Her fingers, with the Scapular also, as in Our Lady of Fatima statue at our home. She spreads Her Hands, and I see the Chalice in Her Immaculate Heart. The Chalice is overflowing, and the Blood of Jesus is descending upon the Souls right now, of whom She is ransoming. And this suffering is united now to that Suffering of Jesus for these Souls. And as this Blood flows now, today all the Holy Sacrifices celebrated everywhere on Earth by the Priests, valid Priests in the Catholic Church, valid, obedient to the Holy Father and obedient to their Bishops, those Bishops and Cardinals that are not in fallen state - those in fallen state of Grace are exempted for not being obedient - but obedient to the Holy Father, today the reigning Pope His Holiness Pope Francis I.

Saint Michael now comes forward and He speaks:

"I am Saint Michael the Archangel, who stands in the Presence of God, once again this day presenting Myself before you, little one of Jesus Our Divine Saviour and Our Blessed Mother, Cleophas, beloved sister.

I have come now to receive the suffering you have endured, its merits - to ransom the Souls that Our Blessed Mother will lead me to - and to bind Satan, who is inflicting them with confusion - those of the Hierarchy who desire to follow God and have repented for even thinking of accepting the vaccine containing the aborted foetus of a child made in the image and likeness of God. Now Our Blessed Mother will receive this suffering. I present before you Our Sorrowful Mother - agonizing for what will come to be! Amen"

... and He steps back.

Holy Mama comes forth, standing on a little cloud. The moon is under Her, and under the serpent that She crushes. She bows in greetings to us, and She speaks:

"Little one of Mine and My Jesus, Cleophas, I thank you, I thank you immensely for consoling My Sorrowful Heart, which is so afflicted by the arrows that are piercing It, of those in the Hierarchy who once were faithful and now have rejected Me and rejected the teachings of the Magisterium of the Holy Catholic Church!

Know and understand, this day, through this little suffering of yours, I will ransom many who desire to not follow those who have decided to become unfaithful. This I speak of the Hierarchy, those in different Orders - Religious Orders - many

Priests, and many of the Churches who will lead the faithful astray in their thinking, of accepting this vaccine which now will bring about what Satan is waiting for ... *Ah!!! ... Oh, my heart is heavy ...* to set into place mass, mass murder! That this abortion now will rise to a higher scale and human cloning will become the trend of the new man, the new world, as he[254] is planning to do so - the *one world order,* the *one world government,* the *one world religion* – that God will allow.

Yet you, My beloved children - I speak to all of you - remain faithful through your consecration to My Immaculate Heart, entrusting all into My Immaculate Heart, consecrating yourselves, your families and all that you have to My Immaculate Heart! In this way I am able to protect you against these forces! Here, many of you will undergo martyrdom, and yes, many of My Priests who will take the stand to reject this form of healing and restoration of human life[255] will undergo martyrdom.

Pray, pray, much prayer for your Holy Father! A terrible weight will befall him in the days ahead, for many in the Hierarchy in the Vatican will try to persuade Him to think differently in the terminology ... *Oh, what is that Mama, my eyes are burning ...* known as the 'Pilgrim Church'. *(2ⁿᵈ Friday of the month, January 9ᵗʰ, 2021)*

132. GOD'S WAYS CANNOT BE CHANGED. GOD'S TRUTH STANDS AS TRUTH!

Know and understand, God's ways cannot be changed. God's Truth stands as Truth! This Truth must be upheld to uphold each child made in the image and likeness of God. Amen."

"Now, little one of Mine and My Jesus, Cleophas, you will fall into a very deep sleep in the hours of the new day. This

---

[254] Satan

[255] This is in reference to Human cloning and to a whole new world vision.

sleep is necessary, it is like the withdrawal of an anesthetic, and then when you wake up, you will feel pain in different parts of your body which will leave you weak. Be on guard, and carry out your duties slowly and lightly, only those that do not strain the body. I will be with you through this week. I thank you, and I love you, little one of Mine and My Jesus."

... Now She pauses and speaks again:

"I also desire with great desire to thank all those praying for you, who knew about this moment that you would undergo this day. I thank them immensely! I bless them for keeping in solidarity with you, to undergo this suffering to ransom Souls back, and I accept all their intentions that they have also placed as they pray for you, and I will help them!

I desire with great desire only to make known to remain faithful to the teachings of the Catholic Church, the Magisterium, the Holy Catholic Church, founded on the Rock, known as Peter, today the reigning Pope, His Successor, Pope Francis I. Pray for Him! Pray also for the *hidden Pope*, His Holiness Emeritus Pope Benedict XVI, carrying the Church in these times through His suffering and prayers.

I Am the *Mother of God*.

I Am the Mother of all humanity.

I Am Your Heavenly Mother, *Mediatrix of all Grace*, *Co-Redemptrix* and *Advocate* in Heaven, interceding for those who invoke Me under this title, awaiting to be proclaimed on Earth. Through your prayers it will come to be.

I love you all dearly. Amen.

The vision closes. I see Holy Mama no more. (2nd Friday of the month, January 9th, 2021)

JESUS PRAYS IN GETHSEMANE, Painting by Iveta

"In anguish, He prayed more earnestly,

and His sweat became like great drops of blood on the ground."

"Could you not keep awake one hour?"

As Jesus appeared, He allowed me to capture (draw) Him.

O, look at those loving eyes of Our God, calling us to Him!

Such love even while we cause Him such agony.

Original Painting Blessed by Rev Fr Duffy, March 2005

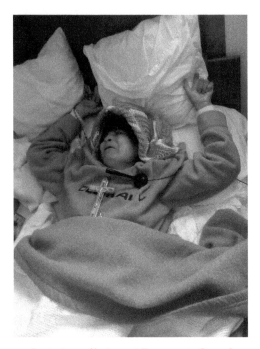

Iveta in suffering at Foymont, Canada

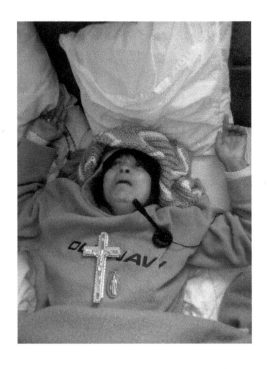

Saint Simon and Saint Jude Church at Mount Batim, Goa, India

The Miraculous Well at Mount Batim, Goa, India

Our Lady' Statue at Mount Batim   St Michael's Statue at Mount Batim

246

Iveta during Our Blessed Mother's Visitation at Mount Batim

Felix and Iveta in Goa

THE THESIS OF PURGATORY

Sources:

Treaty of Purgatory of Catherine of Genova: https://www.saintsbooks.net

Catechism of the Catholic Church:

https://www.vatican.va/archive/ENG0015/_INDEX.HTM

250

THE FINAL PURIFICATION, OR PURGATORY

ACCORDING TO THE CATECHISM OF THE CATHOLIC CHURCH

All who die in God's grace and friendship, but still imperfectly purified, are indeed assured of their eternal salvation; but after death they undergo purification, so as to achieve the holiness necessary to enter the joy of Heaven.

The Church gives the name Purgatory to this final purification of the elect, which is entirely different from the punishment of the damned. The Church formulated her doctrine of faith on Purgatory especially at the Councils of Florence and Trent. The tradition of the Church, by reference to certain texts of Scripture, speaks of a cleansing fire.

As for certain lesser faults, we must believe that, before the Final Judgment, there is a purifying fire. He who is truth says that whoever utters blasphemy against the Holy Spirit will be pardoned neither in this age nor in the age to come. From this sentence we understand that certain offenses can be forgiven in this age, but certain others in the age to come.

This teaching is also based on the practice of prayer for the dead, already mentioned in Sacred Scripture: "Therefore Judas Maccabeus made atonement for the dead, that they might be delivered from their sin." From the beginning the Church has honored the memory of the dead and offered prayers in suffrage for them, above all the Eucharistic sacrifice, so that, thus purified, they may attain the beatific vision of God. The Church also commends almsgiving, indulgences, and works of penance undertaken on behalf of the dead.

Let us help and commemorate them. If Job's sons were purified by their father's sacrifice, why would we doubt that our offerings for the dead bring them some consolation? Let us not hesitate to help those who have died and to offer our prayers for them.

- Catechism of the Catholic Church, n.1030-1032

133. THE HISTORY OF THE MYSTICAL PAINTING

The Holy Images and its understanding were received by a little Soul[256], on Holy Saturday, 1997 (between 1:00pm. -3:30 pm)

First, the "little Soul" heard the Voice of Jesus, her Saviour.

Jesus speaks:

"My Peace I give you. I have conquered death, and now you shall no longer be captives. I have won for God His people and created for Him a Nation. Rejoice, for even those who are asleep, have risen! For I Am the resurrection and The Life. Amen."

External vision: Embedded in the miracle picture are other many unexplainable faces and images of Holy men and women. John is the artist who drew and painted this beautiful Image.

*

Explanation of the Mystical Painting: See Page 250.

I see the Risen Lord. He could faintly be seen. He is all Light. The Holy Spirit gave me the grace to run my pencil back and forth, as if in a tracing, and the Face appeared by itself, on its own. Since the painting is not by me, this would not be so, as in the original you only see the traces of the Holy images made known to me; and all my part was to run the pencil back and forth, while we were in prayer and the Holy Images appeared. Amen.

The Lord calls St. Michael, His Glorious Prince, the Defender of His Heavenly Army, the Defender of Souls. In this vision, the Lord gives St. Michael the Archangel, the Ladder that was used to lower His body down from the Cross. The Ladder

---

[256] Iveta Fernandes

is placed on the right shoulder of Saint Michael as the Souls climb up from Purgatory.

His Redeeming Cross goes before Him as He appears in all His Glory. Amen.

From the Lord Jesus' Sacred and Merciful Heart appear so many rays of red, blue and gold colour falling upon the Souls who seek His Mercy. Amen.

His left hand is outstretched and falling from it are like gold dust or sand-like granules of gold colour to reveal victory over death. Amen.

Now also seen is Our Lady. Our Lady's right hand appears as though holding those baptised in a pool of water, a spring in the Earth on rocky ground, like that one seen at Batim[257] (India), the place of Our Lady's Visitation.

Our Lady is seen helping these Souls climb the Ladder, the Way of Jesus, Her Divine Son. Amen.

St. Michael is seen here very different from the many pictures painted of him. He appears like a Royal Prince prepared for battle. Gentle, are the features of his face, but fierce like the one who would tolerate no nonsense, only the Truth!

The Truth as revealed to him, by none other than God as he would say: "Who is like unto God? None but Thee, none but Thee, O God! Amen."

---

[257] Located in the Goa, Mount Batim is a hill on which stands the church dedicated to Sts. Simon and Jude. It is said that this was the place where Saint Francis Xavier S.J. baptized hundreds of Goan inhabitants. It is also the place of the 'Visitations' of the Blessed Virgin Mary related to Iveta and Felix Fernandes. These visitations have yet to receive Church approval.

134. THE UNDERSTANDING OF THE THREE STAGES OF PURGATORY

Iveta: She speaks to me Soul to Soul.

"Little one of mine and My Jesus Cleophas, Co-Redeeming with Me, the *Co-Redemptrix* united to the *Redeemer*, this Good Friday. Here I desire to make known the understanding of the three stages as it would be called, made known to you of Purgatory. Here My Jesus, Our Saviour falls, in the understanding of the Souls who suffer in Purgatory. You are now offering this suffering of yours; it will be the torments of your Mind.

These are for the sins when a Soul does not rebuke the thoughts and allows these thoughts to enter the mind, the conscious, subconscious and unconscious thoughts.

You will understand more as I will make known in the days ahead. Here you are offering this suffering for the Souls in Purgatory. This suffering I will take, as you co-redeem for them, and for those sinners who do not repent, to save many and bring them to repentance. Those who desire to stop these thoughts, sinful thoughts, uncharitable thoughts, I will help them with this Grace so that they will not enter the second fall. Here you must understand that I will apply this Grace tomorrow when I will gather all the prayers for the Souls in Purgatory and apply them when Our Divine Saviour, the *Redeemer* rises as He foretold. Amen."

*

I am the Mother of God. I am the *Mother of God*, I am your Heavenly Mother suffering this day, Co-Redeeming and obtaining all the Graces necessary for you to sustain yourselves. You will understand My role as *Mediatrix of all Grace* in the days ahead Amen." *(Good Friday, April 14ᵗʰ, 2017)*

135. THIS IS THE SECOND STAGE OF PURGATORY AS IT IS KNOWN

"… now to the second fall of Jesus. Jesus is exhausted. He looks at His Mother.

"Mother, Mother" … and He takes a heavy fall. He falls as though on His face but His face rests on the Cross, a part of the Cross. They are trying to pull Him up, but they cannot!

Redeemer to Co-Redemptrix:

"Mother help Me, save those who will continue in their sins and will not repent."

Here Holy Mother reveals another understanding:

"Little one of Mine and My Jesus, Cleophas, Co-Redeeming with the *Redeemer,* through Me the *Co-Redemptrix.* Your heart is breaking! It is very heavy!

Understand now, this is what sin does when it enters the heart. This is when they, who do not rebuke it in the beginning and ponder; and now it has entered the heart to contaminate it. This is the second stage of Purgatory as it is known. Those suffering for these sins have passed into the Resurrection by paying Divine Justice, for they have repented at the last hour! Know now, you are co-redeeming in suffering for those who are pondering on this sin. It is a grave offence, the sins of the flesh to defile the Temple of God! Here you will redeem many, many, My little one. I will use this Grace to open and cut through their hardened hearts for they will ponder no more!

Now rest a little bit, your heart is heavy, rest in My Motherly Mantle, rest in My Immaculate Heart! Amen."

... He (Jesus) sees all the women lamenting and weeping for Him. In spite of all His suffering and pain, He raises His head, and stops, and looks at them and He says: "Do not weep for Me, but weep for yourselves and weep for your children."

Soul to Soul, Heart to Heart, He speaks to His Mother: "Mother, Mother, help these children of mine. They see Me in this manner and do not understand it is for their sake I am enduring this, and so are You. I love Thee, Mother, Blessed art Thou among all Women[258], for thou has borne the Son of God. Holy art Thou among all Women for Thou has obeyed the Will of God, Co-Redeeming with me now as *Co-Redemptrix*. Amen. Amen." *(Good Friday, April 14th, 2017)*

136. THOSE WHO COMMIT AND GIVE CONSENT TO THE SIN KNOWN AS EUTHANASIA

Iveta in suffering for Euthanasia

Saint Michael speaks: "I am Saint Michael Who stands in the Presence of God. I come before you this day beloved children of God who are pleasing to God as you keep this fast and prayers and the suffering of this little one, our beloved sister Cleophas, little one of Our Blessed Mother and Our Lord Jesus.

This suffering by no means is little, it is a grave *suffering of silence* and of deterioration of the Soul and of the heart becoming numb and cold towards God, of those who commit and those who give consent to the sin known as Euthanasia, consent to die

---

[258] Luke 1,42

and those who commit this offence is taking the lives of others without consent, discreetly! It is a grave offence before God!

I come before you this day to accept the suffering of this little one and place it in a bowl."

... and now Archangel Saint Raphael rises and He stands at the left Hand side of Our Lady and now He moves in front and He has the bowl of incense brought to him by another Archangel, as though. He is on Earth at this time and He holds the bowl with this incense and the suffering is placed in there and our fast is placed in there, and the prayers from all these Angels and Archangels are placed in there. These Archangels are those of many Priests and Religious who are dying with this same understanding in silence. They have been put to death, even Bishops and even Cardinals.

... Saint Michael Who was silent for a while speaks again: "I bring before you the message of the Mother of our God to understand this grave moment. I Am Her servant here before you, Saint Michael."

Our Lady speaks:

"My beloved children, I thank you for keeping this fast, this day in a total abstinence of meat, the flesh of My animals. It pleases God immensely and having consumed the Living Flesh and Blood of Our Lord in the Holy Eucharist, you have sustained yourselves with that."

"This grave abomination that has come to be known as Euthanasia is the error of Russia not being Consecrated to My Immaculate Heart and now playing God. First the abomination of the consent to kill as in abortion, the innocent who have no right and no voice to speak for themselves! Now the consent to speak by those who have a voice, giving consent to take away their lives because their minds have become distorted with the understanding that suffering is not necessary. They do not understand the grave offence they are committing! Yet, many are Catholics!

Today with this suffering I will prevent many from escaping from suffering, those even who have written a consent form. God Himself will intervene to release them from their bodies and they will enter ... *(now I am shown the last stage of Purgatory)* This is because many are praying against this terrible crime against God, and to those who die in this manner, who are giving consent, *(Iveta: Oh my goodness me!)* many will fall into Hell and through the prayer of many, some will enter into the last state of Purgatory *(where I see a candle burning)* and will not come out of this stage until the last day of judgement, the final judgement! If they only knew this suffering, they would embrace the suffering, that is the Cross that God has given them to carry for their own Salvation, the Salvation of their Souls! And they would rejoice with the Crown that God would place ... upon them, welcoming them Home, having kept the Cross and not seeking to abandon it.

This abomination is spreading to many Nations. I call all My children this day to say 'No' to such evil! Do not give consent! Only God has the right as the Creator of each one of you to release you from the bodies made of clay, to allow you to be released from it, when His purpose is served to glorify Him on Earth and in Heaven. And then you return to dust and some become Saints with this suffering and incorruptible, to show the power of God alone! Amen.

I am the Mother of God, the *Mediatrix of all Grace, Our Lady of Sorrows, (that is why She is clothed with a navy blue and white Garment, but with a red sash that drapes to Her right) Co-Redemptrix*, interceding for you who call upon Me and those who pray for those who are pondering on this manner of death to befall them.

The Mother of God: I warn you of not entering the hospitals unnecessarily. Learn to call upon Me and abandon yourself into My Immaculate Heart and offer this suffering that befalls you for the Salvation of Souls in Purgatory and the Salvation of Souls to be converted on Earth, even members of your own household! There[259] they wait for you, that is My adversary who has entered many Souls now desiring to play God himself. When you hear of such, pray for them! Pray many Rosaries, for many Rosaries are needed! I love you dearly Amen."

*

"I love you dearly, I thank you immensely for consoling My Sorrowful Heart so wounded for the loss of so many of My children. Even the faithful who have kept the law of God in the last stages have abandoned Him and embraced the law of Satan.

I am your Heavenly Mother, the *Mediatrix of all Grace, Co-Redemptrix* and *Advocate* in Heaven, interceding for you and for those who call on Me. I thank all the little ones of Mine who are praying for this beloved sister of theirs. Yes, in this manner I will Bless you. You strengthen her to suffer for these grave offences in this little weak body of hers, and yet it is mighty with the Grace of God. She also prays for each one of you before Me in thanksgiving. I will Bless you and your families. Continue in this manner for much will befall her in the coming days known as the Holy Week. I love you dearly. Amen."

---

[259] In the Hospitals

Now She withdraws, the little scroll is rolled up and St Michael gives it to Our Lady. This message came on a scroll, and now He explains why his sword is downcast.

He has no authority over the human will and so He cannot even rescue their Souls from falling into Hell, but now He raises his sword and holds it above His Head, and He holds the Divine Scales in His left hand and the chain hangs around His left forearm, and with our prayers He is able to thrust the sword - He shows us, when we pray for those who have committed Euthanasia - at Satan himself, and Satan escapes, and the Soul is now placed on the scales of Divine Justice and taken up to Heaven.

This is the first judgement, and through our prayers the Soul enters the last stages of Purgatory, and there it shows me the Angels associated there are of the rank of 'Powers', the last stage of Purgatory closest to Hell ... and there is silence. Now Saint Michael also shows me the understanding of Purgatory:

When we pray for these Souls who have committed Euthanasia, not those who are killing them, but those who die at the hands of Euthanasia - this evil spirit, St Michael stands at the entrance of the last stage of Purgatory and the Angels of 'Power' come and take the Chalice from Him and pours it over them ... relieving them ... of their suffering and the chalice is returned and the door closes. St Michael takes the Chalice and then gives it to Our Lady who stands and watches everything. Amen.

The Vision Closes. (5th Friday of Lent, 2018)

137. REPARATION THAT MUST BE RENDERED BEFORE THE SOUL COMES INTO PARADISE

"Know understand now, you are entering to suffer for the Souls in Purgatory[260]. To you is given an understanding in small portions of the thesis of Purgatory: Jesus[261] descends into the dead and night it is. Here, when He rises *in remembrance of* the first day of His resurrection from the dead, a great Schism took place. He gave the Devil his position, and in Heaven, which is an understanding of a Spiritual World, the World of God, a place was created known as 'Purgatory'[262].

The schism consists of two understandings: Heaven and Hell. Hell is to be understood as below Heaven. The schism must be understood as once the Soul is condemned to Hell it can never enter Heaven[263]; but once in the first Judgement, it

---

[260] Iveta's experience is different from that of Catherine of Genova. To Catherine was given a spiritual personal experience that was similar to the experience of the Souls in Purgatory, that gave her an understanding of Purgatory which her disciples wrote. Iveta tells about her experience of suffering for the Souls in Purgatory within a co-redemptive experience, during which she receives an understanding of Purgatory which her husband did record and write down.

[261] Iveta's experience happened during Holy Saturday. She receives an insight of what will happen during the coming night, during the Eucharistic celebration of the Easter Vigil which celebrates the Resurrection of our Lord.

[262] Purgatory is presented here as part of Heaven. Thus, is underlined the radical difference between Purgatory and Hell. "Since the Souls in Purgatory are freed from the guilt of sin, there is no barrier between them and God, save only the pains they suffer, which delay the satisfaction of their desire." (Catherine of Genova, Treaty of Purgatory, chap. III)

[263] "Those, therefore, that are in Hell, having passed from this life with perverse wills, their guilt is not remitted, nor can it be, since they are no longer capable of change. When this life is ended, the Soul remains forever confirmed either in good or evil according as she has here determined." (Catherine of Genova, Treaty of Purgatory, chap. IV)

enters Heaven and into the stages of Purgatory where God will send it to be purified.

This purification is an understanding of reparation that must be rendered before the Soul comes into Paradise and into the Presence of God, where there is no contamination[264]: an all-Good God, and all is good, Crystal clear! Here you understand the purpose of all Souls: To Praise, Worship and Glorify God unceasingly!

Now, when you understand about your ancestors who are in Purgatory and you fail to pray for them, to release them through your prayers so that they may Praise, Worship and Glorify God unceasingly for you and obtain the Grace and Faith necessary, you see the loss of faith on Earth; yes even in families once predominant in faith, righteous before God!

And yet the understanding of sin that one commits, even a righteous person sins seven times a day, must be understood as a purification necessary for that righteous person when he or she enters Heaven, that is Purgatory. But when the Soul falls into Hell, this is where the Devil - his angels, the fallen angels have been given a place - his own dominion, so to be understood.

Just as you have ranks and the stages of Purgatory, the St. Michael's Chaplet[265] as it has come to be known, reveals the power of Angels. The Devil has the same power in Hell, but not the Power of God above all.

---

[264] But I see that the divine essence is so pure — purer than the imagination can conceive — that the Soul, finding in itself the slightest imperfection, would rather cast itself into a thousand Hells than appear, so stained, in the presence of the divine majesty. Knowing, then, that Purgatory was intended for her cleaning, she throws herself therein, and finds there that great mercy, the removal of her stains. (idem. Chap VIII)

[265] See content of St. Michael's Chaplet in appendix section of this book.

When a Soul falls into Hell - that is to say it is condemned to Hell - it is not God's desire to do so, but this has been brought about for lack of prayer and the Soul's desire to renounce God and choose the Devil - as in the free will[266] understanding, the Gift that God gives each Soul when it is created: The will to choose right from wrong, to choose good from bad, to choose God or the Devil, and to serve God on Earth - as it is created - or to choose to serve the Devil with the help of his fallen angels.

This is the path that Souls are walking, of perdition, and if we do not pray, many Souls are lost in this manner!

More will be given in its understanding in the days ahead of you My beloved daughter, little one of Mine and My Jesus. I who am The *Immaculate Conception* through My Holy Spirit will reveal this understanding to cleanse Souls of bondages and of ancestral temptations. This is the preparation for Souls entering into the Remnant and an understanding for the Constitution known as the Constitution of the Holy Orders dedicated to the *Sacred Heart of Jesus* and *My Immaculate Heart*!

I Am the *Immaculate Conception, the Mediatrix of All Grace, Co-Redemptrix* and *Advocate* in Heaven, the *Mother of God* interceding with your prayers for the Souls even in Purgatory when you offer your prayers for them. Your sacrifice can be offered up for them too! Your good deeds and your actions, your kind words can also be offered up for these Souls! They are paying God's Divine Justice[267] and right it is for they have

---

[266] "It is evident that the revolt of man's will from that of God constitutes sin, and while that revolt continues, man's guilt remains." (idem, Chap. IV)

[267] "Seeing with certainty the importance of the slightest hindrance, seeing that Justice demands that their attraction be delayed, a fire of extreme violence is born in their hearts, which resembles that of Hell." (idem, Chap. IV)

repented[268], even if their many sins have embraced God's Mercy, be it during their lifetime or at the hour of their death. It is through the prayers of many Victim Souls that this Grace is granted unto them, but this also is the Choice of God Who knows the heart."

And now this vision is granted to Me.

"When I received the sword that pierced My Immaculate Heart at the foot of the Cross to reveal to the hearts and the Souls of My children who will Consecrate themselves to My Immaculate Heart and Consecrate all their loved ones and all those dear to their heart, friends, even so each morning by name as I have asked mothers to do so with their children through prayers for their children, they will be granted the Grace like these Souls that are consecrated to My Immaculate Heart to see themselves as God sees them before they take their last breath on Earth[269].

Now you must suffer, little one of Mine and My Jesus, Cleophas with the Lord. I love you dearly and I thank you My beloved of the Beloved, Felix Xavier for helping Me, allowing your spouse to endure this and through your prayers and standing in solidarity with her united even in your tiredness and suffering, you are also co-redeeming and offering your prayers for these Souls! Amen."

---

[268] "They are pure from sins, because they have in this life abhorred them and confessed them with true contrition, and for this reason God remits their guilt, so that only the stains of sin remain, and these must be devoured by the fire. (idem, Chap.V)

[269] This an immense gift of grace: A Soul is given the grace "to see themselves as God sees them before they take their last breath on Earth", and therefore to repent and welcome God's grace before death. The 'normal' path, according to Catherine of Genova is: "At the moment of leaving this life, they see why they are sent to Purgatory" (idem Chap. I).

Iveta: My head is heavy, my body is paralysed, my hands cannot move, my eyes are suffering the worst suffering[270]. They are blind to such a degree! I cannot see anything internal nor external.

My God how long will you keep me in this way? When will you bid me to come unto You? My God do not leave me like this, it is You I long for! I'm surrounded with flames, yet my body cannot be consumed by them nor do I have any worms eating it. I have the Garment of a glorified body[271], but my Crown awaits me still! My God, I long to wear my Crown. When will You declare me righteous and worthy of coming into Your Presence to Praise and Worship and Glorify Thee with all the Angels and Saints! Even if I sit in the last rank, I will be content because I will see You my God. The Beatific Vision I was told on Earth, it is true, it exists! It is You, the Face of My God I long to see, my Creator! Here I can only be and thank Thee for allowing me to be spared the eternal damnation of Hell where I would never see Thee, and where the flames would never go out, burning me with pain!

Now my pain is the anguish of my Soul to see Thee! I love Thee My God, quench my thirst! Amen.

The Vision Closes (Holy Saturday, March 31st, 2018)

---

[270] "It is true that the divine love which overwhelms the Soul gives, as I think, a peace greater than can be expressed; yet this peace does not in the least diminish her pains, nay, it is love delayed which occasions them, and they are greater in proportion to the perfection of the love of which God has made her capable. "Thus have these Souls in Purgatory great pleasure and great pain; nor does the one impede the other." (idem, Chap.V)

[271] See Footnote No. 29

138. JESUS HAS PAID THE PRICE FOR THESE SOULS FROM THE FIRST MAN TO THE LAST MAN THAT WILL BE CREATED

Iveta: Please give me a drop of Holy Water, Bubs[272] ... thank you, thank you.

"My beloved of the Beloved Felix Xavier, do you understand what you have just done? It is in this way when you pray for the Souls in Purgatory, that I Am able to offer them a release from one position to the other[273]: The position is not of a physical nature, it is of a Spiritual understanding and brings relief to their Spirit just as this little one of Mine and My Jesus, your beloved Spouse Cleophas, has received a joy; it is that way I Am able to bring this joy, even if it be for a little moment!

It is a greater joy to move the Soul from one stage to the other, I will make known how they move in days ahead.

This turning, now is an understanding of time taken away from them, lessened[274]!

Iveta: Now a Vision presents itself, and I see Our Holy Mother standing at the door that opens into what appears dark at first. Now Her brightness shines, and then Archangel Michael comes from the rank of an Angel, known as the Choir of Angels of Seraphim. Works of charity; a Soul that was lacking this work, now receives release from one position to the other.

---

[272] Iveta calls her husband Felix this familiar name.
[273] Catherine of Genova also speaks of a path for the Souls in Purgatory: "They experience thence a great and never-failing satisfaction which constantly increases as they approach to God". (idem, Chap.XVI)
[274] "The pain never diminishes, although the time does." (idem, Chap. II)

Our Lady speaks:

I thank you! It will be most fruitful that when the Holy Mother, the Catholic Church celebrates what is known as the Easter Vigil - the Resurrection of Our Lord - many Souls will enter into Heaven! These Souls are those who are in the stages close to Heaven, especially all Souls in the first stages - known as limbo - of little children who have miscarried, aborted an even the Souls who have suffered and died gravely and are paying Gods Justice in Purgatory, paying the price of Divine Justice in Purgatory.

It will be a great moment! All the prayers that you are now reciting and those who are praying, venerating My seven sorrows, these prayers will be applied for this moment. I will use them to ransom Souls from Purgatory. They will rise with The Lord in remembrance of that first day! May you know and understand, the first Resurrection brought forth Souls from the first man created to the last Soul that died that day. Now know and understand, Jesus has paid the price for these Souls from the first man to the last man that will be created. Such is the value of suffering!

The Lord has walked that path! When you offer the Holy Sacrifice, the Holy Mass for Souls in Purgatory, sometimes it will be used only for that particular Soul[275]. But if you pray for the different Souls as the Church prays in every mass, it is in this way these Souls in Limbo are released into all Eternity. They are like little Angels who will Adore, Praise and Worship God and bring great Joy in Heaven[276].

---

[275] The Soul for whom the Holy Mass is being offered.

[276] "Just so, I tell you, there will be more joy in Heaven over one sinner who repents than over ninety-nine righteous persons who need no repentance." (Luke 15,7)

I Am the *Mother of God*. I am the Mother, Co-Redeeming for these Souls in Purgatory through your prayers and suffering, *Mediatrix of all Grace* and *Advocate*, obtaining the Grace of the prayers of those released in Purgatory, of your Ancestors, and applying it to the Souls of that Ancestral line, and giving them the Grace to hold fast to their faith and to pass their faith on to the next generation. *(Holy Saturday, March 31ˢᵗ, 2018)*

139. THE SOULS IN PURGATORY ARE GRANTED THE GIFTS OF THE TONGUES OF ANGELS

Iveta: Bubs[277], can you turn me a little more?

"My beloved children, know and understand!" ...

"Thank you, My beloved of the Beloved. This is the manner you must treat those who are suffering: With Love! Yes, it may appear like it is taking all your time, but it is the most valuable time for your Soul and for the Soul that is suffering!

Know and understand that the Souls in Purgatory do not speak as mortals do on Earth. They are granted the Gifts of the Tongues of Angels. They speak to God crying out all the time in Tongues of Angels. The One that hears their Tongues very clearly is their Guardian Angel who is doing the Adoration for them. And it is their Guardian Angel that often brings a message of prayer. As many times, people have dreams of their ancestors or Souls coming to them. It is not the Soul coming, it is their Guardian Angel bringing their vision as they were on Earth, before the Soul who prays for these Souls in Purgatory, the Soul on Earth! *(March 31ˢᵗ, 2018 Holy Saturday)*

---

[277] Iveta calls her husband Felix this familiar name.

268

140. CONFESSION MUST BE UNDERSTOOD AS EXORCISM AGAINST MORTAL SIN

"Know and understand how valuable suffering is! Here you will understand the meaning of the Gift of the Sacrament of Reconciliation in the Holy Mother, the Catholic Church.

When you go for confession, as you also know it as, as you confess your sins to the Priest, here the reparation is taken by Jesus!

When you confess at the hour of your death and you beg Mercy for all your sins, the gift of Mercy is granted, just as in reconciliation in confession.

Know and understand, it is for the reparation - the Divine Justice -that the Soul now enters into the stages of Purgatory. That is, God the Divine Judge, the Lord Jesus, True God and True Man, now God sitting on the Throne of Judgement will Judge in the first justice as the first Judgement when a Soul comes before God and He renders the sentence according to His Merciful Love and Divine Justice!

It is important, beloved children, for you to enter confession often when you have committed an offence, especially of Mortal nature. Yes even venial sins, it is well for you to confess them, so that you do not compound them, that is repeat them and they become Mortal sins if you do not correct them. Confession is Holy Reconciliation with God through the Priest, the Catholic Priest who has been given the authority by the High Priest to absolve you, taking the reparation, that is! The Lord's and often your sufferings on Earth, will make up for that Divine Justice!

It is a beautiful moment! And even the sufferings that befall you because of your iniquity, will be brought to healing if you believe in this great gift.

Confession must be understood as exorcism against Mortal sin, for here the adversary flees and you are made whole again. If you confess your sins with repentance and do not hide them from the Priest and not being ashamed of them in the understanding that your Soul becomes as pure as you were as when you were baptised, and that your gifts now to help others will be fortified, you now have the courage and strength to exorcise them, to bring Souls back to God! I do not mean that you become a Priest, no one can take that place! That is only for those who have been called in that manner by my Divine Son Jesus, the High Priest." *(Holy Saturday, March 31ˢᵗ, 2018)*

141. PRAY MY BELOVED CHILDREN MANY ROSARIES FOR THE SOULS OF YOUR ANCESTORS WHO THIRST FOR YOUR PRAYER, THEY WILL HELP YOU

"Pray, pray, pray My beloved children many Rosaries for the Souls of your ancestors who thirst for your prayer, they will help you! And yet, many of your ancestors are known to God as daily Saints! You can invoke them to pray for your needs. If you only understand this great gift of The Creator and His desire to reconcile each one of you back to Him, from your fallen state from Original Sin!

You have been given the gift of Holy Baptism. Many are not baptised! Bring this knowledge to them that they may be baptised in the Catholic Church, where Jesus waits for them. It has the full authority of the High Priest, left under the understanding of the seat of Peter the Rock upon which He has built His Church, and no one can take that, not even the

270

adversary[278]! He[279] can bring great suffering and sorrow, but he has no power to take the Authority of the Catholic Church away from Her, for her Head lies in Jesus, True God and True Man! If you understand this gift of your Faith, you will not hesitate, nor will you hide it! You will boldly confess it to others by your love for them and by your deeds of Mercy, Love and Forgiveness!

How easy it is to bring Souls back if you only understood your faith and pray for the gift of faith!

I am the *Mother of God, The Mediatrix of all Grace, Co-Redemptrix* and *Advocate* for you who intercedes for your loved ones through Me under this, My title. It is to be understood as the last title and the first title, the beginning and the end! I Am She whom God brought forth into your world for His Personified Glory, I love you all dearly. Amen." *(Holy Saturday, March 31st, 2018)*

142. IT IS MOST FRUITFUL AND EFFICACIOUS TO RECITE THE ROSARY WITH ITS MEDITATION IN THIS MANNER

"Beloved children, it is most fruitful and efficacious to recite the Rosary with its meditation in this manner:

1. Pray the Rosary for the unborn and for little children miscarried: the meditation is the Annunciation, the first joyful Mystery - the entire Joyful Mysteries!

2. The second for Euthanasia: those who sign them off willingly for this death. Pray the Mysteries of the Luminous Mysteries.

---

[278] Mt 16,18-19

[279] The adversary

3. For the Souls that commit suicide, in the seventy-two hours before the Soul comes before God for judgement, pray the Mysteries of the Sorrowful Mysteries.

4. And for the Souls that die of a ripe old age, pray the Mysteries of the Glorious Mysteries, the Resurrection. Amen." *(Holy Saturday, March 31st, 2018)*

143. THERE ARE THREE STAGES IN PURGATORY, AND IN EACH STAGE ITSELF THERE ARE THREE LEVELS

Iveta: I have entered to suffer in the second stage now where there is mobility. I can move my hands, my fingers - so to say move, but not to the sides. Amen.

I am granted now the Wisdom through our Holy Mother, the Wisdom to understand Purgatory more deeply. This is the Wisdom presented to me now:

"There are three stages in Purgatory[280] and in each stage itself there are three levels. St Michael is the custodian of Souls, and in each level a choir of Angels has been assigned

---

[280] "So rust, that is sin, is what covers the Soul. In Purgatory this rust is consumed by fire. The more it is consumed, the more also the Soul is exposed to the true Sun, to God. Her joy increases as the rust disappears and the Soul is exposed to the divine Ray. So, one grows and the other decreases until the time is fulfilled. It is not the suffering that is diminishing, it is only the time to stay in this pain." (Saint Catherine of Genova, Treaty of Purgatory, chap. II)

for[281]. When we pray for the Souls, Saint Michael who goes with Our Blessed Mother, opens the door of Purgatory, and brings refreshment for these Souls through our prayers. And the Choir of Angels are the Ones Who take them through the different stages when time has been completed according to God's Divine Justice and God's Holy Will and move the Souls to the next stages until they come into Paradise. Here Our Holy Mother greets them and walks with them." ... *there is more to it!*

Having completed the suffering in the first hour[282] *of the third stage in Purgatory,* "... the choir of Angels assigned to that stage at the bottom closest to Hell, otherwise they would be in Hell, are the Choir of Powers. The next level up is the Choir of Dominion, and the next level up closest to the Second Stage in Purgatory are the Choir of Principalities. Amen."

I am going through the second stage suffering now ... I have now completed the suffering of the second stage in this second hour and here is the Wisdom granted to me through Our Holy Mother:

"The choir of Angels assigned to the bottom level of the second stage, that is closest to the third stage are the Choir of Virtues, and above that is the Choir of Thrones, and above that

---

[281] "We spoke of the nine orders of angels because we know that sacred scripture clearly bears witness to Angels, Archangels, Virtues, Powers, Principalities, Dominations, Thrones, Cherubim, and Seraphim. Nearly every page of Sacred Scripture bears witness to the existence of angels and archangels. The books of the prophets, as is known, often speak of the Cherubim and Seraphim. And the apostle Paul enumerated the names of four orders when he said to the Ephesians (1:21) : Above every Principality and Power and Virtue and Domination. Again, writing to the Colossians (1:16) he said: Whether Thrones or Powers of Principalities or Dominations." (Pope Saint Gregory the Great, Sermon 34)
[282] The first hour of Iveta's suffering

level is the Choir of Angels of Archangels, from which level Saint Michael is."

In this level I am granted this wisdom. "There is mobility, that is as if a bedridden person has the ability to move a little. This is only an understanding of the suffering lessened by our prayers, bringing a little relief to the Soul to be a little mobile. One can just move from side to side or move the limbs a little to bring comfort, unlike the third stage with where you have no mobility at all. Immense prayer is required just for mobility!"

I will be granted more on this understanding in the days ahead.

Now I've entered the first stage, that is the stage closest to Paradise.

"I am at the third level, that is the bottom level of the first stage in Purgatory. There is mobility in this first stage, to wiggle, to be like a butterfly. There is also a certain joy from moments to moments, the Soul knows now it is coming closer to see its Creator, and here it is granted the Grace to pray a thanksgiving prayer to God for rescuing it. In this first stage the Soul seems to be in a joyous state[283], knowing that they will soon be with their Creator, constantly thanking God for giving them this gift! Here I understand we can apply our thanksgiving prayers to the Souls in this stage so they will move faster through the levels in this stage, thus lessening their time of serving Divine Justice."

---

[283] There is no peace to be compared with that of the Souls in Purgatory, save that of the saints in Paradise, and this peace is ever augmented by the inflowing of God into these Souls, which increases in proportion as the impediments to it are removed. (Saint Catherine of Genova, Treaty of Purgatory, chap. II)

Once again Divine Wisdom presents itself through Our Holy Mama. Now may we understand as I'm given this understanding:

"In these levels now, the Souls have mobility; not a fellowship mobility, but mobility in a confined area, that is each Soul has like a room, separate from the other Souls, who each have their own room.

There is no light in any of the stages of Purgatory except when our prayers rise and Our Blessed Mother comes with Saint Michael to them with the Light of God shining through Her Immaculate Heart and sometimes through Her Hands that depict the Graces that issue forth, through our prayers for them."

I am granted the Wisdom of the Choirs of Angels assigned to this first stage:

"On the third level of this first stage, the Choir of Angels assigned are the Choir of Seraphim. Above them in the second level are the Choir of Cherubim. Above the choir of Cherubim in the first level of the first stage, are the Choir of Angels. They are the closest level to Paradise.

The Souls of little children are usually in this level closest to Paradise. The Souls of Saints on Earth go to this level and spend three days there, that is the seventy-two hours needed for their purification with all the prayers raised for them before they enter Paradise, and in turn they respond by granting favours requested by us through our prayers for them, through their intercession!

It is an amazing moment to see what God grants these creatures[284], mere dust and yet the Love of God, which is immeasurable, cannot be fathomed! Only Divine Wisdom, known only to God Himself can issue the time and understanding. But most of all, we must understand as Our Blessed Mother has made known, how to pray daily for these Souls as we understand them to be: 'Angels' in Heaven, praying for us and Our World!

It is a lack of prayer and understanding of how important it is to pray for these Souls that have brought down various crimes and great disturbances and bondages on Earth in families who do not understand Ancestral bondage. Here of most importance, it is to offer the Holy Sacrifice for our Ancestors. Do not worry if they have made it into all Eternity with God! All the more they can buy Graces for those, either to be applied to our Ancestors still serving time in Purgatory, or Graces necessary for conversion of their ancestral line who have fallen into deep sin on Earth, to bring this joyous moment on Earth - when we offer the Holy Sacrifice for them. Amen. *(Holy Saturday, March 31st, 2018)*

144. THESE SOULS WILL COME AS GUARDIAN ANGELS TO HELP YOU, TO WARN YOU, TO PROTECT YOU!

Now Our Holy Mama speaks:

---

[284] "I behold such a great conformity between God and the Soul, that when he finds her pure as when his divine majesty first created her he gives her an attractive force of ardent love which would annihilate her if she were not immortal. He so transforms her into himself that, forgetting all, she no longer sees aught beside him; and he continues to draw her toward him, inflames her with love, and never leaves her until he has brought her to that state from whence she first came forth, that is, to the perfect purity in which she was created." (Saint Catherine of Genova, Treaty of Purgatory, chap. IX)

"My Beloved children, how important it is to pray for Souls in Purgatory! Many of you who once practised this manner, even My Priests and Religious, by your many duties have failed to pray for them! Offer those duties up! And many have embraced socialism and have no time to pray for these Souls! It is important for you to shed the foreskin of socialism that you have clothed yourselves with as a garment and a necessary means to reach out. It is most important to reach out through prayer now for the Souls that you even counsel.

It is to you beloved children, that I lay this yoke upon. It is a light yoke carried by Jesus My Divine Son already, now you can carry it with joy in the duties you perform; even the smallest act of Love can be applied to the Souls in Purgatory serving God's Divine Justice. Do not wait, there is very little daylight time! I have made known to you: When the persecution becomes grave, many will have no time to pray for such Souls. It is also for these who will be Remnant and those who will go into the underground Church.

You must raise Holy Sacrifices for these Souls who will come as 'Guardian Angels', to help you, to warn you, to protect you! Yes, this is how important it is to understand the importance to pray for the Souls in Purgatory!

All to you who are brothers and sisters, you belong to a family of God: Jesus, Who laid down His Life as your Brother, Your God, Your Redeemer, I who am *Co-Redemptrix*. Your Judge, The Divine Judge Jesus, is My Divine Son Who intercedes before your Heavenly Father for you. I am your *Advocate* interceding for you before the Divine Judge in your last hours of agony, and even now when you call on Me under the title as the *Mother of God, Mediatrix of All Grace, Co- Redemptrix* and *Advocate*.

I love you dearly, I desire only to bring you to your Heavenly abode Amen." *(Holy Saturday, March 31ˢᵗ, 2018)*

145. WHAT TAKES PLACE AT THE RESURRECTION OF OUR LORD[285]

Now Holy Mama grants me the last vision for this suffering:

"The understanding: I am granted to understand that in the first time of the Resurrection of the Lord, the *first* Resurrection, all Souls were released from the dead. Some went down to Hell; some went up to Heaven.

Heaven was in the preparation where Jesus prepared Purgatory for us. And then, when He ascended into Paradise, to be glorified by His Father who received Him, it was the first time that all the Souls in Purgatory that was created by the Lord, ascended with him, as we understand that the good thief did, as when Jesus said: 'This day you will be with me in Paradise!' And there, it was the Banquet where you could hear the Angels singing, and trumpets and every instrument playing, for the Glory of God shone on them. And then - that is in itself an understanding of how the Saints are ranked and given one could say in human understanding - to aid the Souls on Earth, as in conversion! And their main task is for everyone to Praise and Glorify God and Worship Him day and night!

Now I'm given the understanding of what will take place at the Resurrection of Our Lord[286], in the understanding of that first Resurrection, when the Paschal candle will be lit to give us Catholics the understanding that Christ is Risen. He truly is Risen! With Him the Souls that will ascend into Paradise when He ascends, who now have fallen asleep, will rise and these that will go with Him into the Eternal Banquet.

---

[285] During the Eucharistic celebration of the Easter Vigil, in the coming night.
[286] idem

This also takes place when the Resurrection Mass is offered for Souls and those who have served Divine Justice, that hour only God knows.

As we continue to offer the Resurrection Mass for Souls in Purgatory and when they enter Paradise, Our Lady shows me now they are clothed with a 'glorified' body[287], like Angels. They do not have a human body, only seen are their little hands through these white garments. The white in Purgatory is as white as our snow but the white in Paradise that they are clothed with - that Garment is whiter than snow! One has never seen that kind of White! It is like the Garments in which Our Lady is clothed, Her White! Amen.

Now Our Lady speaks:

"Now my beloved children, do you understand you must hunger and thirst for Heaven. Walk each day with the understanding of desiring Heaven. Use the things on Earth as if you use them not, all for the Glory of God, that you may one day see His Beatific Vision! I will come with Jesus, My Divine Son to call you into the Presence of the Eternal Father, your Father through Jesus, your *Redeemer*. I who will Co-Redeem and bring you to this moment when you call upon Me. Remember only to pray the Rosary! Pray, pray beloved children the Holy Rosary, of Most importance!"

… There is silence …

---

[287] This is not to be understood as the glorified body that will be given to the elect at the final resurrection. It appears to be a "garment". It can either be interpreted as a visibility of the (invisible) Soul that was necessary for Iveta to see and describe what is happening in Paradise before the final Resurrection, or as a real gift of a "heavenly garment" given to the Soul in Paradise while awaiting the final Resurrection and the gift of the glorious body.

"I am the *Mother of God*, your Heavenly Mother Who loves you dearly. Amen."

The Vision closes. (March 31ˢᵗ, 2018 Holy Saturday)

146. THE MANNER IN WHICH YOU ARE TO PRAY

Iveta: … Holy Mama is here. She wants me to tell you, my husband:

Archangel Michael has also come and is prostrated, but He throws the Divine Justice Scale that was in His right Hand and as well as the chains in His left Hand down. Archangel Gabriel is behind me and Archangel Raphael is behind you my husband, and my little Guardian Angel Daniel is at My right side, arming.

Holy Mama smiles and She looks at both of us, while St Michael rises, and He has the Scales in His right Hand and the chains in His left Hand. And now all the suffering that I have borne are like arrows going and forming little crystals, like precious stones, and the scale is full[288] on both sides and it sits perfectly balanced. It's amazing, the scales are so full, yet St Michael is not tired holding it! And now He throws the chains down, and now He binds a lot of spirits - like different little snakes - of the Souls that have departed today, that tormented them at the eleventh hour, but this suffering has brought them Divine Justice through the Mercy of God; and the merits will be used to get them into Purgatory where they will serve Divine Justice of whatever is needed of each Soul. There are countless Souls.

I do not see[289] anybody that I know. And Our Lady speaks as She holds Her hands as in the *Mediatrix of All Grace* Medal[290],

---

[288] Full of Souls

[289] Among these Souls

[290] See: https://www.mediatrixofallgrace.com/medal

and in Her Sorrowful Immaculate Heart are the seven arrows. You can see three on the right and four on the left, and Her Immaculate Heart is bleeding. She has the Pearl White Rosary in Her right Hand and the Mediatrix Scapular in Her left Hand[291].

She speaks:

"My beloved children, I thank you with a Motherly and Joyful Heart, in spite of My many sorrows this day, that you have kept your fast and your fidelity to Me, to pray. And you, little one of Mine and My Jesus, Cleophas, your suffering has brought great joy to My Immaculate Heart to see so many Souls, who will now be lifted at the Vigil of the Holy Sacrifice, known as the Easter Vigil …

Today, in this understanding of Divine Justice, your suffering will be used to bring Souls out of Purgatory, from the different levels they will rise to another level, according to the Divine Will of God for them and with the prayers through which they have come to do so.

Know and understand, it is of great importance that you make known, in what I had made known to you as the '*Thesis of Purgatory*', the manner in which you are to pray. It is very important, beloved children, and this yoke I lay upon your shoulder, My beloved of the Beloved Felix Xavier, to bring it forth. For many do not pray, and there are many who do not believe in Purgatory. This will bring clarity that it exists and that it must be

---

[291] Idem

so, for in Paradise there is not even a speck of dust[292]. It is crystal clear! Such is the purity required to enter into Paradise! Now there are exceptional Souls too, that God grants this Supreme Grace as a privilege on the merits of their suffering. Amen."

Then She pauses and says: "I desire to add to the understanding of the *'Thesis of Purgatory'*, that each stage that has been made known to you and in each level, each level is a hundred years. That is the kind of prayer necessary! So, beloved children know and understand that you must pray all the indulgences that the Church, the Holy Mother, the Catholic Church has made known, to bring these Souls out of Purgatory. And there will be many more coming into Purgatory, through your prayers it will come to be[293] and We shall rejoice as a Family of God into all Eternity and at the last Judgement. Amen."

She pauses and She speaks again: "I am aware of your weaknesses now; the suffering has borne and has beaten upon you a weakness so great! It is well for you to take a little nourishment, little one of Mine and My Jesus Cleophas and you My beloved of the Beloved, Felix Xavier I thank you too, immensely! I am with you through it all, keep in harmony and keep in peace …

Now go and rejoice in the celebration that the Lord will rise, and yes, you too will rise in joyful obedience. You have carried your mission.

---

[292] But I see that the divine essence is so pure—purer than the imagination can conceive—that the Soul, finding in itself the slightest imperfection, would rather cast itself into a thousand Hells than appear, so stained, in the presence of the divine majesty. Knowing, then, that Purgatory was intended for her cleaning, she throws herself therein, and finds there that great mercy, the removal of her stains. (idem. Chap VIII)

[293] The Treaty of Purgatory of Catherine of Genova mentions the help of the militant Church only once: "And if pious offerings be made for them by persons in this world." (idem. Chap XIII)

I love you dearly, I am the Mother of God, the *Mediatrix of all Grace, Co-Redemptrix* and *Advocate* in Heaven; it will come to be on Earth through your prayers. Amen."

The Vision closes with Her rising up, and Saint Michael with Her, and I see no more. Amen. Saint Michael descends, and He comes and stands behind us. (Holy Saturday, April 20th, 2019)

147. SO MANY SOULS IN THE CHURCH ARE WALKING OUT OF THE CHURCH AND DO NOT BELIEVE IN PURGATORY ANYMORE!

Saint Michael speaks:

"Today, this little one, Our beloved Sister Cleophas, little one of Our Blessed Mother and Our Lord Jesus, shall suffer for the Universal Church and the Domestic Church, for the Souls in Purgatory who are lacking prayers to rise into Paradise. These holy Souls are serving Divine Justice. Very little prayer, very little prayer is rising for the Souls in Purgatory for many do not believe in it. And today as the smoke of Satan has entered the Universal Church, in what has come to be known as the new age movement, they do not believe in Purgatory where Souls go to serve Divine Justice, who are faithful to God, who convert even at the eleventh hour pleading for God's Mercy to serve Divine Justice. She will also suffer at the hour of eleven p.m. till twelve a.m. for the Holy Father.

I Am St Michael Who stands at the Presence of God, here to defend God's Elect. Amen."

My body is like a furnace burning with pain, as though I am standing near a fire and it's burning. Amen. I am going into a paralysed state. I cannot do anything except I am lying in wait and my heart has a deep pain of anxiousness. This suffering that is beginning in me is like nothing on Earth, more intense is the suffering than any physical suffering. My eyes are closed, but they are like open eyes standing near a flame of fire, burning with pain. This burning is the longing to see someone I love so much and yet I cannot see. This someone, here in this state that I am, is My God, My Creator[294].

I am now going through the first stages of Purgatory and this suffering will serve to bring many Souls forward, closer to the first stage, and after that into all Eternity, Paradise, with God. Amen.

At this moment I see Saint Michael again. He has the scales of Divine Justice in his right Hand, and in His left Hand He has the long spear with the Cross at the handle of it ... then I see no more. Amen.

"... So many Souls in the Church, baptized as Catholics, are walking out of the Church and do not believe in Purgatory anymore! Their ancestors are in anguish of prayer in Purgatory: Prayers, not words! Prayers as the Catholic Church teaches us with the indulgences that come with it to apply to these Souls serving Divine Justice.

How numerous they are in every stage of Purgatory, especially in the last stages of the third level. And how many are those who would otherwise go to Hell, but through the prayers of the faithful for such Souls, the Mercy of God, the unfathomable Love of God, the Fruit of Divine Mercy has granted them the Grace to enter Purgatory, and they are in the last stage of the third level. Otherwise, they would have been in Hell where the Souls burn in the unquenchable fire forever and ever, and can never ascend into Heaven, nor can they

---

[294] Saint Catherine of Genova had a similar experience: "How, in comparison with the divine fire she felt within herself, she understood what Purgatory was." (Introduction to the Treaty of Purgatory).

descend into Hell to bring them relief[295]. Such is the distancing, the void ..." (*I can't read that word ... long pause ... Amen.*)

"As you[296] sprinkled Holy Water[297] now, many Souls that are called 'Earthbound', who die, especially those who have been killed and those who commit suicide, known as 'Earthbound', you have released them! And through the prayers of the faithful, they come before the Divine Judge." ... *and then I see no more. Amen.*

"As I drank this Holy Water[298], many Souls who drown, who die in the sea, are released, who were bound. And now Saint Michael is seen taking them before the Divine Judge and, through the prayers of the faithful, the prayers for these Souls and this little suffering that I am now enduring, the Mercy of God will grant them to serve Divine Justice in Purgatory. Amen."

It feels like a fever burning - and God forbid, I never go to Hell, for the intensity of this fever burning within me is like Hell. "And the anguish of these Souls who are serving thousands and thousands of years, hundreds and hundreds of years, day after day, are unable to do anything for themselves, even pray for themselves. They are in anguish of the desire that had they wished to have served on Earth, it would have been far easier. All the suffering on Earth of those Souls who are serving would be far less than they would be with the pain they are enduring right now in Purgatory, serving Divine Justice. Amen."

---

[295] "And besides all this, between us and you a great chasm has been fixed, in order that those who would pass from here to you may not be able, and none may cross from there to us." (Lc 16,26)

[296] Iveta is speaking to her husband Felix

[297] The very special efficiency of the use of a sacramental (holy water) here is to be understood in the context of the prayer of suffering of Iveta on that day.

[298] Idem.

From head to toe, it is like a current going through, and that can be described as when you bang your elbow - that sharp pain, it is of that nature from head to toe, but only hundred times worse, yet I cannot cry. I have no tears in me, I can only endure this.

I love you my God, I thank thee my God ... it's like a boxer who takes beating and beating and beating: the body has been boxed in that manner of pain, and I long to just fall asleep. Ah ... Ah ... "This state is endured by the state of the Soul. It is not a physical pain; it is a Spiritual pain, but only can be described by the body, how it would feel! My whole skin feels dried up. It has the pain of a dried skin, where it is about to form wounds that could bleed."

... relief ... I can now hold my Rosary and am with my Guardian Angel Daniel, here beside me. He is at my head now, praying the Rosary with me.

... and the Vision closes.

A vision presents itself with St Michael holding in the like same manner the scales of Divine Justice in His right Hand, and the Sword with the Cross in His left Hand. He's dressed in His full attire as the Defender of God's Elect and He speaks:

"Beloved children of God, I am Saint Michael, the Defender of God's Elect. At the hour of Divine Mercy today, Our Blessed Mother will come to receive this suffering. I will carry this suffering on the scales of Divine Justice and entrust it to Her to apply it to the Souls that have no one to pray for them anymore. Amen."

... and the Vision closes. (First Friday of Lent, March 15th, 2019)

148. SUFFERING FOR THE SOULS IN PURGATORY OF THE RELIGIOUS

Iveta in terrible suffering from head to toe. Fingers numb—Feet numb. Pain in back, Pain in uterus. Abortion pains --miscarriage pains. Canada has legalised marijuana - the drug - and Iveta was in suffering to rescue back Souls ...

There is more but I cannot bring it. My heart is pressing now. It is a suffering I must endure and the intensity of pain running through my body and my Soul is weighing heavy, for this is the pain of Soul to Soul, of each of the brethren now here.

I now see myself in the arms of Our Blessed Mother through this suffering. Amen.

I'm entering severe pain, the pain of the Soul, like the dark night of the Soul. The body is so burnt out with pain that it slips into quietness, till relief comes.

This relief I understand is when the Holy Sacrifice is raised for Souls in this state, brought by our Blessed Mother, the Precious Blood to quench the flames, the burning flames of Divine Justice. Amen.

... and Jesus is in Her Immaculate Heart. St Michael and the other two Archangel's are prostrated with Our Guardian Angels. And there are in this room countless Angels. They are Guardian Angels of all the Souls that will receive the merits of this suffering, united to the numerous, numerous prayers, Rosaries, that are coming - united to my suffering - from the many brothers and sisters who are praying this day all over on Earth.

St Michael rises, and He moves to the right of Our Blessed Mother. Our Lady comes forward. Her hands are joined below at waist level in which She has the *Mediatrix of all Grace* Scapular in Her left Hand and the Rosary in Her right Hand.

She speaks: "I desire with great desire to thank all those children praying frequently. And this their prayer will be applied to their ancestors paying Divine Justice in Purgatory. You do not understand this suffering; it seems so little or unknown and misunderstood. And yet the suffering will bear much fruit, much fruit in the hours from now till the eleventh hour of this day, before the suffering begins for the Holy Father. It is none other than the continuation of this suffering. She will now suffer for the religious orders that have closed down and no one is praying for the Divine Justice that they must pay; those that have passed into Eternity, who failed to live the vows of obedience, chastity and poverty and for those who do not believe. Now this is the heavy cross the Holy Father is carrying!

They do not believe in Purgatory anymore! This is the New Age movement that has infiltrated into many orders, and their laxity to embrace the lures of electronic devices that I have warned, that will be given freely to them, as if the instrument needed to bring Souls to God. No, my beloved children, no, this is not the way! You are only opening yourselves to fall deeper and deeper into the jaws of Satan and making it easier. For when martial law is declared all over the world, they will round you up and imprison you, My Priests and my beloved Daughters, the Religious, to easily to put you in the chambers of death. How will you then provide?

Many of you here will abandon your faith because you have not prayed. For faith is needed now, and in faith you must do all things to lead others through Me to Jesus, My Divine Son, Your Master."

"I love you dearly. I am the Mother of God, the *Mediatrix of all Grace, Co-Redemptrix,* and *Advocate* in Heaven. Many of you mock this title of Mine and do not pray for it. I speak of the Religious and My Priests. You do not understand. How then will you teach and lead others to Me, as it is the desire of our

Heavenly Father 'to Jesus through Me' and 'in Jesus, with Jesus, and through Jesus', to the Heavenly Father perfectly! This way has been traced by God our Father, and it shall not be otherwise!

Pray, pray, pray, many Rosaries for this My intention and for the Souls serving Divine Justice in Purgatory, who will help you when your hour befalls you."

Now, as I come out of this - a relief from head to toe, the suffering now begins of another nature for the Souls in Purgatory of the religious; the orders that have closed down. Amen. This suffering is beginning from my heart to waist down ... This reparation is enormous, and my heart is fluttering. When you are anxious and fearful of a wrong you are about to do, and you are knowingly going to do this wrong, that is the kind of feeling it is. But this is a grave offence, since these are sins against the Author of Life, that these Religious and Priests are about to commit. It is for this reason that their orders have been closed down, and many more are closing. There is no vocation, God is not allowing vocations! Amen.

With the Grace of God, I now repeat the suffering that befell me earlier which has consumed my body.

I hear this supplication. I'm not clear where it is coming from. It's like a prayer one would say when walking and remembering these Souls in Purgatory, of the Souls dying that might never understand the Mercy of God.

Jesus, Mary, Joseph, pray for me.

Jesus, Mary, Joseph, assist me and the many Souls dying and have no one to pray for them.

Jesus, Mary, Joseph, I offer Thee my suffering for the Holy Souls in Purgatory. Amen.

It is a prayer of one experiencing the coldness of the Church, the Mother Church, the Holy Mother - the Catholic Church.

My God, My God, have Mercy on the many Souls who are abandoning their faith and have no faith in Thee and in the teachings of the Catholic Church. Amen.

A cold tempest now befalls me, and I am consumed with chills with a fever burning within me, and now my body is consumed with the pain and afflictions that would come at the eleventh hour of one, as when the Soul is about to leave the body. Amen.

The vision begins with an hourglass and above it is the Holy Spirit. There is a little sand left and the bottom is almost full, one eight left to fill.

Now the Vision closes ... and another one begins as it presents itself, where Holy Mama has come, and She has Saint Joseph next to Her and Saint Michael is next to Saint Joseph. And now She extends her Hands, and She has the Rosary in her right Hand- the Pearl White Rosary, and the *Mediatrix of all Grace, Co-Redemptrix* and *Advocate* Scapular in Her left Hand.

She extends Her hands as though to receive something and then withdraws them and places them Criss Cross on Her Immaculate Heart, and Saint Joseph smiles, but says not a word. St Michael is holding the scales of Divine Justice in His right Hand and the Sword with the Cross at the handle in His left Hand, dressed in an attire for battle. And that what Mama has received is as though placed on the Scales of Divine Justice held by St Michael. It does not have any figure, but it has tilted the scales where you would put the item and on the other side are the merits of my suffering. It reads 'Merits of suffering'.

This will be applied to the different stages in Purgatory, as I understand it is written. And at the Vigil - the Easter Vigil, many Souls will rise into Eternity. Many Souls will move from one state to the other, except the last stage closest to Hell in the third level of Purgatory, those serving Divine Justice till the Judgement, the Final Judgement day. Amen. *(First Friday of Lent, March 15th, 2019)*

149. HOW I WILL PROTECT BOTH, THOSE NOW ON EARTH AND BRING RELIEF TO THE SOULS IN PURGATORY

Saint Michael now speaks to Felix Xavier:

"My beloved brother Felix Xavier, you who are beloved and chosen by the Hand of God, your Mission has been made known through Our Beloved and Blessed Mother. Her beloved son you are, and beloved of the Beloved, our Divine Saviour. I desire to press upon your heart to bring forth what has been made known of the Chaplet dedicated to Me, and the understanding of Purgatory, and the prayers to be recited, for there is little devotion to Me!

In this way, many Souls will be released and the devotion and understanding of Me for these times will be made known, of how I will protect both, those now on Earth and bring relief to the Souls in Purgatory, and protect the Souls of the faithful departed, to render them before the Divine Judge and then into Purgatory, where they will serve Divine Justice.

You must also understand the times of St Joseph, the Holy Pure and Just Man, known to you as The Herald of these times. Amen." *(Friday, 1st week of Lent, March 15th, 2019)*

150. THEY WILL BE COUNTED AMONG THE SAINTS AND WILL ENTER PARADISE DURING THE EASTER VIGIL

Now Our Lady speaks - She bows in greetings:

"My Beloved Children, I thank you immensely for responding to my request, specially you, little one of Mine and My Jesus, Cleophas, who will undergo the suffering for the Souls in Purgatory, during which in each hour you will recite the nine choirs of Angels, the Salutation Chaplet that Saint Michael has made known[299]. He is the Guardian Angel who brings them safely, their Spirit; and in this moment they have been entrusted to Me as *Mediatrix of all Grace, Co-Redemptrix* who suffered and is suffering for them united to the *Redeemer*, and as *Advocate*, now pleading before The Divine Judge who will rise this day in the understanding: who descended into Hell[300] to release these Souls who were Earthbound now and to grant them Mercy and Divine Justice. Now, there will be many who have washed themselves with the Blood of the Lamb[301], that is: Knowing that they could contact this Virus yet gave themselves to the service of others and died as Martyrs in this Plague, offering themselves up! They will be counted among the Saints and will enter Paradise during the Easter vigil.

Beloved Children, know and understand: You must also pray invoking Me under *'Our Lady of the Seven Sorrows'*. These prayers will be used now for them to satisfy Divine Justice. It is the Mercy of God for them who have embraced it. Even to those who were walking the path of perdition[302], like the good

---

[299] See Appendix

[300] 1 Peter 3,19

[301] Rev 7,14

[302] Mt 7,13

thief who pleaded, and to the many who called out to Me, who only knew Me as Mother Mary - and yes, I responded!"

She has a smile; it is a great moment for her. The smile represents the Resurrection that She is waiting for, to see Her Divine Son Jesus[303] now Her God, fully aware that He is God in the Second Person united to the First Person and in Whom the plenitude of the Holy Trinity dwells. This is the understanding She gives me of Her Smile. Amen.

She pauses and She speaks:

"My beloved of The Beloved Felix Xavier, you please Me much, yet I know I am laying heavy yokes on you. Know and understand, it is not without My Grace for you to fulfil them. I desire with great desire - with a sorrowful Mother's Heart, for many have no one to pray for them - to bring forth that what I had made known of the understanding of the 'Thesis of Purgatory', the 'Chaplet of Saint Michael and the nine Choirs of Angels' marking the nine levels in the three Stages of Purgatory, each one having three levels.

This little one, now, your spouse, will undergo suffering. Be not anxious, be not troubled! I am with her. There will be moments where she will be paralysed, and there will be moments where she will lament for those who have no one to lament in their last hours of agony. She will even plead Mercy for them, as if pleading Mercy for herself. I thank you immensely. Only do what I have asked, and work in communion with your other brothers and sisters to bring everything in order quickly. You will understand why.

I will receive this suffering at the hour of twelve noon (12:00 p.m.), this day after Angelus - the recitation of the Angelus prayer. Amen.

---

[303] The Blessed Virgin Mary on Holy Saturday is longing to see Her Divine Son

293

I Love you dearly, I am the *Mother of God,* The *Mediatrix of all Grace, Co-Redemptrix* and *Advocate* in Heaven, today interceding under this title for those who have no one to pray for, who died in this terrible agony, but were united to My Divine Son Jesus and Me in the Easter Triduum. Amen. I Love you dearly Amen."

The Vision closes.

I only see the Angels gathering, and more and more are coming. They are all around and above me. I do not see the other Angels who have descended from Heaven and who will ascend at the Easter Vigil. Amen.

Cough!! Cough… and I'm as though gasping for breath. I know I had my medicine this morning, and this could not have happened, but yet this is happening to me.

OK, the Pieta book is underneath here to pray the Saint Michael's Chaplet. I won't be able to pray all of it, but I will join you. Amen.

" … with their babies in their wombs, and little children, innocent children have also perished un-mourned and unaccounted for. These are among the poor in remote areas like Africa, India, like China, Korea, Japan, and wherever poverty is. Amen."

… a scene I saw. "The Crucified Jesus hanging on the Cross in the Amazon Jungle where this virus has entered among the people. The men are killing the women. As soon as they realise they have the virus, they kill them and they cut their throats and they burn them up. It's a horrible state! And the men kill the men too. It is their way of dealing with it. Now those Souls are Martyrs; they have prayed to an unknown God. Here, there are also women, pregnant, and the baby is alive in their womb. Yet they are killed now, and the baby struggles inside" *… crying … Ah!!! …*

… I see Saint Michael.

"He is standing on the head of Satan, His spear is pierced down from His left Hand – very, very faint. His sword is in His right Hand up. As Hell opens, then it's a wildfire, and Souls are perishing as bodies are thrown into Hell, while their Guardian Angels are forming a ring around Earth weeping for them. These are those that have cursed God and have embraced Satan as their god in their last hour of agony.

Can that be true, Saint Michael? "Yes, it is true, this is Truth."

He says this is truth, what you are bearing witness to now. Not even prayer can save them, because they have chosen the evil one for their god ... and now last, Saint Michael closes the bottomless pit, and He throws the evil one down to Earth again!

Satan tries to enter the last stage of Purgatory under the disguise of a creature that he possesses and as that creature's Soul was to enter this last stage, he started swearing blasphemous names at God, and Saint Michael throws him down and He pins Satan down, till all those Souls entered into Hell.

Jesus is crucified in this scene ... and these Souls even after seeing Jesus, did not want to go to Heaven, having chosen Hell[304].

---

[304] "As the purified spirit finds no repose but in God, for whom it was created, so the Soul in sin can rest nowhere but in Hell, which by, reason of its sins, has become its end. Therefore, at that instant in which the Soul separates from the body, it goes to its prescribed place, needing no other guide than the nature of the sin itself, if the Soul has parted from the body in mortal sin. And if the Soul were hindered from obeying that decree (proceeding from the justice of God), it would find itself in a yet deeper Hell, for it would be outside of the divine order, in which mercy always finds place and prevents the full infliction of all the pains the Soul has merited. Finding, therefore, no spot more fitting, nor any in which her pains would be so slight, she casts herself into her appointed place." (Saint Catherine of Genova, Treaty of Purgatory, chap. VII)

Now they are screaming for help, but no one can help them! This bottomless pit closes! "The Mercy of God is for all, though not all can enter, for not all choose to enter. Saint Michael, Defender of God's Elect. Amen."

The Vision closes.

Holy Mama has come to receive this suffering with Archangel Raphael who has a bowl of incense. St Michael is holding the scales of Divine Justice. All the Angels are with their hands joined, suspended as we recite The Angelus. (Holy Saturday, April 11th, 2020)

Appendix 1: ADDENDUM TO THE THESIS OF PURGATORY

151. THIS MANNER OF MERCIFUL KILLING

"I Am Jesus of Nazareth, your Merciful Saviour, your Redeemer, beloved children of God.

My beloved children be aware of this Merciful killing[305] as it comes to be known. It is an offence against Me, the Creator as God-Man and Man-God. I have traced the path of suffering that you may understand that this is the requirement of reconciliation with God the Father, to pay the debt of Divine Justice that sin requires. I have paid the major part of your debt, but you are required to do reparation for some of the offences in a small amount known as Divine Justice[306].

Those who embrace to you My faithful, this manner as merciful killing, you will receive the sentence of being in Purgatory, should you receive under My Mercy the Sacrament of the Sick anointing before you die. You will be in Purgatory till the last day when Divine Justice will come to be under the last judgement.

And to those I speak of, who perform this act, to you faithful that directly offend the Creator by playing the role of The Creator, it is not yours! Yours is to constantly provide loving care and Mercy to those who are in suffering, in times when they are in doubt and agony as I was in the garden of Gethsemane.

---

[305] Euthanasia

[306] Luke 23, 41, Saint Paul's experience after his conversion, Saint Mary of Magdala's penitent life according to the Tradition,

I have said a 'life for a life', know then to you who perform such an act, you will die mercilessly at the hands of the ruthless hardened hearts possessed by Satan. I will allow such, to those who kill by the sword, they will die by the sword[307]! (*Fifth Friday of Lent, April 7th, 2017*)

152. SOULS LIVING IN SIN, DEFILING THE TEMPLE OF GOD

Jesus speaks to My Soul, Soul to Soul:

"Little one of Mine and My Blessed Mother, Cleophas, Co-Redeeming with me through My Blessed Mother, the *Co-Redemptrix*. Now understand the suffering you will be offering for the Souls in Purgatory who rest in what is called the "third stage" made known to you. These are those who have committed the deed. And through My Blessed Mother as their Advocate, you will bring conversion to many Souls living in sin, defiling the temple of God and living in abomination and you will ransom their Souls for Me.

Your heart is heavy yet understand you will not die. It is only the weight you are carrying with Me. How I love you, I thank you. I am your Jesus receiving consolation from you, My little vessel Amen. Amen." (*Holy Thursday, April 13th, 2017*)

---

[307] Mt 26,52

Appendix 2: THE CHAPLET OF ST. MICHAEL THE ARCHANGEL

The Chaplet of St. Michael[308] is a wonderful way to honor this great Archangel along with the other nine Choirs of Angels. What do we mean by Choirs? It seems that God has created various orders of Angels. Sacred Scripture distinguishes nine such groupings: Seraphim, Cherubim, Thrones, Dominations, Powers, Virtues, Principalities, Archangels and Angels (Isa. 6: 2; Gen. 3: 24; Col. 1: 16; Eph. 1: 21; Rom. 8: 38). There may be more groupings, but these are the only ones that have been revealed to us. The Seraphim is believed to be the highest Choir, the most intimately united to God, while the Angelic Choir is the lowest.

The history of this Chaplet goes back to a devout Servant of God, Antonia d'Astonac, who had a vision of St. Michael. He told Antonia to honor him by nine salutations to the nine Choirs of Angels. St. Michael promised that whoever would practice this devotion in his honor would have, when approaching Holy Communion, an escort of nine angels chosen from each of the nine Choirs. In addition, for those who would recite the Chaplet daily, he promised his continual assistance and that of all the holy angels during life, and after death deliverance from Purgatory for themselves and their relations.

The Chaplet of St. Michael

O God come to my assistance. O Lord make haste to help me. Glory be to the Father, etc.

---

[308] See: https://www.abbaye-montsaintmichel.com/actualites/
chapelet_saint_michel

[Say one Our Father and three Hail Marys after each of the following nine salutations in honor of the nine Choirs of Angels]

1. By the intercession of St. Michael and the celestial Choir of Seraphim may the Lord make us worthy to burn with the fire of perfect charity. Amen.

2. By the intercession of St. Michael and the celestial Choir of Cherubim may the Lord grant us the grace to leave the ways of sin and run in the paths of Christian perfection. Amen.

3. By the intercession of St. Michael and the celestial Choir of Thrones may the Lord infuse into our hearts a true and sincere spirit of humility. Amen.

4. By the intercession of St. Michael and the celestial Choir of Dominations may the Lord give us grace to govern our senses and overcome any unruly passions. Amen.

5. By the intercession of St. Michael and the celestial Choir of Virtues may the Lord preserve us from evil and falling into temptation. Amen.

6. By the intercession of St. Michael and the celestial Choir of Powers may the Lord protect our Souls against the snares and temptations of the devil. Amen.

7. By the intercession of St. Michael and the celestial Choir of Principalities may God fill our Souls with a true spirit of obedience. Amen.

8. By the intercession of St. Michael and the celestial Choir of Archangels may the Lord give us perseverance in faith and in all good works in order that we may attain the glory of Heaven. Amen.